# Life Writing Series

# Life Writing Series

In the **Life Writing Series**, Wilfrid Laurier University Press publishes life writing and new life-writing criticism in order to promote autobiographical accounts, diaries, letters and testimonials written and/or told by women and men whose political, literary or philosophical purposes are central to their lives. **Life Writing** features the accounts of ordinary people, written in English, or translated into English from French or the languages of the First Nations or from any of the languages of immigration to Canada. **Life Writing** will also publish original theoretical investigations about life writing, as long as they are not limited to one author or text.

Priority is given to manuscripts that provide access to those voices that have not traditionally had access to the publication process.

Manuscripts of social, cultural and historical interest that are considered for the series, but are not published, are maintained in the **Life Writing Archive** of Wilfrid Laurier University Library.

*Series Editor*

Marlene Kadar
Humanities Division, York University

# Be Good, Sweet Maid
# The Trials of Dorothy Joudrie

by Audrey Andrews

**Wilfrid Laurier University Press**

We acknowledge the support of the Canada Council for the Arts for our publishing program. We acknowledge the financial support of the Government of Canada through the Book Publishing Industry Development Program for our publishing activities.

Canada

**Canadian Cataloguing in Publication Data**

Andrews, Audrey, 1935-
  Be good, sweet maid : the trials of Dorothy Joudrie

(Life writing)
Includes bibliographical references and index.
ISBN 0-88920-334-2

1. Joudrie, Dorothy – Trials, litigation, etc. 2. Trials (Attempted Murder) – Alberta – Calgary. I. Title. II. Series.

KE229.J68A52 1999          345.71'025          C99-931278-2
KF224.J68A52 1999

© 1999 Audrey Andrews

Cover illustration: *Cold Cream, 1983* by Mary Pratt, reproduced courtesy of the artist. Pencil and oil on gesso on masonite, 48.3 x 41.9 cm. Collection of the Canada Council Art Bank, Ottawa. Photograph by Ned Pratt.
Cover design by Leslie Macredie, based on a concept by Patrick Andrews with a facsimile of notebook excerpts by Audrey Andrews.

Wilfrid Laurier University Press
Waterloo, Ontario N2L 3C5

Printed in Canada

"There's rue for you, and here's some for me;
we may call it herb of grace a' Sundays. You
may wear your rue with a difference . . . . "
William Shakespeare, *Hamlet* IV, v.

# Contents

# Preface

It should not surprise me, I suppose, that writing a preface to this book is a kind of reckoning. Most prefaces, introductions, or addresses to the reader are written when the project is finished. I think of the times, reviewing books, when I have held writers to account, and not always generously, for their explanations, their justifications of what they have done. So I sit here looking out my workroom window, looking away from my desk. The world around me this morning is white; the snow is new, pristine; the air is dense, hazy. The sunlight on this cold, still, bleak day is diffused.

On January 21, 1995, Dorothy Joudrie was arrested for attempting to murder her estranged husband Earl, a successful Canadian corporate executive. On that sunny winter Saturday morning, as Dorothy waited for her husband to visit her, she could not have imagined the turmoil she experienced that day and has continued to experience since then. In a few moments that morning, Dorothy changed her life and the lives of her husband and their four children forever.

I think of how I have spent the past four years—reading, thinking, remembering, talking, listening, watching, and writing, writing. I think of the afternoon in 1995 when I sat in a quiet corner in a coffee shop at the University of Calgary with Penney Kome, an established writer and an editor of *NeWest Review*, while we discussed an article I wanted to write about Dorothy Joudrie. When I had asked her if *NeWest* would be interested in my article, we talked of my concern about Dorothy, my interest in her, my sense of identification with her, partly because we had been schoolmates when we were children. Dorothy and I experienced the same societal expectations of girls and women during the years immediately following World War II, the years that prepared us for our adult lives. Most girls accepted these expectations, as we did. But I discovered, as I matured, that they were unrealistic and unreasonable, and I knew that some women had been seriously damaged by them—that in the process of becoming ladies, wives, mothers, they had lost all sense of owning themselves. I wondered if, for Dorothy Joudrie, embracing society's role may have been part of the cause of the tragedy in her life.

Penney understood what I wanted to say about Dorothy. That day she offered me a spontaneous, lively lesson about how to write a magazine article, and we entered into a relationship that has sustained me throughout the past four years. I decided, finally, to put my article in the form of a letter to Dorothy, which I have revised somewhat and use here to begin my story. The letter was published in NeWest Review shortly before Dorothy's trial began in 1996. During the trial, CBC's Sunday Morning presented an edited version of it, read by the Canadian actor Eve Crawford.

After my article had been accepted for publication, Penney suggested to me that I should write a book about Dorothy. I had decided in 1994 that after the summer session the following year I would stop teaching as a sessional instructor in the English department at the university, partly because I wanted to write. But a book was a new and daunting undertaking for me, and one I had not for a moment considered. Nevertheless, I continued to write, and without really making a conscious decision, I found myself thinking about and planning a book, until finally, I recognized not only what I was doing, but what I was determined to do. Penney, who was now officially my mentor under the auspices of the Writers' Union of Canada, continued to guide, encourage, and advise me. My husband listened, endlessly, to what I wrote. Also, he, our family, and the small group of women, The Wednesday Circle, with whom I meet weekly for coffee, prompted me with astute comments and questions, and allowed me much more than my fair share of time to test my ideas. All of these people supported what I wanted to say about Dorothy Joudrie. But I discovered others who did not agree with what I was doing.

During the first days after Dorothy was arrested, the media both reflected and created the public's shocked reaction to her violent act. The corporate community, to which the Joudries belonged, was silent. When a publication ban was put in place a few days after the shooting, and Dorothy was released on bail, the news stories stopped and did not begin again until her trial in April 1996. But people continued to talk. Occasionally when someone discovered that I was writing about Dorothy, they were not reticent in telling me that it was beyond their comprehension that anyone would want to read a book about a wealthy woman who, in a fit of rage, had shot her husband six times in the back, as news reports had told us many times, and still had not managed to kill him. When I heard such remarks, which reflected much more than cruel humour, I was disturbed, but not deterred from what I had decided to do. In fact, this attitude was exactly what I wanted to examine, to try to understand, and to counter. I didn't know where my pursuit of Dorothy Joudrie's story would take me, but I became increasingly sure that writing about it was valid.

Until I attended her preliminary hearing in October 1995, and her trial in April 1996, I knew nothing of the real story of Dorothy Joudrie's life. While I wanted to get to the bottom of the story I was writing, to tell the truth, I had learned from experience that truth is especially vulnerable to the subjective reach of the reporter of human lives. I wondered, not for the first time, but perhaps more analytically than I had before, if truth really exists, although most of us use the word easily every day.

During the long, silent months between Dorothy's arrest and her trial, and especially after I stopped teaching, I began my research in earnest. I wanted to learn about the lives of women of Dorothy's socio-economic class, and I discovered that while a few women were willing to talk with me, such information is scarce. The silence surrounding the private lives of wives of corporate executives is like a sacred trust. Women who break this code of secrecy are seen as reckless and dangerous, not only with respect to their families and their husbands' careers, but to the corporate community generally. The propriety, the decorum, and the obedience and silence that Dorothy and I had learned is required of ladies is an integral part of the ethics of women of wealth and privilege. After Dorothy's preliminary hearing, when I found out about Earl Joudrie's abuse of Dorothy, I sought out as much information as I could find about spousal abuse. I found abused women who were willing to talk with me, to tell me about their lives, as had a small number of privileged women. And I discovered that Dorothy Joudrie is not the only woman who belonged to both groups.

I had thought that I was reasonably sophisticated about our society and women's place in it, but my research, my presence at Dorothy's preliminary hearing, her arraignment, her jury selection, her trial, and my occasional conversations with her provided me with one revelation after another. One of the most important was my realization, finally, that the story I wrote would be my version of Dorothy Joudrie's experience, and my reaction to it. Only she can tell what she believes is her story. I know this, because in writing my memories of myself as a daughter, a wife, a mother, all of which I think are an essential part of my story about Dorothy, I was surprised sometimes at what seems to me to be my own life, my experience as a woman. While I know that memory is not always reliable, and that truth is often elusive and subjective, my story is, nevertheless, supported by both. There are contradictions in this true story.

But my realization that I can never know exactly what Dorothy has experienced did not alter my determination to show that her plight is the result of the complexity of her personality, which is both strong and fragile; her extraordinarily difficult and painful and costly capitulation to her husband's treatment of her, and to society's demands on her; and her desperate act of resistance and self-defence, which her conscious mind simply could not embrace. In some ways, Dorothy Joudrie's life epitomizes the unreasonable demands our society places on women, and its frequent failure to support and help them. I knew that I must show as carefully and accurately as I could the effect on one woman, and on others, of the myths, prejudices, traditions, and institutions that are still at the foundation of our lives every day. I knew this because I believe that women can help each other, and the men we know and love, and our society. We can do this by trusting ourselves, and by telling our life experiences. This is what I have tried to do.

# Acknowledgments

I could not have written this book without the many people who were willing to talk with me about themselves, and to encourage me. There are more women than men in this group because it was women I sought out, but I am equally grateful to the men who approached me voluntarily to offer their support. These people do not want to be named, but they know who they are.

At Wilfrid Laurier University Press, Sandra Woolfrey's wise, patient editorial direction, the response of the two readers of my manuscript, and Carroll Klein's scholarly and sensitive editing gave me confidence, especially in their recognition of what I was trying to do. I am very grateful to Mary Pratt for giving WLU Press permission to use her painting *Cold Cream*. Long before its completion, when I imagined holding the book in my hands, it was this painting I saw on its cover. Professor Chris Levy, in the Faculty of Law at the University of Calgary, was most generous as he listened to me and answered my questions soon after the trial; later he directed me to Virginia May, Q.C., for a legal vetting of my manuscript. Virginia May offered me more than legal counsel, for which I thank her.

Thanks also to Kim Pate, executive director of the Canadian Association of Elizabeth Fry Societies, and the research librarians in the Calgary Public Library and the law library at The University of Calgary for whom no question was too minor, or too difficult. Karen Blasé, director of the Calgary Women's Shelter, gave me sound advice at the beginning of my project and referred me to the Older Women's Long-Term Survival Project (OWLS). These women welcomed me, and talked with me, and I will never forget what they said. Dr. Ken O'Brien took time during a brief visit from Australia to listen to me, answer questions, and direct me to books that provided further assistance. I am also grateful to Dr. John Brooks for permission to visit the Helen Hunley Forensic Unit 3-1 at the Alberta Hospital Edmonton.

During the trial, several journalists went out of their way to share information with me and to include me in their conversations. This was true particularly of Bob Beaty, Rick Mofina, Alanna Mitchell, and Brian Hutchinson. I am also grateful to Penney Kome, Gail Youngberg, and Terry Pugh at *NeWest Review* for their support in the publication of my initial article about Dorothy Joudrie, and to Verne Clemence, editor of *NeWest Review*, for giving me permission to include it here. My brother, Jim Allison, directed me several times to sources of information that were most useful. Susan Toy remains a constant friend and advisor.

I know that I could not have written this book without the example, insight, and inspiration of my friends, JoAnn McCaig, Donna Coates, Elaine Park, and Roberta Jackson, and our weekly meetings of The Wednesday Circle.

Although Dorothy Joudrie knew that I would include in my book some of what she said to me, she did not know exactly what my story would be, and I thank her for her acceptance of that. She never questioned my right to tell my version of her story, which I consider remarkably generous, as I do, also, the time she spent talking with me. She has helped me to interpret myself, and to accept the surprises I discovered sometimes in this long, continuing process.

Our family, Stephen, Patrick, and Karen, not only endured me during the past four years, but offered practical assistance and unfailing optimism.

Finally, I dedicate this book to Doug, my husband, my partner.

---

GRATEFUL ACKNOWLEDGMENT is made to the following publishers for permission to reprint selected materials: lyrics from *Miss Otis Regrets* (She's Unable To Lunch Today), by Cole Porter. Copyright 1934 (Renewed) Warner Bros. Inc. All Rights Reserved. Used by permission of Warner Bros. Publications U.S. Inc.; excerpt from "The Babysitters" from *Collected Poems by Sylvia Plath*. Copyright 1960 by the Estate of Sylvia Plath. Copyright renewed. Reprinted by permission of Faber and Faber Limited. Excerpt from "The Babysitters" from *Crossing the Water* by Sylvia Plath. Copyright © 1961 by Ted Hughes. Copyright renewed. Reprinted by permission of Harper Collins Publishers, Inc.; excerpt from "Käthe

Kollwitz" by Muriel Rukeyser. Copyright 1968 by International Creative Management Inc., All Rights Reserved. Reprinted by permission of International Creative Management Inc.; "What are little boys made of?" from *The Oxford Dictionary of Nursery Rhymes*, 1996, edited by Iona and Peter Opie. Reprinted by permission of Oxford University Press; "On the mountain stands a lady" from *Children's Games with Things*, 1997, edited by Iona and Peter Opie. Reprinted by permission of Oxford University Press; excerpt from "Overview: The 'Wife-Beater's Wife' Reconsidered" by Elaine Hilberman, M.D., from *American Journal of Psychiatry*, 137:11, 1336-1347, 1980. Copyright 1980, the American Psychiatric Association. Reprinted by permission of the American Psychiatric Publishing Group; excerpt from "The Prodigal" from *The Complete Poems 1927-1979* by Elizabeth Bishop. Copyright © 1979, 1983 by Alice Helen Methfessel. Reprinted by permission of Farrar, Straus & Giroux, Inc.; excerpt from "Silence of the Lions" by Mike Woloschuk, from *Elm Street,* October 1996, 16-20. Copyright 1996. Reprinted by permission of the author and Stevie Cameron, Editor-in-Chief of *Elm Street*; excerpt from "It's Her Job Too" by Betsy Morris. Excerpt on pages 66 and 71. Reprinted from the February 2, 1998 issue of *Fortune* by special permission, copyright 1998, Time Inc.; excerpts from "High Society Shooting" by Tom Fennel, with Carla Turner in Calgary, from *Maclean's*, February 6, 1995, 44-45. Reprinted by permission of *Maclean's*; excerpts from "Joudrie Verdict Raises Issues" by Kirk Makin, from *The Globe and Mail*, May 11, 1996. Reprinted by permission of *The Globe and Mail*; excerpts from the following articles in the *Calgary Herald*: "Gulf Canada Chairman Shot" by Wendy Dudley and Gordon Jaremko, January 22, 1995, A1, A2, "Accused 'had and ideal life'" by Helen Dolik and Vicki Barnett, January 23, 1995, A1, "Joudrie Hearing Set for June" by Daryl Slade, February 1, 1995, B2, "Socialite's Hearing Adjourned" by Daryl Slade, June 16, 1995, B6, "Nanny Recalls Family Violence" by Bob Beaty, May 2, 1996, B1, "Six Shots Can Change a Life" by Don Braid, May 2, 1996, B1, "Corporate Plumber: The Business Side of Early Joudrie" by Gordon Jaremko, May 4, 1996, A1, "Joudrie Taking Leave of Absence" by Gordon Jaremko and Anne Crawford, May 11, 1996, D1, "The Joudrie Affair: Legal Top Guns" by Kim Lunman, May 10, 1996, A15, "Trial Split Calgarians Along Gender Lines" by Don Braid, May 10, 1996, A23, "Not Responsible" by Bob Beaty and Rick Mofina, May 10, 1996, A1, "Dance of Death Is Over" by Catherine Ford, May 10, 1996, A23, "Behind Locked Doors" by Helen Dolik, May 26, 1996, City and Life 2. Reprinted by permission of the *Calgary Herald*; excerpts from "Oil Patch: Gulf Exec Back on Job" by Leif Sollid, *The Calgary Sun,* May 4, 1995, News 4, "Socialite's Trail Weighty Responsibility" by Licia Corbella, *The Calgary Sun*, April 19, 1996, News 5, and "Forgiving But Not Forgetting" by Licia Corbella, *The Calgary Sun*, May 8, 1996, News 21. Reprinted by permission of *The Calgary Sun*; excerpt from "Hard Lessons: What We Learned from the Joudrie Trial" by David Coll from *Calgary downtown*, June, 1996, 5. Reprinted by permission of David Coll. The discussion arising from "R. v. Joudrie – Automatism: Legitimate Defence or Legalized Irresponsibility" by Noel C. O'Brien, Q.C., is printed with the permission of the author.

# Part One

# Before the Trial

# Dear Dorothy

May 1995

Dear Dorothy,

Do you remember a late winter afternoon after school when you and Ann and I sat at your kitchen table eating graham wafers? You urged us to spread them liberally with honey, showing us by elaborate gestures of pleasure how much better they tasted that way. It was 1944; we were in grade three. The light in the kitchen created a bright warm contrast to the cold Edmonton dusk gathering outside. I remember that as we talked and laughed I looked at you—your clear olive complexion, your thick gold-brown hair, the exotic air of your Icelandic heritage, your delight in entertaining us—and thought how happy I was to know this girl for whom life seemed to be so easy and such fun.

After my family moved to another neighbourhood two years later, I seldom saw you. But I did occasionally see Earl Joudrie, who lived near us. He seemed quiet and serious as I saw him riding to school, alone, on his bike. I knew that he was a good student. I also knew that you and he dated when we were in high school, so perhaps I saw you more frequently than I remember now. I lost touch with many of my childhood friends when I went away to university and stayed for several years in Ontario. Eventually I married, and moved with my husband and children back to Alberta, and finally to Calgary.

Although my domestic life and my teaching provide me with ordinary problems and minor crises, most of the time, in my day-to-day existence, I am relatively comfortable with the choices I have made, and with myself

3

as a woman. But suddenly one Sunday morning last January a news report about you ripped open a dizzying kaleidoscope of memories of the past fifty years, and a shocking new realization of the struggle some women of our age have experienced in their efforts to own themselves.

I could hardly believe that you had been charged with attempted murder after allegedly shooting your husband, Earl, six times with a small-calibre handgun. According to the police, Earl's visit to you, "his estranged wife," the previous morning, had degenerated into a bitter dispute. I learned that when the police arrived at your home Earl was lying on the floor and you were there as well. The police arrested you.[1] One photograph of you handcuffed was particularly disturbing.[2] I tried to interpret the expression on your face in the photograph, and I still do as I look at it now. But I cannot.

A publication ban, requested by your lawyer at your court appearance the following Monday, prevents an announcement of the terms of your release on bail that day, and any other pertinent information. But there were media reports of your appearing in court again on January 31, when you entered no plea, and chose trial by judge and jury.[3]

I hadn't known that you live in Calgary, nor that Earl had become an important figure in the Canadian business community—chairman of Algoma Steel, Canadian Tire, and Gulf Canada, and a director of nine other Canadian companies. I discovered that you were married in 1957 after you both graduated from the University of Alberta and that you have four grown children.

In news reports friends and associates of Earl praised him and his outstanding skills as a "diplomat and deal-maker" in business. They also described him as reliable, trustworthy, and "old school." They were surprised by the alleged shooting because he is a private man, they said, and they knew little or nothing about his personal life.[4]

How did you react, I wonder, to these descriptions of your husband, and to your friends' and neighbours' descriptions of you? You noticed, I'm sure, that speaking of you, their tone differed, tactfully, cautiously, from the lavish praise Earl's associates offered about him. Some of your neighbours said that you are a "fine person," "a lot of fun to be around," "good hearted," generous.[5] But for the most part, people spoke not about you, but about your luxurious home, your membership in exclusive golf clubs, your yearly winter vacations in Arizona, the parties you like to give. They said that as Earl's career prospered you had "stood at his side," an accomplished

and gracious hostess. "It seems like she had an absolutely ideal life,"[6] someone said. This curiously inappropriate comment to the press is a good
example of the public reaction to your alleged behaviour. You are the good
wife gone suddenly, mysteriously, awry. Why, they seemed to wonder,
would you attack the one person who provides your very comfortable life,
the one person who defines your cherished wifely role.

I know almost nothing about your marriage, and what I have discovered about the events of the past few years is puzzling. According to an article in *Maclean's*, since 1990, Earl has petitioned for divorce more than once,
and each time you have contested the petition. On at least one occasion, you
sued for half of his assets, including sole ownership of your family home on
an acreage west of Calgary. Your divorce lawyer said that although a negoti-
ated settlement over property was concluded, there was never a divorce. At
one point, the *Maclean's* reporters said, you sought a civil restraining order
which would prevent Earl from going near your present home on Country
Club Lane. What fierce struggle was behind all this?[7]

You knew, I am sure, that at the time of the shooting Earl wanted no
one to speak to the media. He was flown by helicopter to a Calgary hospital, where medical personnel respected his wish and made no public
announcement about his injuries. But the RCMP told newspaper reporters
that his condition was "stable and not life-threatening."[8] A few days ago,
while attending the Gulf Canada annual meeting in Calgary, Earl told newspaper reporters that he has recovered from the gunshot wounds. He said
about the incident in January, "It's a difficult thing for the family. I mean,
this whole thing is a family tragedy."[9] Here was the private man, whose mas-
tery of negotiation and diplomacy is, as his associates claimed, "not restrict-
ed to corporate boardrooms,"[10] breaking the silence he imposed.

Earl knew that as soon as he appeared in public he would be questioned. He was not caught off guard by the reporters. I suspect that his
comment, and particularly his making any comment at all, reveals not
only his own perception of his position in relation to you but also his confidence that his having the authority to speak publicly is quite acceptable.
He is in control—or perhaps more accurately, he has resumed control.
Things are back to normal. And, unfortunately, too often what is normal
in our society, and especially in the socio-economic class to which you
belong, is that wives are expendable, replaceable, invisible, and silent. You
may not speak about the shooting, but apparently he may. And Earl
believes that he can define exactly what this "whole thing" is.

All of us, you and Earl and I, born in the mid-1930s, came to early adulthood in the 1950s, a decade which was probably the most difficult period for women in the twentieth century. Postwar women were directed to find fulfilment as the highly valued, necessary, but nonetheless, as Simone de Beauvoir named us, second sex.[11] Marry, and marry well, many mothers told their daughters. These mothers knew that we would find our future, our security, even our identity, in our husbands.

Only a very small proportion of women pursued graduate studies at universities, or worked outside the home. We regarded single professional women with ambivalence: our admiration was mixed with pity. We regarded "working" mothers with the disapproval we had learned from society generally, and from child psychologists in particular.

Do you remember how women's magazines burgeoned with articles featuring wedding plans, home furnishings, and recipes to keep our husbands healthy and to serve at dinner parties designed to help them get ahead in business? We were constantly urged to acquire material possessions to demonstrate success. How naively we acquiesced in this crude strategy to pump up the economy!

My senior classmates at university spent every spare minute knitting argyle socks for their boyfriends, and collecting recipes which they would use to convince these young men of their domestic skills when they took them home for the weekends. Frustrated couples dreamt of romantic trysts which were rarely realized, or in their realization fraught with secrecy and guilt. Sex outside marriage was officially forbidden. Reliable contraception was inaccessible. More brides than we knew were pregnant when they married. The disgrace of an unwanted pregnancy destroyed some relationships. Abortion was illegal, dangerous, and very expensive.

If we were not engaged to be married by the time we had completed high school or, at the latest, an undergraduate degree, we had failed. Most young people were married by the age of twenty-five and had at least one child, and eventually, at least three children. You, apparently, more than met these expectations.

In 1959 I was a graduate student and a don in a women's residence at the University of Toronto. There were seven dons, each responsible for a house filled with women students. Two of the seven dons were preoccupied with impending marriages; the remaining five quickly formed a tightly knit group who talked together at meals and over endless cups of coffee. We believed that meeting the expectations of our families and society generally was secondary to our dedication to our studies and our determination to have careers. We regarded our pursuit of self-development essential to our lives as rational beings.

The Dean of Women, who had never married, advised us often that the further we pursued our studies, the fewer chances we would have to marry. Men, she assured us, did not want to marry women who were smarter than they were. Behind her back, we laughed at her concerns for us, and rather cruelly pitied what we saw as her need to satisfy vicariously what we thought may have been her own unfulfilled romantic dreams. But the truth is that while we wanted professions, we also wanted husbands and children, and we worried secretly that not all of our dreams would be fulfilled. This fear had been bred in us, nurtured by every expectation of us that we had ever known. Yet, while we were aware that we were living outside the norm for women of our day, our heady spirit and energy, the opportunity to share it with each other, and our busy days, satisfied us—almost.

I wonder if you had a similar experience of intellectual confidence and freedom while you were at university. I know that you taught high school for a while. Did you have reservations about giving up your profession to become a wife and mother? My husband believed quite adamantly that when we married I would stay at home and be a "chatelaine." We laugh about that now—how willingly we conformed to the expectations of us then, my husband's innocent arrogance, and my naive complicity. But the reality of homemaking and motherhood could be and was, for many women I knew, a life of cruel isolation and dependence that was sometimes very frightening. I have never forgotten that in those days the only money I possessed which was in my name was the monthly family allowance cheque from Ottawa.

In 1963, when Betty Friedan named this postwar phenomenon which thrust women into a narrowly defined wife/mother role the "feminine mystique," she released the second wave of feminism in this century.[12] I wonder if you read her book and reacted to it with the surge of excitement and recognition I had. Not all women, and certainly not all men, were prepared to accept the ideas of what was labelled, in the mid-1960s, "women's liberation."

Ten years after Friedan's book appeared, one of my neighbours, who often walked with me and our preschool children, would wait patiently on the sidewalk each month, rather than be seen with me, while I went into the only store in a small Alberta town that sold my eagerly awaited copy of *MS* magazine. She thought *MS* was dangerously radical and improper, and she did not want to be associated publicly with someone who read it. *MS* and the books it recommended about women were ballast in the unsteady ship of my domestic existence then.

In some respects women's lives, and our position in relation to men, have changed dramatically during the past thirty years. In some respects society has accepted women's insistence upon an equal position in relation to men. Some women of our generation broke free from the accepted expectations by leaving their marriages, by getting more education and finding successful careers, or by finding independence within their marriages. At the same time, however, many old attitudes are so deeply ingrained that our society seems not to have changed at all. The reactions to your alleged behaviour demonstrate this.

Women like you, who apparently did exactly what society demanded of them, and who helped to create their husbands' power and privilege certainly deserve to share it. Your wanting half of your husband's assets is quite reasonable. You devoted more than thirty years of your life to Earl and your children. Money can ensure both a certain position in society— what some of your neighbours consider an ideal life—and certain kinds of power, including, perhaps, your release on bail after a charge of attempted murder. But for a wife, this power and privilege are, in the end, second-hand, an illusion, a minefield of vulnerability, jealousy, rage, despair, and guilt. Worse, if women lose themselves in the process of "standing at their husband's side," the cost is too great. This is a personal tragedy endured silently by many women of our age. And this is why you terrify some women whose identity is dependent on others, and whose private selves have all but disappeared.

A few weeks ago, I taught Sylvia Plath's poem "The Babysitters"—perhaps because without realizing it, I was thinking of you. In the poem a woman recalls herself and another teen-aged girl in the 1950s, who were babysitters of children of affluent families at summer homes in Swampscott, north of Boston. The girls love the elegant "richness" of the "handsome houses in Swampscott," but they are spiteful and feel "put-upon" by the domestic duties expected of them—cooking, ironing, managing the fussy children. They are jealous of their employers, the "sporty wife and her doctor husband," the "big people" with their rose gardens, guest cottages, cabin boys, and maids. On one of their days off the girls lift "a sugared ham and a pineapple from the grownups' ice box," rent an old boat, and row out to the deserted "Children's Island." They beat off the gulls who seem now to own it all, as they step down the steep beach and into the ocean. Then, floating on the buoyant, salty water, they kick and talk. The woman who recalls this summer experience thinks, "I see us floating there yet, inseparable—two cork dolls./ What keyhole have we slipped through, what door has shut? . . . / Everything has happened."[13]

I know now that my admiration of you when we were children rested on your intelligence, and energy, and your apparently happy realization of yourself. This was many years before "everything" happened—before you became a wife, a mother, a member of a privileged class in a society whose expectations of women have often controlled and demeaned them and betrayed them. You are charged, now, with breaking society's rules. And the terrible irony is that your alleged behaviour has put you firmly under your husband's and society's control. They, again, may determine your fate.

Oh, Dorothy, how innocent we were—laughing, talking, eating graham wafers with honey, so long ago, in 1944.

Sincerely,
Audrey

# Waiting

The lie of the "happy marriage," of domesticity—we have
been complicit, have acted out the fiction of a well-lived life,
until the day we testify in court of rapes, beatings, psychic
cruelties, public and private humiliations.
           Adrienne Rich, *On Lies, Secrets, and Silence*[14]

He was always saying how his mother said, "What a man
wants is a mate and what a woman wants is infinite security,"
and "What a man is is an arrow into the future and what a
woman is is the place the arrow shoots off from," until it
made me tired.
           Sylvia Plath, *The Bell Jar*[15]

Today, June 16, 1995, there was a brief public announcement that
Dorothy Joudrie's preliminary hearing, which was scheduled for this
month, has been postponed until October—four more months.[16] What is
the reason for this delay? I wonder about her reaction. Does it cause her
relief, frustration, anxiety?

I am sure that like most women, Dorothy has learned what it means
to wait. I remember when I realized with anger and resentment that the
act of waiting, like many expectations of women, was imbued with
patience, virtue, and romance, and that those who expect it of us consider it proof of our true feminine natures. "Keep the home fires burning" we
sang with our mothers when we were children and our fathers had gone
to war, and who would have argued with that? During World War II our

mothers, as women had always done during wartime, stayed at home and waited. But many of them also returned to professions they had abandoned when they married, or they found jobs to support the war effort and, no less important, themselves and their children. They carried on, and they were praised for their courage and stamina. They tried not to complain about their exhaustion, their loneliness, their fears for their husbands' lives, their anxiety about their futures. And when the war was over and the men came home, most of these women, as they were expected to do, gave up their jobs to the men. They resumed their traditional submissive positions as wives and mothers. Some were so happy to be relieved of their solitary responsibilities that it was some time before they realized that they had also given up their independence.

When I was in my teens—curious, expectant, and filled with romantic dreams of my future—I read about the mythical Penelope, who waited twenty years for her husband, Odysseus, to come home from his wars and adventures. This myth of married love and the faithful wife thrilled me, and it was years before I realized that like most myths about women, ancient and modern, the story of Penelope is a male paradigm and that women should reexamine such unreasonable and often cruel models of female behaviour. The late British writer Angela Carter believed that "all the mythic versions of women, from the myth of the redeeming purity of the virgin to that of the healing, reconciling mother, are consolatory nonsense."[17] What a relief, these words, for me.

Many women, quite apart from the extraordinary circumstances of war, suffer the pains of waiting for too long before they discover how destructive and demeaning it can be, that they are fools not to get on with their own lives, and that to do so is not unfaithful, or unfeeling, or unwomanly, but sensible and reasonable. I remember the importance of the job of phone duty in the women's residence during my undergraduate years at university. The designated person was never to leave her post between the hours of six and ten o'clock each evening. She sat by the telephone in a small office, which was part of the formal, English-style vestibule of the residence. We had a buzzer system. She buzzed our rooms once if we had a phone call and twice if we had a visitor. One buzz sent us running to the single phone at the end of the corridor on our floor. Girls told the person on phone duty that they were studying in their rooms, and they were. But they were also waiting, hoping that at any minute their buzzer would signal a call from the young man who was important to them. In those days, nice girls, good girls, never called boys—never. I used to marvel at the girls sitting smoking and playing bridge—relaxed, happy, confident—in the Blue Room, far from their rooms, from their buzzers. I longed to be like them, to have such confident control of my life, not to be so willing to accommodate myself to the capricious nature of a young man who would fit me into his schedule when it suited him. For years after I graduated from that university, the sound of a buzzer like the ones in our residence caused my heart to leap, my stomach to clench. I also remember many evenings, years after I was married, singing softly to a restless, sleepy baby in my arms, as I walked and half danced near the window in the darkening bedroom of our house in Montreal, watching for the lights of our car, waiting for the sign that my husband was safely home. I can't count the nights, many years after that, when I lay awake, listening for the sound of a Volkswagen turning into our street, stopping in front of our house, and my older son's step on the front porch, his quiet, careful turning of the lock on the front door. By the time our second son was in his teens, I had become preoccupied with my own work, which was partly a deliberate exercise in self-protection. I would never have survived our children's teen years if I had not been able to shut my door and set my mind exclusively on Chaucer's Wife of Bath, or George Herbert's "Love Bade Me Welcome." I was too tired after my evening's work to stay awake. Also, I had finally learned that waiting anxiously would not prevent a car accident, or any other imagined disaster. But I always heard my son come into the house. Then I settled, finally, into a sound sleep. Dorothy waited for four teenagers. I wonder how she managed it.

I don't remember my husband ever actively waiting for either of the children. When we discussed this once he said that I did it so well, he didn't need to bother. This remark was facetious, of course, but it was also, implicitly, a traditional assumption about women. Women wait. Men are expected to get on with their lives, or the sleep they need to face a new day.

Still, all people—men and women—must wait sometimes. Dorothy, now, has no choice. This recent postponement to which she is subjected prolongs her ordeal, and also the silence imposed upon her. Perhaps she welcomes the delay and the possibility inherent in it that she will escape the whole legal process which, she may hope, might not be inevitable. Perhaps she welcomes the silence. Yet surely going about her day-to-day life while a decision about her actions is suspended and beyond her control must be very difficult.

Sometimes during my weekly grocery shopping I think of Dorothy. I'll admit that occasionally I wonder, if I had been charged with attempting to murder my husband, would I have been kept in jail for only two days and then be allowed to live in my home as she is, free to attend to these mundane but necessary duties. Could I have paid the bail, and hired one of the most skilled and expensive lawyers in Alberta? This freedom is one of the benefits of her social position. Then I realize that some of her "freedom" may, in fact, be very costly. Grocery shopping, even in a large city and especially in the suburbs, has about it aspects of village life. I almost always meet other women and men whom I know. We chat in a desultory and pleasant manner, catching up on news about our work, our children, our neighbours and friends. We also complain, and commiserate, and then move along with our task, reassured somehow by this membership in a community. What is it like for Dorothy now? What does she talk about with the people she meets when she shops for groceries? Does she belong, still, in her community of neighbours? If I were Dorothy, I would dread this most ordinary of tasks. I realize now, having talked with others about her, that I might very well find it impossible.

I sought out the opinions of well-educated, thoughtful people whom I see from day to day because I thought that their reactions to Dorothy's behaviour would be different from those reported initially in the media. I thought that their reactions would reflect a more benevolent and wise awareness of women, and particularly of women of our age. But for the most part, I was wrong. I could not have anticipated the number of apparently enlightened, sophisticated women who express no sympathy for her. One such woman said scornfully, "What does she think she is doing, living out the plot of a soap opera?" A prejudice against her wealth was foremost in this woman's mind, along with the moral judgement that Dorothy lives in a fantasy world, a world in which she must believe that she can get away with anything. Another woman was very uncomfortable talking with me. She seemed cross and impatient with the scandal, the vulgarity of Dorothy's family crisis, and she made it clear not only that she did not want to discuss Dorothy, but that behaviour such as hers would never occur among the affluent people she knows and with whom she aspires to belong. Like Scott Fitzgerald's Gatsby, this woman believes that wealth and moral superiority are inseparable. She and a few other conservative, decorous women let me know, usually indirectly, that they thought my interest in Dorothy and what would become of her was strange, even rather perverse, as if my being concerned about her perpetuates what they consider to be her aberrant and disgraceful behaviour and brings it down upon the heads of all women. These women are suspicious of "feminists" like me, who, they believe, stir up controversy and discontent among women, and justified criticism from men. Their emotional reactions seem to me to reveal a fleeting sense of identification with Dorothy, but one which they cannot allow themselves to examine. My conversations with them caused me to remember, with relief and affection, a friend who once said to me with her usual jokey/serious candour, "I've never considered divorcing my husband, but I have seriously thought of murdering him." We laughed, enjoying a reckless moment of exasperation.

Men's reactions to Dorothy's behaviour are more cool, detached. Men often laugh slightly when they talk about her, almost always mentioning the six bullets, none of which hit home. There is a suggestion here, I think, of her having invaded the male territory of guns, even the mystique of guns, which are not traditionally female weapons, and which women, obviously, cannot use properly. But men also appreciate the violence of the act of shooting, because some of them use guns. They know their danger. One man gently, softly sang for me Cole Porter's song "Miss Otis Regrets":

> When she woke up and found that her dream of love
> was gone, Madam,
> She ran to the man who had led her so far astray,
> And from under her velvet gown
> She drew a gun and shot her lover down.
> Madam, Miss Otis regrets she's unable to lunch today.[18]

There was a romantic and almost tender respect for Miss Otis and for Dorothy in this man's wry humour, but he could afford to spend this much emotion, which included some condescension, because he was simply the teller, or singer, of an old, an eternal tale of a woman's crime of passion. He felt quite separate from Dorothy Joudrie, but he enjoyed his clever comparison of her plight to the sad and shocking tale of Miss Otis.

Of course none of us knows more than the barest details of Dorothy's story. My husband had more imagination and insight than many people. When the newspaper arrived on the day after the shooting, he and I stood silently, side by side at the kitchen table, reading the headline, looking at the photos, and skimming the lead article about Dorothy and Earl. As my husband moved to the stove to rescue the boiling kettle, he remarked,

"What did he do to her to cause this!" Surely, we both thought, she must have been desperate to risk giving life such a fierce, wild shove.

I did discover a few responses, which reflected both my husband's and mine. My search for them inspired some unforgettable conversations with women, and about women and their place in society. I recently talked about Dorothy with a friend as we walked early one morning, enjoying the damp, green spring. I was telling her about a review I was writing of *The Promise of Rest*, a new novel by Reynolds Price that I found both troubling and very moving. I had decided that I would probably refer to it as a male novel, a distinction I had never made in more than ten years of book reviewing. I was trying to justify my decision to do this, despite the fact that Reynolds Price sometimes writes with beauty and insight about women. I told her about a passage in which Price describes "the bountiful meal" that the protagonist's friend Emily "had worked on since nearly dawn," picking vegetables from the garden, walking a mile down the road to get fresh cream, frying corn cakes, baking strawberry pies.[19] My friend put her hands on her solar plexus, shutting her eyes, as she was overcome with memories of herself and other women who forever, with deft, loving, silent dedication to their task, fulfilling the traditional expectations of them, have prepared similar bountiful meals.

Dorothy Joudrie is well known as a gracious and generous hostess. I wonder what her reaction would be to Price's Emily and her role in relation to her husband and her friends—and their expectations of her. Dorothy's parties, I hear, are sophisticated, quite elaborate, and fun. The fact that her guests enjoy them suggests that she does too. Earl's business skills and aspirations carried them into a socio-economic class which was surely strange and new to both of them at first. Neither of them came from homes of the wealth and privilege that became an important part of their marriage. Those of us who live in a different socio-economic class than hers often think how simple life would be if we didn't have to worry about our yearly taxes, unexpected repairs on the car, our childrens' student loans, or exactly how much our budget will be stretched if we entertain friends for dinner. And while this may be naive on our part—the idea that life would be simpler if we had more money—the difference between the Joudries' wealth and the economic position of most of the rest of society is already an issue in Dorothy's legal case, and I suspect that people's attitudes will become more testy as time goes on. Is she ready for this?

A sad truth is that some women of Dorothy's class suffer acutely from their subservience to the men in their lives. This is a fact that is still not commonly known, and seldom recognized openly by wealthy women themselves. But some women are beginning to talk and to write about this now. They say that while they share the money and prestige and privilege their husbands provide for them, they also are expected to learn their place, their assigned role, quickly, and without questioning it. They are expected to manage the household; the children—their performance at school, their participation in other activities suitable to their family's position, their behaviour generally; and frequent and elaborate entertaining, whether or not they have hired others to do the practical work. They are expected to stay at home while their husbands travel, often for prolonged periods of time. They are also expected to sit as volunteers on boards of social agencies, hospitals, art galleries, and orchestras. Although this is beginning to change as more wealthy women have the courage to speak out, the fact is that most of this volunteer work and few of these charities have little to do with the plight of women in our society. It is a sad comment on the lack of social sophistication of many of these women, and on the extent to which they submit to their husbands' moral and ethical sensibilities, their political affiliations, and their corporate allegiances. Even more important, the reluctance of such women to align themselves with controversial issues is a reflection of their loyalty to their husbands, and in some cases their fear of undermining or threatening their husbands' professional or corporate images. Some women—and Dorothy knows about this because she has done it herself—give money generously but silently to help other women. Women of Dorothy's socio-economic class say that they are expected not to upset or criticize their husbands, but to ease their busy lives. Above all, they are expected to be quiet, and to wait.

The corporate world is very powerful. All of us know this. Why then should we be surprised that many of the men who control the economic affairs in our society expect to control their families in a similar manner? Occasionally we hear about feuding wealthy Canadian families—the power struggle between the brothers Wallace and Harrison McCain, of McCain Foods, for example. But the problem is almost always between, or among, fathers, brothers, sons, nephews; we rarely hear about the wives, daughters, sisters. They do as they are told. They say nothing. If, like Margaret McCain, Wallace's wife, who was chancellor of Mount Allison University, and in 1994 became lieutenant-governor of New Brunswick, they do speak out publicly, expressing their own views, or their disapproval or concern about family or business matters, they are soundly criticized not only by their families, but by friends of their families. Margaret McCain decided quite early that she would stay in her marriage to Wallace only if she could maintain what she considered to be an acceptable degree of independence. Some friends of her brother-in-law, Harrison, are merciless in their criticism of Margaret:

> God, she's an obsessive woman. All the things she says about Harrison can be directly applied to herself. Look, she's terribly ambitious, very focused, and plenty egocentric too. She calls Harrison a megalomaniac, but you know, the shoe's on the other foot . . . . Wallace is really not a bad fellow, you know. I always liked Wallace—it's just that he's the weak sister in the thing . . . . Margie really controls him. Family nourishment means nourishing Wallace in the direction she wants him to go. She just manipulates Wallace like a toy doll. My God, she drove a stake into Wally's scrotum. She is so full of shit . . . . Harrison has become a monster in her eyes. She's political right up to her god-damned tits. All this stuff about Harrison playing politics is just such a crock of bullshit . . . .[20]

So Margaret McCain has paid dearly for her refusal to be quiet, but she does not apologize for being strong and independent. Her greatest strength is her rejection of the traditional role of the wife of a wealthy and powerful man.

Dorothy Joudrie, and other women like her, whose husbands' power and wealth provide the advantages and luxuries they enjoy, are caught. If they challenge their subservience to their husbands, they also challenge the security of their position, the superiority of class that they enjoy. Many women like Dorothy have decided that the cost of achieving equality with their husbands, or admitting honestly that their marriage is a failure, is not worth the loss of their privileged lives.[21]

Some rich women have begun to talk about their loneliness, about the fact that they do not know how much money they—or their husbands—have; about how little money they can decide, themselves, to spend; about sexual and physical abuse in their families; about their dependence on alcohol and prescription or recreational drugs; and, most important, about their fears of what will become of them when their husbands die, or cast them off, divorce them, to make room for a second, usually younger wife. Some of these abandoned first wives—more than we know officially—succumb to depression, and finally suicide. I'm sure Dorothy knows of such women in Calgary. One woman with whom I talked about Dorothy said quietly, "At least she pointed the gun at someone else."

So, I think about Dorothy, and I wonder how she will manage the next four months of waiting, and the directions, which I am sure her lawyer has given her, not to talk with anyone about the day she created havoc.

# Preliminary Hearing

Mrs Bridge . . . was seated before her dressing table in her robe and slippers and had begun spreading cold cream on her face. The touch of the cream, the unexpectedness of it—for she had been thinking deeply about how to occupy tomorrow—the swift cool touch demoralized her so completely that she almost screamed.

She continued spreading the cream over her features, steadily observing herself in the mirror, and wondered who she was, and how she happened to be at the dressing table, and who the man was who sat on the edge of the bed taking off his shoes. She considered her fingers, which dipped into the jar of their own accord. Rapidly, soundlessly, she was disappearing into white, sweetly scented anonymity. Gratified by this she smiled, and perceived a few seconds later that beneath the mask she was not smiling. All the same, being committed, there was nothing to do but proceed.

Evan S. Connell, *Mrs Bridge*[22]

Although Dorothy's preliminary hearing is over, I am frustrated by the fact that the publication ban is still in place. It means that I still may not talk with her. This is a usual procedure in criminal cases, I have discovered, and there are serious legal consequences for anyone who contravenes this ban. Because of Earl's position in the business world, and their family's social position, there are some rumblings and accusations of privilege and special measures to protect the Joudries' privacy. Nevertheless, until the trial, the media may not report the shocking revelations they heard during those three days. But I think of the people who do know: the police in Calgary and Cochrane; members of the Calgary emergency medical team; Earl's doctor and some of the staff at the General Hospital; the staff at the Betty Ford Center in California, which Dorothy has attended since her arrest last January; the psychiatrists and psychologists who have been examining and treating her in Calgary; Mr. Justice M.C. McDonald, who presided at the hearing; Jerry Selinger, the Crown prosecutor, and some people in the Crown prosecutor's office; Noel O'Brien, Dorothy's lawyer, and his advisors and office staff; Dorothy's family and the friends in whom she confides; and those of us who were present at the hearing. No doubt there are others who belong on this long list. At first I was surprised when I overheard strangers discussing the hearing, sometimes not accurately, but certainly with authority. Despite the legal publication ban, people seem to have a perverse and irresistible need to spread bad news, shocking news. Not many people can keep secrets.

Dorothy is an exception. For almost forty years she has kept secret the true nature of her marriage: her husband's violent physical abuse of her, her children's vulnerability, her alcoholism, her loneliness, her feelings of inadequacy and self-blame, her terror of being divorced. It is quite apparent now that she took very seriously the expectations of the 1950s that no matter now fiercely fraught her family relationships might be, they must be locked behind a façade of domestic peace and bliss. No wonder she was desperate. The revelations of the witnesses at this hearing were more shocking than any of us had imagined they might be. Some people claim knowingly that they were not surprised. I don't believe them. None of us was prepared for what we heard and saw.

Because I have not attended any other criminal trial—I wonder if Dorothy has—I learned that the main function of a preliminary hearing is to allow the Crown to establish reason for a trial. The hearing also allows the defence to observe the Crown's examination of its witnesses, to cross-examine these witnesses, and consequently to see what the Crown's position is likely to be. So there is a chance, theoretically, that this case might not proceed to a trial. I did not realize until the end of the hearing, as I read over the notes I had taken, how desperately Dorothy must have hoped that this hearing would be the end. In fact, as I think of what I have learned about her marriage, and her skill at simply denying reality, I suspect that she may actually have believed that it would be the end.

Dorothy seems to have a good relationship with Noel O'Brien. He appears to treat her as an equal, but gently and respectfully. There is no obvious sign that he patronizes her. I noticed that she touched his elbow once or twice as she talked with him and laughed with him. This physical gesture appeared to be rather flirtatious, but perhaps it is simply friendly affection. It did not seem particularly inappropriate to me. But he did not touch her. He is careful. He allowed her to move about freely before the sessions began, but he kept his eye on her inconspicuously. He intervened quickly when any journalist approached her. I wonder what she thought of his performance—the manner in which he cross-examined Jerry Selinger's witnesses. I admired his cool authority; it was evident that he had done his homework, especially about battered women. I was relieved, I think, that O'Brien seemed not to hide the animus which appeared to me to be aroused in him during his cross-examination of Earl. The fact that he was not performing for a jury made this show of emotion even more reassuring.

I could not tell what Dorothy thought of Jerry Selinger, the Crown prosecutor. They were obviously very much aware of each other, but they both avoided any expression of this, and particularly any eye contact. Selinger seems to have little of O'Brien's aplomb. His almost agitated physical movements, his smile, which appears and disappears in an instant, and his apparent tendency to call attention to himself seem to reveal a nervous lack of assurance which does little to inspire confidence in the minds of any observers—fortunately for his sake, not a jury at this time. Because of the nature of the preliminary hearing, there was little opportunity to see Jerry Selinger's behaviour in a confrontational position. I suspect, however, that Noel O'Brien is a formidable opponent.

Dorothy and I have reached an age when, if we need professional help, the people on whom we must rely are almost always younger than we are. Both O'Brien and Selinger are in their mid-forties. They are mature, experienced lawyers. I wonder what they think of people who are in their sixties.

The pomp and ceremony of the court room is not quite so formal during a preliminary hearing as it is in a trial, but the procedure has the aura of theatre nonetheless. The lawyers did not wear their gowns and tabs. But the judge, wearing a gown, sat on the bench, and there was a witness box, a prisoner's dock, and the commanding "All rise!" from the clerk of the court each time the judge entered and left the room.

The atmosphere was bizarre at times. Despite the intense seriousness of the hearing, the sheriff and the officers in charge of Dorothy stood together during adjournments, telling stories and laughing rather loudly. One day while we waited for the judge, the court clerk told everyone, incidentally, that she shouldn't have gone to the gym that morning, but we did not hear why. Sometimes before the court was in session Noel O'Brien and Jerry Selinger stood at their tables laughing and talking quietly. When the judge entered, they stood apart. But I found this behaviour before the curtain rose, as it were, disconcerting and inappropriate somehow, suggesting that they were working in tandem. In fact, this chatting together was probably simply professional decorum. I discovered that there are people who pass their time attending trials and preliminary hearings. They wander about the court house looking for a case that interests them. They enter and leave the courtroom with an assurance few of the rest of us, who are strangers in this environment, can muster. When the police were there to testify, the clean, stiff, synthetic fibre of their uniforms made a sharp swish as they moved. The military stance of the female officers, with their large pistols in leather holsters strapped at their hips is a disturbing image that stays in my mind. And Dorothy. Dorothy stays in my mind.

A sophisticated young lawyer said to me recently, "The Joudrie trial, you realize, will be Calgary's social event of the year." Perhaps. But I was surprised at how few people attended the preliminary hearing. There were never more, and often fewer, than fifteen people in the courtroom. A journalist and I speculated about the identity of three men, one of whom sat each day as inconspicuously as possible in the back corner, taking copious notes. The other two talked together occasionally; one of these two, we realized soon, was Earl's corporate lawyer, Len Sali. The other man, tall, grey-haired, sturdy, and pleasant looking, was a sign of Earl's imminent appearance. "Earl's body-guard," the journalist said.

The only person who was present for Dorothy, every day, was her brother, Ken Jonason. When Mr. Jonason was interviewed by a newspaper reporter just after the shooting, he said that he hadn't seen Dorothy since they had lunched together at Christmas time. He also said that he and his sister "don't mix in the same social circles."[23] The implication was that they do not see each other regularly or often, but also that their lives are different in many ways. So I was interested not only in his faithful presence in court, but also in the fact that he was so obviously a comfort to Dorothy. When she could, she sat next to him, talked with him, and after a very emotional afternoon, he embraced her sympathetically. I know that he is her only sibling.

When I saw Dorothy on the first day of the hearing, I recognized her immediately—her large eyes, her high, wide cheekbones, the same clear olive complexion she had as a child. The gold-brown hair of her youth is silver now, stylishly cut and set. She wore a dark silk pantsuit and black patent leather flat-heeled shoes. Each day she wore a ring on her wedding-ring finger; one day it was a stunning cluster of diamonds. As she moved near me, I caught the scent of her perfume. She carries herself with dignity and grace and she moved about the room almost as if she were the hostess at a gathering she had arranged. This was the only inappropriate, even rather startling aspect of her behaviour. There was nothing timid or fragile about her appearance, but her quick, rather wheezy breathing and her sighs revealed her anxiety, her nervousness. As I listened to the revelations of her life from her husband, one of her sons, and her daughter, I realized something of what it has cost her to achieve her practised outward composure.

Two thoughts came to my mind almost simultaneously. At the time of the shooting, one of her neighbours described Dorothy as a "lovely churchgoing lady."[24] I had scorned that description initially, especially the word "lady," which I dislike, but I understand now why a man would say this about her. Everything about her outward appearance during the hearing made it almost impossible to imagine her attempting to murder her husband. My other thought was, at first, more difficult for me to understand. As I watched her, she made me think of my mother. My mother was a proud woman, who drew a very distinct line between her public and her private selves. I used to marvel at her public presence, and how different it was from the woman I knew at home. To some extent we all do this, of course. And there is little doubt that when Dorothy's trial begins, it will be the revelation of Earl's private self which will be most shocking to those who have known him only publicly. Still, there is something about Dorothy's demeanour that epitomizes the women of her class and of our generation who really took seriously their mothers' advice and society's admonitions to women, and who learned to be quiet, to wait, to listen—especially to men—to hide their thoughts and emotions, even to the extent that they no longer know who they are.

When Dorothy and I were children, little girls were often given autograph books in which we collected good wishes and wise comments about life and ourselves. Our friends wrote silly messages and riddles. Teachers and relatives and other adults we knew provided the words of wisdom. A frequent entry, often made by women, was the admonition by the nineteenth-century writer Charles Kingsley: "Be good, sweet maid, and let who will be clever." I was always a little puzzled by this advice. I knew, as every child does, that I should be good. To be addressed as a "sweet maid" was rather flattering. But what was wrong with being clever? I knew that I was clever, and to their credit, my parents had always encouraged me to be proud of that. What they had not taught me, and this is even more to their credit, is that I should hide the fact that I was clever. As I grew older and observed other girls and women, I realized that many people thought clever women were dangerous, unwholesome, and most important, unfeminine. I realized, finally, that ladies learn how to let men be clever, and that deception is an important part of being a lady.

During the hearing Dorothy sat in the prisoner's dock, watching and listening to the lawyers and the witnesses. We could see her face, which was often a pale, still, guarded mask. When the testimony of some of the witnesses was profoundly disturbing, she turned her whole body away from the observers in the room, leaning forward, resting her elbows on her knees, absolutely absorbed by what the witnesses said, and not allowing any of us to see her tears, and her private emotion. After the hearing one of her neighbours asked her how it had been for her, and according to this neighbour, Dorothy said, "Fine. It was just fine. Everything went very well."

# Polished Brass Doors

Now, sitting and waiting on the bench in this little chamber,
which already seems like the dungeon it could change into
at any moment, I wonder whether this conclusion could
have been avoided. Whether it's really the case that a chain
of circumstances I was powerless to alter has driven me to
my place on this bench, or whether perhaps something
inside of me I didn't have control of has forced me to go in
this direction.

Christa Wolf, *Medea: A Modern Retelling*[25]

At Dorothy Joudrie's arraignment today we learned that her trial will begin
on April 22, 1996. Her jury will be selected on April 18.

This was a bitterly cold November day—windy, and the snow after rain
last night made walking and driving treacherous. I slipped and fell as I
walked along the icy sidewalk on 8th Avenue. I had thought that the street
was almost deserted, but a man and a woman were there suddenly. They lift-
ed me gently to my feet, commiserating, enquiring about my well-being.

Dorothy's case now is in the Court of Queen's Bench, a solid building, with two huge polished brass doors that signify the solemnity, the dignity, the authority of the legal decisions made here.

The courtroom was filled with people waiting their trial dates. At the
front of the room eighteen lawyers, in full regalia, gathered with the noisy
flourish of a society of magpies. Ten minutes before the proceedings
began, Noel O'Brien ushered Dorothy in to a seat in the front row. People

had to squeeze together to make room for her and her brother, Ken, who sat beside her. Her name was called first and her charges were presented so quickly and quietly that some people, distracted for a moment, would not even have noticed that she was there.

# Memories

On the mountain stands a lady,
Who she is I do not know,
All she wants is gold and silver,
All she wants is a very fine man . . . .
                    Skipping song (Coventry, 1970)[26]

Women have often felt insane when cleaving to the truth of
our experience. Our future depends on the sanity of each of
us, and we have a profound stake, beyond the personal, in
the project of describing our reality as candidly and fully as
we can to each other.
          Adrienne Rich, *On Lies, Secrets, and Silence*[27]

At the edge of every experience is the refracted light of
recollection, snagged there like an image in a beveled mirror.
          Carol Shields, *The Stone Diaries*[28]

Once a week I meet with four friends in a small coffee shop where we
draw our chairs close around a table just large enough to hold our mugs
and bowls of coffee or tea and the occasional muffin or cookie. In the winter we arrange our coats, scarves, purses, and books carefully, near our
chairs. As women who are both assertive and respectful of others, we claim
without ceremony a certain allotment of space, but not too much in relation to the other customers. Otherwise we are unaware of anyone else,
except in hindsight, when we might recall the facial expression of someone

who was listening to us—amused, or curious, or surprised. Our discussion of language and literature, specific texts and theories, is sometimes quite intense, since this is the formal intellectual interest we share. The youngest of us is in her mid-forties. We rarely discuss our domestic responsibilities. When we are together we put aside, for the moment, these homely burdens. Our talk is lively, interspersed with laughter. Here, we have no ties. We are free to be ourselves. Our conversation fills us up, reassures us, rejuvenates us.

At sixty, I am the oldest. I wonder if Dorothy finds it as difficult as I do to believe that she is on the verge of old age. I hate to admit that there are moments when I am aware of a sort of phantom of old age that hovers annoyingly around me. This prescience is aggravated by the fact that society, generally, includes people of our age—Dorothy's and mine—in the category called "seniors." I am not ready yet to be a senior, but I cannot escape the fact that it is fifty years since she and I knew each other. Fifty years.

Thinking of Dorothy as I have during the past year has caused me to remember specific details of my childhood in Edmonton, many of which I thought I had forgotten. I realize that I am remembering what we have in common, and also how different our lives have been. I think of how we both embraced and resisted the expectations of us as we were growing up, and our discovery of the complexity of women's lives. Since her daughter Carolyn testified at her preliminary hearing, I find myself thinking of our mothers, of relationships between mothers and daughters. I have two sons, but I do not have a daughter. When my second son was born, I discovered that I was relieved not to have a daughter. My relationship with my mother was difficult in many ways, and I think I was afraid of the responsibility of bringing up a daughter.

Does Dorothy remember, I wonder, the airplane we built as an enterprise project in Miss Tyner's grade three classroom at Queen Alex school? It was built with thin strips of light wood and bumpy grey construction paper which we coloured with poster paints. The body of the plane must have rested on chairs, because two students could sit in it and it was so large that our desks had to be pushed back against the walls of the room to accommodate it. Some of our fathers were flying planes like this, we imagined. But both men and women built the real planes, in factories. And, in grade four, Miss Twiss's cozy gabled room, up the narrow stairs, on the third floor? She had her own piano in that room, and I used to imagine the struggle it must have been for the janitors to get it up there. She encouraged us to borrow her books. "Jean Twiss" she had written on the flyleaf, which made her seem not like a teacher at all. I would stare at that signature as I sat on my bed at home, with the book in my lap, more fascinated by my dreamy speculations about her than by the book itself. I think I loved Miss Twiss. But I loved books too, even then. We had books at home, which I read and which were read to me, but other books seemed more exciting somehow.

Miss Auxier, the librarian at the Strathcona Public Library, taught me how to borrow books with my own card. I suspect she taught Dorothy as well, because I remember that Dorothy's friend Ann was Miss Auxier's niece. My mother took me to the library the same day that I ran home from school to announce that I could read. Learning to read had been a matter of contention between my mother and me. She resisted my curiosity, my coaxing for help, because as a former teacher, she believed that children who could read when they started school were a nuisance. But during my first month at school it happened suddenly; like magic, the words came alive. I remember resting my chin on my arms as I leaned on the curved counter at the library, watching Miss Auxier print my name, my full name, including Elizabeth, which I liked better than Audrey. I remember the style of her printing, the round-square letters, announcing firmly, officially, that this card was mine. Perhaps the reason I recall this incident so vividly is that I was seeing my name, recognizing what identified me, for the first time. During the next twelve years I became so familiar with the stacks and the little side room in that small library that I was sure I had read every book. I also remember the smell of the library—musty, warm, exciting. Miss Auxier and the other librarians—all women—often brought bouquets of flowers, and I remember that the strong sweet scent of lilacs in the spring, the peonies in early summer, and later the delicate scent of sweet peas and baby's breath could not mask that other enticing smell of the books.

These quiet-spoken, gentle, unmarried women were the guardians of knowledge. They did their job well—a job fit for women probably only because the pay was so meagre. But what freedom they gave us to choose! I remember when I first began to choose books from the adult section, starting discreetly, I hoped, with one of Zane Grey's adventures from a long shelf of his books at the back of the stacks. There were other books I wanted to borrow, books we didn't have at home, or at school. I had read parts of them as I stood between the stacks as unobtrusively as possible, looking, sampling. But there were no objections when I finally got the courage to take to the desk *Anna Karenina, Gone with the Wind, A Tree Grows in Brooklyn*, Gabrielle Roy's *The Tin Flute*, Edna St. Vincent Millay's poetry, George Orwell's *1984*. I remember sitting on the big rock at the end of the library sidewalk talking about *Nineteen Eighty-four* with my CGIT leader, Mrs. Lang.

I think that Dorothy, also, belonged to CGIT, although at another church than the one my family attended. I was surprised when Earl mentioned CGIT quite casually during his testimony at the preliminary hearing, when he told that Dorothy's second cousin, Lynn Manning, who became the "other woman" in Dorothy's life, had stayed with them, years ago, when she came to Calgary to attend CGIT conferences. CGIT was an important influence on many young girls. "Canadian Girls In Training—for what?" smart boys liked to ask. CGIT was dedicated to helping girls to learn about themselves and about the world, and about "knowing God," and "seeking Truth"—lofty ideals. For several years I was absolutely committed to CGIT, and I don't regret that. I learned how to think rationally, and how to talk with other girls and women, and if that was all I learned it would have been enough. I also learned self-confidence, and how to speak in public, and that it was important not only to think about others but to do something for them. I loved the summer camps. I sang the hymns and said the prayers with a fervour that I realize now was inspired more by a teenaged girl's love of ceremony and sentimentality than by what I thought then was a sophisticated commitment to Christian beliefs.

My mother stood silently in the background during my CGIT years. She never expressed overt disapproval, but I knew that she was not quite comfortable with what I was doing. She came to the yearly mother-daughter banquets with me, and any other events at which I had an important role. Very early I had learned to iron my own blouses because I didn't like the way my mother did them, but she continued to wash and iron my CGIT middies. They were beautifully white, and without the tiniest wrinkle, and she knew that I appreciated the results of her practiced hand. When I was older, I realized that my mother couldn't have imagined herself leading girls in activities like this. I think she believed that women who did this were caught, themselves, in a kind of everlasting adolescent fog of romance and sentimentality, a silliness, that ought to be outgrown, not nourished, as it seemed to her to be by the women who were our leaders, and who were willing to spend so much time with us. In this respect, my mother was like the young Del Jordan's vision of her mother in Alice Munro's *Lives of Girls and Women*. Del remembers her mother at the house at the end of the Flats Road: "I would watch her walk across the yard to empty the dishwater, carrying the dishpan high, like a priestess, walking in an unhurried, stately way, and flinging the dishwater with a grand gesture over the fence."[29]

This description, and especially the "flinging," remind me of my vision of my mother when I was a child—my mother, who often seemed simply consumed by worry and anxiety, but who could also be quite self-possessed, even snobbish, and about some things, absolutely confident.

But these qualities I thought I saw in my mother did not endear her to me then. They embarrassed me and disappointed me. They caused me, instead of listening to her, to listen carefully to my CGIT leaders and my home economics teacher when they told us how to be ladies. For in the end, that was what all girls must be. It was what all girls wanted to be. Our home economics teacher taught us about personal hygiene, the importance of wearing a girdle and a brassiere, stylish pencil-slim skirts and sweater sets, and that our hair would shine only if we used shampoo, not the melted Ivory soap that I used at home. My mother's aura of self-possession and confidence created a distance between us, and very early on I learned not to tell her everything I did. From about age thirteen, I went every week to the Varscona Theatre to see movies with my friend Muriel. My parents knew where I was, of course, but it never occurred to me to tell them that the film *Waterloo Bridge*, with Robert Taylor and Vivien Leigh, was a film I considered more romantic than any other I had seen during those early years of adolescence. Vivien Leigh, consumptive and desperate, became a prostitute while she waited for Robert Taylor to come back from the war. How soiled, how filled with shame she was when she saw her pure, clean, courageous warrior, safely home! My heart broke for her—because I thought I knew then, very well, what it meant to be a lady.

But, like many other children, I had a private life long before I was in my teens. When I was in grades five and six I knew a quiet, rather sad and solitary girl, Ruth, whose home was much more luxurious than those my family and friends' families could afford. It was a large house, with shiny, new, white appliances in the spotless, tiled kitchen; soft rugs throughout the rest of the house, even on the stairs; heavy velvet drapes and deep cushioned furniture; and a new record player in the living room. Ruth's sister was at university. She had a car, and beautiful, stylish, scented clothes, which Ruth showed us proudly and let us try on. Ruth's sister and her mother had mink coats. Her mother, who was never there except when a number of us stayed overnight once or twice and whom we saw briefly on her way out for the evening, seemed kind and generous, and rather amused by us. She was quite stunning, with her long blond hair pulled back in a chignon. We never saw Ruth's father. When Ruth invited us occasionally to her house after school, we were always alone. We closed the drapes, took off all of our clothes, put her sister's newest Frank Sinatra records on the record player, and accompanied by that sweet sexy voice, we danced, by ourselves, on the luxurious carpet, perfectly naked, and as free as birds. We did not laugh at ourselves. We were very serious. And what we were doing was unbelievably thrilling, sensuous—and innocent. We never talked about these afternoons with anyone else, or even among ourselves. We felt no shame or embarrassment, but we sensed that others, especially our parents, would not understand. We didn't know, of course, about Isadora Duncan: her dancing, her independent spirit and wild pursuit of freedom, her diaphanous gowns and veils, and huge, flowing shawls—her fatal, red tasselled shawl.[30] But I think of her now as I recall our perfect, uninhibited pleasure. We were children who one day would be women, some of us wives and mothers. How would we pursue our freedom? I wonder what has become of Ruth, and the others. I wonder if they, too, remember those magic afternoons.

I imagine that Dorothy's home, in many ways, was like mine. Our mothers taught us by example the importance of an organized household: general tidiness; beds always made in the morning; clean sheets; clean bathrooms; meals at the same time every day when everyone sat together at a small family ceremony, the tablecloth and serviettes freshly ironed, the cutlery set carefully at each person's usual place. At Sunday dinners, after church, our fathers carved the roast; our mothers served the vegetables; we had washed our hands and faces not only for the sake of our health but out of respect for others. Our mothers organized the daily and yearly activities in our families. We learned from them, and not only from society generally, the importance of the gracious wife, the nurturing mother, the healthy, happy, safe home.

My mother, like Dorothy's, was a teacher before her marriage. She was in her mid-thirties when she married; by that time she had established herself as a high school Latin teacher and a musician, and she was well aware of her professional identity and her independence. Yet, married women were not allowed to teach in those days, and when she married, she submitted, happily she said, to her new role as a wife and mother. It was many years later, of course, that I realized that a pleasantly ordered household was important to her because it was what defined her, identified her in her new, real life.

As a child I was glad that my mother kept our house as she did, and I realize now, of course, that the order she created provided me and my brother, and my father too, with an important sense of security. She was not obsessed by her housework; she seemed to do it unobtrusively and if there was any apparent emotion about doing it, I think it was pleasure. She never complained about it or railed at us, as some other mothers did, for walking with wet feet on a clean kitchen floor. Also, my mother was a good cook, and she seemed to prepare meals easily—no small accomplishment I have learned. She always welcomed our friends as guests. She often sat in the kitchen as she waited for everyone to arrive home for lunch or dinner. I remember one day when I was about twelve, when she and I were waiting together, talking, and I said impulsively that I would like to sit on her knee. We laughed at my childish request to be held, comforted, especially since we were about the same size. But she opened her arms and took me on her lap, embracing and rocking me, still laughing, but also recognizing that I needed her love and attention.

But there were other things about my mother that did not make me happy, and that disturbed me for years. It wasn't until I was in my forties that I realized why my mother was so hurt sometimes by my behaviour, why she seemed so critical of me. I knew that I hurt her because she told me that I did. It is interesting that I cannot remember what I did that upset her. But as a child and a teenager it seemed to me that there was something wrong, something particularly selfish about her being hurt by the way I behaved. If she had felt angry or concerned I think I could have accepted that. But I felt confused and very resentful about her being hurt, and consequently I did not feel sorry. What's more, I vowed that I would never tell my own children, if I had any, that they had hurt me. It was a dramatic revelation when after all those years, I understood, finally, that from her point of view everything I was and did was a reflection of her. If I wasn't the person she wanted me to be, or expected me to be, or the person she thought others expected me to be, then she didn't matter.

When my mother was at university she had a close friend who became a teacher, too, and later a professor at a university in another province.

Because she lived so far away, and also because she didn't marry and have children, she and my mother grew apart somewhat, and visited only occasionally, but they wrote to each other several times a year. I liked this woman. She was gentle and feminine, intelligent and independent. She was one of my heroes—all of whom, I realize now, were professional women who were not married. When she was in her fifties, my mother's friend announced suddenly that she was going to be married to a widower who had grown children. My parents seemed very pleased for her and sent her and her husband a gift and good wishes, and she and my mother began to correspond more frequently. About three years after her marriage, my mother's friend died. Not long after her death, my mother and I were talking one day about marriage—I was in my early twenties, not yet married, visiting my parents during a university break—and I said how sad it was that this woman had died when she was so young and before she had really had time to enjoy her marriage. I asked my mother what had caused her death. "I think she died of unhappiness," my mother said. "She found being married very difficult. It made her very unhappy." I realized at that moment that my mother knew more about life than I had thought she did—things she and I had never discussed.

Lately, I think often of what it has cost some women to be good and sweet, but not too clever; to be attractive—even sensuous—but not brazen and dangerous; to manage households, raise children, and be good wives, but not lose ourselves. I think of how we learned from the time we were little girls the importance of discretion and keeping private not only our hopes and dreams and pleasures, but our fears of failure, disappointment, and loss of love and respect. I think of the awful secrets hidden in closed drawers, locked behind shut doors. Certainly Dorothy Joudrie learned the importance of discretion and privacy and secrecy very well—too well.

On two or three occasions women have asked me to tell them when I became a feminist. These were mature women whose discovery of feminism changed their lives suddenly and dramatically, almost like a religious conversion. I had difficulty answering their question, and I remember saying quite seriously to at least one of them that I must have got it with my mother's milk. This was a lie. Male obstetricians during the 1930s persuaded many women, including my mother, not to nurse their babies.

My mother and I never discussed feminism and I suspect she might not have considered herself a feminist. Nevertheless, it was she who taught me the importance of getting a good education, of having a profession, of earning my own money, of cherishing women friends. She also taught me by example to like men, not to diminish them, or to use them, or to flirt with them. She told me many times that it would be better not to marry at all than to marry a man who did not love and respect me as much as I did him. And my father taught me, also, by example, what I should expect in the man I chose to be my husband. Dorothy's father and mine were gentle, wise men whom we loved.

Despite all this, if my mother had suggested to me on the eve of my wedding, as Dorothy says her mother did to her, that I could cancel my wedding, that it would be better for me not to marry than to marry a man about whom I had serious doubts,[31] I suspect I might have done what she did, especially if I had been as young as she was. Dorothy knew, even then, and apparently her parents did too, that Earl could be possessive, jealous, impetuous, and sometimes cruel. But I understand why she went ahead with her wedding. I can imagine many reasons for her decision. She couldn't face the embarrassment of cancelling it, and the inevitable scorn and pity. She worried about Earl's reaction, if she were to reject him. Also, she loved Earl, and thought that she knew him better than her parents did. She was sure that when they were married he would change. Above all, she wanted, as almost all young women did in those days, to be married. She couldn't possibly have imagined that her marriage would end as it did. And as I write this, the image of Earl walking through the door of the courtroom during Dorothy's preliminary hearing is vivid in my mind.

The provincial court building where the hearing took place is an example of 1960s architecture gone wrong: an open bare concrete structure that seeks to let light in, but only obstructs it. The physical darkness is compounded by the building's juxtaposition to the police station, and the north windows giving out on a dreary, ugly, treeless street. As I sat each day in the waiting area before I could go into the courtroom, I thought how depressing this gloomy atmosphere must be for the people here who are frightened and troubled and lost.

That afternoon when we were finally seated, waiting for the session to begin, the air was electric with tension and nervous expectation. We had discovered during the lunch break that Earl would testify in the afternoon. The same few people who were there each day were present, as well as a man and woman who I assumed were related to Earl, and armed policemen, whom we had not seen before. They were there to protect Earl from Dorothy. Len Sali, a corporate lawyer, and one of Earl's party, slipped quickly, several times, in and out of the courtroom through a private door at the side. He looked at Dorothy, the people in the gallery, the empty witness box. He appeared anxious, uncomfortable, self-conscious. I watched him, fascinated. What was his purpose here? Dorothy seemed to be very nervous, not sure where she should sit as she waited. For a few moments she sat directly in front of me and she made a rather derogatory but humorous comment about Mr. Sali. Suddenly the clerk was present, we rose while the judge entered, Dorothy took her place in the prisoner's dock, and Earl, accompanied by his "bodyguard," was entering the room.

The expression on his face at that moment seemed almost triumphant. All of us turned to watch his entrance, and the grandiosity exuded by the presence of this corporate executive was extraordinary. "Where are the trumpets!" I wanted to ask the journalist beside me. Everything was happening so quickly. Mr. Selinger arranged for a chair to be put in the witness box, saying that Mr. Joudrie was rather "unsteady." Mr. Selinger asked him how we should pronounce his name. Mr. Selinger asked him to tell the whole story. Such deference! This witness—Earl Joudrie himself, the man Dorothy says she will always love, the man she tried to murder—began to speak.

I recognized Earl just as I had Dorothy. His hair is thinner, his face has broadened, as men's faces do as they age, and he has gained weight which is exaggerated somewhat by the way he stands. He pushes his chest and abdomen forward. He declined Selinger's suggestion that he sit. As he spoke, and was questioned by Selinger and then O'Brien, the people in the courtroom sat in shocked silence. All of us knew that Dorothy had shot Earl, not once, but six times. We had read about it in the papers and now we had listened to the police tell us the details of her actions. We had seen the gun, the bullet casings, the bullet holes in Earl's jacket, photographs of his blood on the garage floor. His telling about the incident made it more dramatic, more real. But that was not all he told.

I have known since I was a child that some men beat up their wives. My mother had warned me not to go near a house in our neighbourhood where the husband was known to be dangerous. But now I was sitting ten feet away from Earl Joudrie as he described how he beat Dorothy. Both lawyers had to urge him to give the details, and O'Brien, especially, had to insist, sometimes unsuccessfully, that he tell about particularly violent incidents. Earl wept once or twice when he talked about "the good times" in their marriage and as he described Dorothy shooting him. But when he told about beating her, there were no tears. He was in complete control. His dispassionate use of the passive voice was breathtaking: "Dorothy was struck."

When the court was dismissed, some of us continued to sit, silently, unable to gather ourselves together to leave, trying to absorb not only what we had just witnessed, but also our reactions to it. How could I have been so unprepared to hear this? I had known all along that something had driven Dorothy to her act of violence. What Earl had done to her was brutal, and the way he talked about it made it worse. As we sat, she seemed quite unaware of us. She left the prisoner's dock and stood, alone, at the window, weeping silently, looking out at the desolate street.

# The Jury

What are little boys made of?
What are little boys made of?
    Frogs and snails
    And puppy-dogs' tails,
That's what little boys are made of.

What are little girls made of?
What are little girls made of?
    Sugar and spice
    And all that's nice,
That's what little girls are made of.
              Iona and Peter Opie, *The Oxford
              Dictionary of Nursery Rhymes*[32]

As I looked at the 135 potential jurors who were summoned by a court order to appear on this sunny April afternoon, I saw few grey heads. The average age was about thirty-five to forty. Perhaps a third of the group were in their twenties. About 90 percent seemed to be middle-class Caucasians, and although I did not count them I thought there were more women than men. It is from this group of people that Dorothy Joudrie's jury was chosen today. At last, after fifteen months, the final and crucial part of the legal process of judging her actions has begun.

Jury lists are prepared annually from a random selection from census or voters' lists. In Alberta these people must be residents of the province

41

and Canadian citizens who are eighteen years of age or older. Anyone who has been convicted of a criminal offense for which they could have been imprisoned for twelve months or more cannot be a juror. Others also are exempted from this duty, including lawyers, government employees, and members of the police force. Members of the pool of potential jurors, if they are chosen to serve on a jury, may ask the judge to excuse them because of severe illness, inability to understand English or French depending on the language of the accused, travel obligations, economic hardship, inability to see or hear, if they are a friend or relative of the accused, or if they have personal knowledge of the case. All that is known about potential jurors is their name, age, address, and occupation. We learned all of this from the sheriff and from a short film, which explained the history of the jury system since the time of Socrates—a slick, upbeat promotion of our legal processes, and only incidentally of our colonial position in relation to Great Britain. In Canada, the film explained, the jury system is regarded as "a cornerstone of democracy." The fact that scholars have debated the efficacy of this system for as long as it has existed was, of course, not part of the presentation. Within seconds of the conclusion of the film we witnessed a test of the democratic nature of our justice system.

Dorothy was not in the room during this initial presentation. Consequently she did not hear the presiding judge, Justice Sal LoVecchio, explain that he knows the Joudries, but that if O'Brien and Selinger agreed, he would not feel obliged to disqualify himself from this particular impersonal procedure. I was staggered by this announcement. No doubt this judge had decided, or he had been advised, that he should be honest about his relationship with the Joudries. I commend him for that. But the media reminds us constantly that Dorothy and Earl are different from most of the rest of us, and now we know that Justice LoVecchio may, perhaps, be an acquaintance or a friend. I suspect that there were others in that room who have friends, acquaintances, and relatives who are lawyers or judges, and this fact says nothing, necessarily, about them. But because Dorothy has been charged with committing a serious crime, and she is in the public eye, her relationship to this judge adds to the public's information, or misinformation, about her and the people she knows, and it prompted one journalist to remark in print, again, about the "powerful circles" in which she moves.[33] Isn't it strange, I wondered, that Justice LoVecchio did not think that his presence on the bench, even for this one occasion, might disturb Dorothy, embarrass her? More important, I wondered if he realized the inevitable implications of what he was doing? Some people may think that there is a possibility that her trial, even though it is in a court of law, is simply a formal exercise performed for show by friends inside the "powerful circles" to which she belongs.

Neither O'Brien nor Selinger objected. The damage was done. Justice LoVecchio was smiling casually, kindly, as he explained this unusual coincidence. There were no smiles from O'Brien and Selinger as they urged the proceedings along as quickly as possible. And Justice LoVecchio, apparently unconcerned, assumed his traditional and paternalistic position in the courtroom, speaking to everyone briefly, expressing the hope that the chosen jurors would find the experience "interesting and rewarding."

Dorothy's case was not first today. Lawyers for two young men chose their jury from the pool before Noel O'Brien and Jerry Selinger began. Shortly before the end of this first case, O'Brien brought Dorothy into the room and seated her among the potential jurors. I was sitting on the side, just a few feet away, facing her. I was shocked by her appearance. She was dressed as carefully as she had been at the preliminary hearing, but she seemed to have gained weight, her hair was wind-blown, and her face was rather puffy. She looked strained, anxious, even haggard. When it was time, she entered the prisoner's dock quickly, but she kept her head down. She was breathing heavily, and sighing. As her charges were read—attempted murder, aggravated assault, use of a hand gun—she looked embarrassed, ashamed. In fact, her appearance and behaviour today seemed more suitable to the occasion, more fitting for a person charged with these crimes than it had seemed to be, sometimes, during the preliminary hearing. She behaved as people expected she should. I suspect that since she had now accepted the inevitability of a trial, she was experiencing a great complexity of emotions, perhaps including anger. There were no tears, no signs of self-pity.

Now, at this final stage, the jurors are chosen by lot. In the presence of this assembly, the clerk of the court draws individual names from a box. The box itself appeared to be a relic from the Middle Ages—an old, varnished, wooden, slatted tub, resting horizontally on fulcrums at each end, with a handle on one end which the clerk used to turn the tub and tumble the names inside. From an opening in the tub, which must be closed securely as she turned it, she drew the names. Surely this is one of the most cherished props of the lawcourt/theatre. Certainly it is significant. From it come the jurors who determine the fate of people charged with serious crimes. Yet when I asked a clerk what this box is called, for an object of such age and importance must have a name, she didn't know.

The clerk draws the names of small groups of people, who walk to the front of the courtroom where they are introduced to the lawyers. Each lawyer is allowed twelve peremptory challenges. No conversation takes place between the lawyers and the potential jurors. The lawyers scrutinize these people one at a time. They make their decisions surprisingly quickly. What have they seen, I wonder, that tells them they should choose one person and not another? The process reminded me of a cattle auction I attended once. How does the potential juror feel, standing there, stroked, patted, poked, prodded, weighed by the eyes of these two men? Can the very substance of their selves be seen?

Observing the jury selection interested me for several reasons, not the least my reservations about trials by juries, and particularly the belief that people are judged by "juries of their peers." Before the procedure began I looked over this gathering of people and picked out only one woman who I thought might be Dorothy's peer. As it turned out, her name was drawn from the box, she was accepted by both lawyers, but she exempted herself because she knows Dorothy and plays golf with her.

Both Selinger and O'Brien used their full quota of twelve challenges and Dorothy's jury consists of eleven women and one man. This unusual gender imbalance will be the topic of controversy no doubt. But on the basis of my conversations about Dorothy with women, I am not sure that a majority of women on her jury will necessarily work in her favour. Also, all of the jurors are younger, some much younger, than she is. I wonder if any of them is a member of her socio-economic class. As their names were called some of them looked worried, perhaps due to adjustments they will have to make in their private lives during the absence from their normal activities. They may be absent from their jobs and homes for long periods, even though this jury will not be sequestered until the end of the trial. They also looked resigned. Both the sheriff and the judge did their best to make the atmosphere at this gathering pleasant and comfortable. They expressed confidence in these people who will fulfill their duty as citizens. I suspect that at the end of her trial Dorothy's jury will look back on this day and marvel at what they didn't know: the weight of their responsibility is an experience none of them is likely to forget. But obviously the serious nature of their task did not escape them even on this day.

Dorothy looked at each juror as they were chosen, but I could not tell what she was thinking. I am sure that she was as puzzled as I was by the lawyers' choice of some people and their rejection of others. She seemed preoccupied, probably by the weight of her situation generally.

It is Thursday. Dorothy's trial begins on Monday. However much she has dreaded it, and hoped that it would not happen, she must feel some relief that finally it is about to begin.

# Women's Voices

What would happen if one woman told the truth about
                her life?
    The world would split open
          Muriel Rukeyser, from her poem
          "Käthe Kollwitz"[34]

But I have been taken aback sometimes to hear her speak of
her own sex with a kind of contempt. "Women are always so
jealous," she told me once, with a grimace.
          Kennedy Fraser, in conversation with Nina
          Berberova, in Kennedy Fraser, *Ornament and*
          *Silence: Essays on Women's Lives*[35]

The winter of 1995-96 in Calgary was unusually cold and long. Many days in March seemed as bitter and dreary and uncomfortable as those in December. I had begun to realize for the first time in my life how important it was for me to watch my step in the snow and ice, that falling might have serious consequences now. I longed for spring, and warmth, and the freedom to step out confidently, taking pleasure in my usual stride.

    Several years ago I taped on the wall of my workroom a snapshot of two women at a summer picnic. The women are sitting side by side, eating their lunch, laughing, and they have put their foreheads together, looking each other in the eye, as children do to get the optical distortion of one eye. When I did this as a little girl with other children, at the moment of contact we would shriek, delightedly, "Owl!" One of the women in this snapshot is about twenty years younger than the other, and when I used to look at this picture, I always looked at her. Now I look more often at the older woman, who leans her whole body towards the other. Her back, her neck, are not so pliable as the younger woman's.

I found myself looking often that winter at photographs of women. I looked at photos of my grandmothers—both beautiful, proud women, posing modestly, graciously, for an unseen photographer; a picture of my mother, wearing her academic gown, walking in her parents' garden on the day she graduated from university; another of my mother with a good friend—both are laughing and posing in woolen bathing suits and a parasol on a narrow sandy beach at the edge of trees and shrubs. The photographer was the third member of their group, when the three of them took a boat trip to Alaska in the 1920s. Some of the photographs I looked at are from the collections of professional photographers. There are pictures of women alone, but I was more interested in photos of women with a friend, or in a group. I looked at their facial expressions, their hands, the position of their bodies as they sat or stood, their appearance of comfort or discomfort, of joy or sadness, where their eyes rested—on the others, or on the camera. When I was with my women friends, I watched them carefully—their expressions of pleasure, excitement, affection, and sometimes pain, or irritation, or frustration. I seemed to be endlessly fascinated by women's relationships with each other.

During that winter I spent many hours talking on the telephone with other women, most of whom I didn't know and never met. This was part of my research. I was surprised that I found so many women who would talk with me. A few of these women accepted my invitation to meet, and we continued our conversations over lunch or coffee. Some I met inadvertently, or I was introduced to them at social gatherings, and we talked quietly, undisturbed for a few minutes. But most of the women talked with me only on condition that they would remain anonymous, that I would not use their names in my book about Dorothy, if I repeated what they told me.

But I wanted to talk not only with wives of corporate executives, but with women who are, or were, corporate executives themselves, women who belong, or have belonged, in what are known as "executive suites." I know a few women who have senior or administrative positions at the university, and I talked with some of them, but I knew almost no women in the corporate world. So I began by calling a woman whose name I had been given by a friend. I introduced myself, told her about my project, and after we talked at some length, she gave me the name of another woman she thought would be willing to talk with me. And so it went. Most of these women seemed to be very candid when they talked about their professional lives. They are engineers, geologists, geophysicists. Some have MBAs, or are specialists in departments such as human resources. Some of these women have been very successful in their work; they enjoy the competitive atmosphere of their professional lives; they are stimulated rather than threatened by the challenge of being the only woman at a boardroom table. Yes, they admitted, there are sometimes difficulties surviving in what is still a man's world, but they are prepared for this and satisfied that they can hold their own. Most of these women were cautious in expressing any opinion about Dorothy Joudrie, but some were very outspoken. A small group who have left their jobs talked bitterly about their experiences. All but one woman in this latter group were compassionate in their views about Dorothy. The one woman who was the exception had no kind words to say about the Joudries and "the whole disgusting mess," as she called it.

As Dorothy's trial date approached, gossip about the Joudries was rife in Calgary. It was during these weeks that a woman who is authoritative, confident, and successful in her profession announced to a group of women, at a social gathering, that there would be no Joudrie trial. She explained that the compromises, the plea bargaining, the procedure to avoid a trial was quite simple, quite discreet. What was happening was for Dorothy's benefit. I had heard that there were such rumours about, but this was the first time I had been confronted with this directly. As I listened to her, I remembered Dorothy at her arraignment, pleading not guilty to three criminal acts. Then, her trial dates were announced. But partly because my own knowledge of the law is not sophisticated enough to withstand much debate—my mind was spinning with a search for plea bargains that might be advantageous to Dorothy—and also because I do not underestimate the behind-the-scenes influence of powerful people, I did not want to argue with this woman. But I had one question. Where had she got this information? From two judges, she said, at a small dinner party that week. She was quite assured that powerful men, including Earl—the alleged victim of Dorothy's assault—would fix her up, would look after her. It did not seem to occur to this woman, or at least she did not say, that by avoiding a trial, Earl would also look after himself, his own reputation.

My first reaction to this announcement was to remind myself that judges had a right to their private opinions, and perhaps even to gossip among close friends and colleagues at an intimate gathering. Then I began to think of all of my conversations about Dorothy during the past fourteen months, of the complexity of people's attitudes, and particularly women's attitudes, towards Dorothy and her trial. I thought of the many and often contradictory roles Dorothy and I, and other women, have learned to play in our society.

One day I realized that the women I had talked with fell into two groups. The first group were women who were thoughtful, sometimes tentative initially, but finally confident in their own views, which were sometimes, but not always, generous about Dorothy. The second group, when they expressed an opinion, were pleased to say that their information had come from male lawyers, judges, doctors, CEOs, and that, therefore, it carried an authority beyond their own judgement. They were apparently quite proud to defer to men of a certain position, and to announce to me, another woman, that these men had confided in them. It occurred to me now that these are women who know how to be one of the men, or more crudely, "one of the good old boys." Perhaps I had not realized this sooner because, while I know about such women, I have never bothered to try to understand them. I have never felt accepted by them. I feel intimidated by them. I feel betrayed by them. But for the first time, I began to think about how women do this. I wondered if they knew that they were acting out the oldest, even legendary, competition among women—the competition for the attention of men. They seemed not to realize that they are compromising their integrity, and other women's as well, as they reinforce the worst expectations of women, and for that matter of men.

I began to realize that although it seems to be contradictory, such women earn their place among men, their welcome and comfort in executive suites, in faculty clubs, in confidential conversations with male judges at dinner parties, by exploiting their traditional roles as ladies. They play a clever game of just the right amount of flattery, flirtation, subservience, and complicity. On its darker side, this can be a game of perverse manipulation, a cruel game of trickery, deception, and careful, deliberate control. It is the old game of power; many men and women know it. Despite its ruthlessness, some people seem to enjoy it. Society has taught us how to play it. Not many men are threatened by this game when they play it with women: they believe, and with some justification, that in the end they will have the upper hand. Women disappear suddenly from senior positions in corporations, and their objections, if they are prepared to fight, fall on deaf ears, but not necessarily because the majority of their colleagues are men. Their female colleagues do not come to their aid. Too much is at stake. They are silent. Some other women disappear as wives of corporate executives. Their objections, if they are brave enough to make them, are ignored. To object is pitiful, unseemly, unladylike, and some of these women, as I have said before, turn their anger against themselves. The social milieu in which they once belonged no longer embraces them. They read about their former husband's "golden handshake" in the newspapers. It is their husband's second wife who stands beside him on the platform, sharing this corporate tribute to him. No one even mentions his first wife. It is as if the years that she devoted to him and their family, and even she herself, have simply vanished. Feminists today would say that these women have been "erased."

Of course some men fall, in the power game, and when they do, it is often women who are blamed. As Dorothy knows too well, in extreme cases—of spousal abuse, for example—some women do bring down their men, literally. Society parodies these so-called "dangerous" women as a warning to men—and to women. Think of Clytemnestra, Medea, Medusa.

The lack of sympathy some women express for Dorothy, especially some women of her socio-economic class, is sad and disturbing. When I ask these women to explain their reaction, and the reaction of their friends, they tell me that women are jealous. Jealous of what, I want to know. This question often causes a sour facial expression, arms raised in exasperation, scorn, and accusations that I am being disingenuous. Everyone, everyone but I, apparently, knows that women are jealous. But they explain to me that women are jealous of Dorothy's money, and privilege, and social position. Are they jealous of Earl's abuse of her, of her dependence on alcohol, of Earl's abandoning her, of the chaos of her life now? Well—they would have managed their lives differently, they say. But I am not convinced that this is the real reason that these women offer her little or no support. I believe that some of them feel compelled to join their husbands or their colleagues in the corporate silence about Earl's behaviour, and Dorothy's. More important, I believe that many wealthy women are terrified by Dorothy and what she did because they know that her fate could be theirs. Because they cannot admit this, or even think about it consciously, they must reject her. Even the mention of her name is more than some of them will tolerate gracefully.

For most of Dorothy's adult years she has presented herself publicly as an authoritative woman. Most of the people who know her would describe her as such. Her appearance, her intelligence, her social skills, her manner, her privilege and position in society, all convey this quality. But the irony—and Dorothy's story is so filled with irony—is that this demeanour is not to her advantage now, in this most public time of her life. I am sure that at least part of her lawyer's defence will be to present her as a victim of her husband's power and control over her. After a lifetime of struggling to accommodate herself to Earl's behaviour, of learning to appear to be self-possessed, confident, in control of her emotions and her world, at great cost to herself, now it would be better if she were to appear to be fragile, sensitive, unsure of herself, even damaged—all aspects of herself that she has learned to hide. Because there is so little precedent in our laws to defend women who are driven to the very edge of endurance by their husband's abuse of them, it is unlikely that O'Brien will argue that Dorothy Joudrie acted out in self-defence. So it would be better if she were to appear to be what people expect of a lady who was driven to the point of losing control of herself, who, in perhaps mad desperation, has succumbed to a crime of passion. This is how the police refer to acts like hers. Our society refers to her behaviour, and Earl's behaviour toward her for many years, as "domestic violence"—a startling oxymoron.[36]

At Dorothy's preliminary hearing, her composure was balanced by the shock and sadness of the exposure to her, and to the people in the courtroom, of the reality of her life. But now, after all this time of emotional strain, of hoping for the impossible, of examinations and preparations, of waiting, she must be worn out. I suspect that she is frightened. I suspect, also, that she is angry. Two of her children have abandoned her—for the present, at least. Her former husband, who defined her as Mrs. Earl Joudrie, has divorced her. He is living with another woman whom he may marry. His rejection of Dorothy is public, final. I wonder if O'Brien, as he prepared Dorothy for the trial, in an honest effort to support her and assure her, told her just to be herself. And I wonder how she can know who that is.

———————

All this was on my mind as I drove downtown and then walked to the Court of Queen's Bench on the first day of Dorothy's trial. Photographers were beginning to gather outside the doors, hoping to record her arrival. They are not allowed inside. The stairs to the lower level of the court house were roped off, directing people upstairs. The commissionaire, smiling, told me before I could ask, that Dorothy Joudrie's trial would be in room 504. This man, polite and helpful, quite correctly anticipated the purpose of my being there. What identified me, I wondered, as a spectator at Dorothy's trial and not at one of the others scheduled for that day. Obviously, the court house was prepared for this event—Calgary's social event of the year, as my friend had predicted. As I reached the main level and stood waiting for an elevator among the clerks, and lawyers, and others going about their usual activities, I began to feel the air of authority in this building. Involuntarily I steeled myself against an atmosphere in which I was a stranger. Also I felt concern about the time. It was still more than an hour before the court would be in session, but if this commissionaire had directed others to the fifth floor, perhaps I would not be one of the first people to arrive. I knew that no seats would be reserved for writers or journalists, and it was very important to me to sit where I could see Dorothy, the judge, the lawyers, the witnesses, and the jury. But this is ghoulish, I thought, feeling a sudden wave of panicky doubt about my motivation for being in court at all.

There were seven people in the fifth floor waiting area when I stepped off the elevator. Three were seated, casually, reading newspapers. The others were collected in a small group near the door of the courtroom, talking quietly. They looked relaxed, sensible, purposeful, not at all like the idle spectators I had imagined, who, having heard and read the reports of Dorothy, were attracted to the trial of a "socialite" who is charged with attempting to murder her husband. But I wasn't ready yet to be part of this group, to be asked, perhaps, to explain my presence.

I went into the washroom and stood looking at myself in the mirror. Why am I here, I wondered. I had thought that I had a serious purpose in attending this trial. Did my interest in Dorothy and my concern for her as a woman—my concern about women of our age, about women of wealth, about women who are abused by their husbands, about women who attempt to kill and do kill their husbands—and my wanting to write about all this, justify my presence? Why had I felt some identification with Dorothy Joudrie almost since the day of the shooting fifteen months ago? One of the dramatic discoveries I have made during that time is how different we are in many ways, how different our lives have been. And now, on this morning, in this building, how presumptuous it seemed to me even to try to imagine what she must be feeling.

I have never been charged with committing a crime. Until Dorothy's preliminary hearing, I had never seen a real gun. During more than thirty-five years of marriage, which for the most part have been stable and sometimes very happy, my husband and I have struggled through periods of strain, and disagreement, and anger, but I have never been the victim of spousal abuse. I do not live in a "high end" condominium in Calgary, or own a home in an "upscale" suburb of Phoenix, Arizona, or drive a "tony" Lincoln town car. In fact, I had had no interest at all in the "powerful circles" of the upper socio-economic class in Calgary until I read about Dorothy and Earl. This is how journalists have described her and her life. These are the words they use. They know that the wealth and position, hers and Earl's, the tragedy in lives that most of us can only imagine, are what really interest their readers. This was a revelation to me—the importance of the Joudries' wealth—but I'm discovering that Dorothy's money is the main source of many people's fascination with her, and also, of much of the negative emotion both men and women express about her and the expectations of what will happen to her at this trial—that because of her position of privilege she will not be punished for what she has done. Already, the word "socialite" has been used so often it has created a minor semantic phenomenon. I wondered why the people writing about Dorothy cannot think of another word to describe her. But then I realized that the word socialite is the key, the signal of a story of scandal in "high places." Labels to identify Earl are endless: "the chairman of several corporate boards," "a powerful business executive," "a corporate giant," "a highly skilled negotiator in corporate affairs." Socialite is such an empty word. Dorothy must find it insulting, demeaning. It says nothing about her except that her former husband is wealthy, and she, still, is a reflection of him. What word would she use, I wondered, to identify herself.

In the washroom at the Court of Queen's Bench that morning I held my hands under the hot water, taking comfort from the warmth, the ordinary act of washing, and thought wryly of the figurative meaning of this act and how often it has been used in literature to signify a need to cleanse, to purify not just the hands, but human behaviour, the conscience, the heart. I took my notebook out of my purse. And I went to join the others waiting at the door of the room which would become very familiar during the next three weeks.

# Part Two

# At the Trial

# 911

'Ferry me across the water,
  Do, boatman, do.'
'If you've a penny in your purse
  I'll ferry you.'

'I have a penny in my purse,
  And my eyes are blue;
So ferry me across the water,
  Do, boatman do.'

'Step into my ferry-boat,
  Be they black or blue,
And for the penny in your purse
  I'll ferry you.'
                    Christina Rossetti, from *Sing-Song*,[37] c. 1872


As Dorothy Joudrie stood in the prisoner's dock on the first day of her trial, listening to the charges against her—attempted murder, aggravated assault, illegal use of a handgun—and pleading not guilty to all three, she seemed breathless, very nervous, very much aware of the people, many of whom she knew, watching her and listening to her. She looked directly at no one, and she spoke quietly. The gallery of the courtroom was full, and among approximately forty spectators, there were at least fourteen journalists.

The bar, separating the central figures in this drama from the spectators, is the edge of the stage on which only the players belong. During the trial, as Dorothy sat on the bench in the prisoner's dock, just inside the bar, and directly in front of the spectators, she faced the two lawyers at their separate tables—their backs much of the time—the judge on the bench, the jury in their box on her right, and the court reporter, who sits in front of the witness box, to the left of the judge. Two officers of the court, in uniform, were also allowed inside the bar, and at strategic moments—moments when someone had decided that she might lose control, or need assistance—one of them sat directly beside the prisoner's dock. Without the judge's permission, no one else is allowed on the stage. I suspect that O'Brien either brought Dorothy to see this room, or explained its arrangement to her before this first day. I wondered if she realized that the wall at the back of the prisoner's dock is so high that it was impossible for spectators, seated behind her, to see her. There were few seats from which anyone could see her face. It was to these few seats that the experienced journalists and I, too, went directly when the clerk opened the door. The centre of the gallery was furnished with wooden pews, similar to those in churches, and people in the audience were expected to squeeze together, if necessary, to make room for others. The weather that day in Calgary, April 22, 1996, was appropriately spring-like. No one was burdened with heavy, bulky clothing.

It occurred to me that the design of the prisoner's dock provided Dorothy with a small amount of privacy from the gallery. But there was also something dispassionate and even cruel about the physical separation of the accused from everyone else. If we really believe that this person is innocent until proved guilty why do we isolate her in this manner, making an object, a spectacle of her? When the jury, who like most of the rest of us have watched American courtroom dramas on TV and in films, asked why Dorothy was not seated beside her lawyer, Justice Arthur Lutz, the judge presiding at the trial, explained that it is tradition in Canadian courts to seat the accused in the prisoner's dock primarily so that they, the jury, can see her at all times. The expressions of skepticism and resignation on the faces of some of the jurors suggested that they were aware that the full weight of the word "tradition" was the real answer to this question, because it was apparent to them that had Dorothy been seated beside O'Brien, their view of her would be quite clear. Also, she would be able to communicate with her lawyer during the proceedings, which in this seating arrangement she could not do. But Justice Lutz made this explanation in a kindly, slightly patronizing, didactic tone and I looked at Dorothy, wondering how it made her feel. She listened carefully, missing nothing in what he said. Then she shut her eyes, resigned. His brief explanation, and the physical arrangement of the room, embodied the purpose of this whole exercise: judging her.

On the first day of the trial, I wondered for a while if Dorothy had been sedated. She seemed sleepy. Often she let her head fall forward, she shut her eyes, and for a minute or two she appeared to be quite apart from the activity around her. Then I realized that she may be using some relaxation technique, as I saw her loosening the muscles of her neck and shoulders, letting her head fall forward, shrugging, moving her shoulders in a circular motion, and breathing deeply and evenly. Twice, during breaks in the proceedings, when she was not with O'Brien, I saw her sitting alone in the almost-empty gallery. I was startled by the sight of her there, how vulnerable she seemed, and I recalled the voice of a woman seated near me earlier: "I hope she gets everything she deserves. The works." Dorothy seemed beyond being able to steel herself against this experience. Or perhaps someone had helped her to realize that trying to resist this assault might be catastrophic physically and psychologically and that she would endure it only by allowing it to happen, which was what she appeared to be trying to do.

Everything seemed so slow getting started, beginning with several minutes of waiting for Justice Lutz. We did not realize, that day, that arriving late is his usual practice. One woman said that she kept track of the number of minutes we waited for the judge and that by the end of the trial it amounted to a day and a half. Before the jury was present, O'Brien made two applications to Justice Lutz. Of the three charges— attempted murder, aggravated assault, and the use of a firearm to commit an indictable offence—only the last would result in an automatic sentence of at least a year in jail. Although the maximum sentence for attempted murder could be life in prison, both of what appear to be the more serious offences carry no minimum sentence. The accused, if convicted, might be considered, for example, for a period of probation. O'Brien argued that the firearm allegation should apply to one, not both of the indictable offences. O'Brien's second request was for permission to address the jury before any witnesses appear. This is a complicated case, he said, and he wanted to do everything possible to assist the jury to understand. O'Brien's arguments were quietly eloquent, but after a recess, during which Justice Lutz consulted legal precedents, he denied both applications. A seasoned journalist, upon whom I came to rely for accuracy and careful investigation, commented to me that O'Brien's challenge of the usual procedure was the first sign at this trial of his being one of three or four of the best criminal lawyers in Canada. The fact that Dorothy, but not the jury, was allowed to be present during such requests and discussions was interesting to me, and an endorsement of her inclusion in the process of judging her, despite her physical isolation on the stage and her enforced silence. The jury was sworn in; the alternates were allowed to leave; the judge addressed the jury; and the court was adjourned until three o'clock. So this is the procedure, I thought: a traditional, formal, intense pageant, punctuated by intermissions—some short, some very long—and waiting, while the judge and the lawyers prepare, rehearse, consult precedents behind the scenes.

---

Dorothy seemed to be prepared for Jerry Selinger's assault in his opening address. He said that he would "prove beyond a reasonable doubt" that she is guilty. He said to the jury, but without looking directly at them, that from the evidence provided by each witness they must make their own interpretation based on their experience, background, and common sense.

Selinger named his witnesses, all but one of whom had appeared at the preliminary hearing. When he announced that Earl Joudrie would be present tomorrow, he described Earl's relationship with Dorothy in January 1995: that they had separated in 1989; that Earl lives in Toronto; that since 1993 Earl has been living with Lynn Manning, Dorothy's second cousin; and that Earl had come to Dorothy's house, at her invitation, on January 21, 1995, to get papers he needed to "finalize" their divorce. After Earl and Dorothy had coffee and a brief conversation at the kitchen table, Dorothy directed Earl to leave through the garage and as she followed him, she shot him in the back. After he fell to the floor, she continued to shoot him "approximately two more times" and then, standing over him, "approximately three more times." Earl was still conscious, and after a conversation with him, Dorothy called the police and the Emergency Medical Services several times. Earl was taken by air ambulance to the General Hospital. Selinger ended his address by telling the jury that they should pay careful attention to the evidence which will be provided regarding Dorothy's appearance and her conduct that morning, and what led up to this incident.

Selinger suggested that the impending divorce led to Dorothy's rage, her vengeful act. He said that there would be questions regarding Earl's relationship with Dorothy, but he did not mention Earl's abuse of her during their marriage. And this, of course, is why O'Brien wanted to be able to address the jury before Selinger's witnesses appear. I wondered how anyone else can really know what transpired between Dorothy and Earl that morning. I wondered how anyone else can really know what has transpired between a man and a woman in a relationship that has existed for more than forty years.

Selinger seemed to have difficulty speaking to his audience, capturing them either emotionally or logically, and his opening address was the first example of this problem during the trial. He appeared to lack imagination, or the capacity to put himself in another person's shoes. I thought that his opening statement was competent, but certainly not compelling, partly because he appeared to be addressing the whole room and not the jury specifically. Selinger seemed to have difficulty looking directly at anyone, looking them in the eye. His pacing distracted me, and I found myself wondering if he would be able to find the pertinent spots in his notes when he came back to them, as he needed to periodically.

His choice of Dr. Joyce Wong as his first witness was not only the logical thing to do, it was clever and dramatic. Dr. Wong, the vascular surgeon at the General Hospital who had admitted Earl on the day of the shooting and treated him, testified that in X-rays they found four bullets in Earl's upper body (which are still there) and evidence of two bullets fired through each of his upper thighs: altogether, seven wounds, from "about six shots." Dr. Wong showed in X-rays and photographs that one bullet, which entered from the front, broke Earl's upper right arm and lodged in his chest, causing his lung to collapse. Another bullet entered his left chest and lodged near his shoulder. Another passed through his upper back and lodged near his lower right spine. And another entered his left side, lodging below his front rib cage. Dr. Wong said that all of these injuries—including the bullet wounds in his thighs, but especially those in his arm and lung—would have been life-threatening if they had not been treated. Also his heart rhythm was affected and required both electric shock and medication. Nevertheless, when O'Brien cross-examined Dr. Wong, she noted that when Earl arrived at the hospital he was breathing on his own, his heart and blood were normal, he did not lose consciousness, and he was able to give his medical history. O'Brien defused, to some extent, the intensity of emotion in the room. But he could not undo the powerful effect of Dr. Wong's testimony.

Several members of the jury watched Dorothy very carefully during Dr. Wong's testimony. As she looked at the X-rays and photographs, and listened to Dr. Wong, she wept silently, and nodded. Her reaction suggested that she was as shocked as any other observer in the courtroom. I was sure that no one in that room, including Dorothy, doubted that what she did that morning fifteen months ago is truly astonishing.

An RCMP sergeant from Cochrane, a town west of Calgary and near Dorothy's home, was Selinger's second witness that afternoon. This man was the first of four RCMP officers and two Calgary police officers who testified intermittently during the next few days. He showed the jury thirty-four photographs of Dorothy's house in Bearspaw: the front of the house, with her car parked in the driveway to the two-door garage; the interior—entry, hall, living room, dining room, bedroom, kitchen, laundry room; and inside this undisturbed, tidy, clean, bright, domestic environment, a black purse which had been in the bottom drawer of the bedroom dresser, a .25 calibre handgun which had been in the black purse, red stains on the stairs to the garage, red stains on the floor of the garage, a pile of Earl's clothing on the floor of the garage, an empty plastic glass found on a shelf in the utility room cupboard, another glass containing alcohol and ice, and several "metal objects"—two spent bullets and six casings—found scattered on the floor, under a rug, and among coffee grounds in a garbage compactor.

There was never more than a very cursory discussion of how three metal casings got into the coffee grounds in the garbage. These casings were pressed down into the coffee grounds, and both lawyers left whatever compelled Dorothy to try to hide this evidence to the jury's "experience and background and common sense." Selinger did ask one of the expert witnesses, a psychiatrist, if a person in a state of automatism, the key to O'Brien's defence of Dorothy, would try to hide bullet casings. The psychiatrist said that yes, such an act by a person in a state of automatism was possible.

There were photographs of items on the kitchen table, among them a binder, which we learned later contained a collection of Christmas letters that Dorothy wrote and sent yearly to their friends; a photograph album of pictures of Earl as a child; and their "wedding album." Dorothy had gathered together these things—mementoes of their years together—to give to Earl, along with a certificate of their joint ownership of the "ranch house." The day before the shooting, Earl had signed the final papers for the divorce settlement, and the "ranch house," as Earl calls it—the Joudries' former family home on an acreage west of Calgary—was now his. Dorothy calls their former home the "big house."

During his cross-examination of one of the RCMP officers, O'Brien established the fact that this policeman was present when the cocked pistol was taken out of the dresser drawer in the bedroom. The police removed the empty magazine and found a bullet still inside the chamber of the gun.

Only one police officer testified on the afternoon of the first day of the trial. It was a long day. Several spectators wandered out of the courtroom during the afternoon, tired, and probably bored by some of the details of what the police found and which were not, apparently, what they had come to see and hear at this trial.

Selinger interspersed his examination of the police and the staff of the Emergency Medical Services with evidence from other witnesses during the next few days. I wondered if this break in the testimony of the police and the medical unit was an accommodation to the witnesses' schedules, or if it was planned deliberately by Selinger. What we heard from the police and the EMS after Earl testified seemed more dramatic than it would have been before. In fact, some of the evidence the police and the EMS provided seemed to undermine Selinger's argument. I began to realize the importance of the sequence of the appearance of witnesses. Also, as the trial progressed, I realized that some spectators chose to attend the testimony of some witnesses and not others, which gave them a skewed version of the trial and probably supported their biases, although they may have been unaware of this when they talked with their friends about having attended the trial.

On the third day of the trial, after Earl's testimony and cross-examination, Selinger asked an officer of the Emergency Medical Services to play a transcript of the tape of Dorothy's 911 calls after the shooting. As the tape played, Dorothy leaned forward, holding her body perfectly still, straining to hear every word she and the EMS operators said. Spectators in the courtroom suppressed any audible reactions to what they were hearing. They, too, remained still, silent.

Dorothy called first at 10:57, saying, in a voice that was urgent, distinct, and controlled, "I have an emergency here."[38] She needed to give directions to her home, on Country Club Lane, which is on the western outskirts of the city. When the dispatcher asked her why she needed help, she said, "Well, somebody's been shot." Here was an echo of Earl's "Dorothy was struck." I could not help but hear this echo, this denial of personal responsibility, even though Earl's comment was made in hindsight, and Dorothy's in the midst of certainly the worst emotional chaos and confusion she had ever experienced. It is common for a person not to remember the details of such a traumatic event; it is so common, in fact, that when someone can describe elaborate details and their sequence, the police and other experts may suspect that they are not telling the truth. But not everyone stands back from their actions, making them impersonal, even when they do something so terrible they want not to own it. On the contrary, admitting responsibility is often an immediate act of contrition, repeated over and over—by a driver, for example, who has struck someone accidentally, unintentionally. The shock and regret and guilt are relentless. But the evidence in the long, sad story of the Joudries' marriage, and studies by experts in wife abuse, suggest that Dorothy's act was not accidental. The evidence suggests that Dorothy's actions when she shot the man who had abused her, betrayed her, and abandoned her, were fuelled by rage, or fear, or loss, or a need to defend herself—emotions so intense that her conscious mind neither controlled nor registered what she was doing. Listening to this tape, all of us could hear her distance from herself, and we could also hear, at the same time, her confusion, her anger, her fear, her need to save her husband's life, and her good manners, which persisted despite her final outbursts of desperation and frustration.

The dispatcher repeated the word "shot?" and asked if it was accidental, and what happened. Her answer was "Yes. Five. Yes."

Dorothy answered correctly the dispatcher's questions about the age of the person who had been shot and whether he was conscious and breathing. When he asked her "What was the weapon?" she said, "A gun." But the dispatcher wanted to know more: "A gun? A rifle? What was it, ma'am?" She said, "No. Just a gun." The dispatcher persisted, "A handgun?" "Yes," she said.

When the dispatcher asked her to tell him where the wound was she said, "I don't know." When he asked if she could get close to the wounded person with the phone, she said, "No, I can't." She did not explain until she was asked specifically if she was in the same room with him, that Earl was in the garage and she was in the house. The dispatcher asked her again if she knew where the person had been shot—in the chest, in the arm, any idea where? She said, "I don't know."

Dorothy said "thank you" when the dispatcher said he had lots of help on the way. But he still wanted to know the status of the patient and he wanted her to leave the telephone and find out, suggesting, "If they're conscious . . . " that he would tell her what to do. But she interrupted him. She said, sounding impatient and exasperated at the suggestion that Earl might not be conscious, "Well, he's still talking to me." We could hear Earl shouting in the background. The dispatcher was obviously startled, and he said, "Is he right there with you now?" Again, we heard Earl in the background, and Dorothy conveyed his message, carefully censoring the profanity, to the dispatcher: "He said 'Hurry up and come.'" The dispatcher assured her that they were on their way. She shouted to Earl, "He says they're on their way." So the dispatcher took advantage of the obvious proximity of this wounded person to suggest that Dorothy ask him where the wound is. She turned away from the phone and shouted, sounding angry, "Where's the wound?" We could hear but not comprehend what Earl said, and she told the dispatcher, in the same tone of voice she had used with Earl, "He doesn't know." It would not be surprising if the EMS dispatcher was having difficulty understanding what, exactly, was happening at 143 Country Club Lane. But he told Dorothy how to cover and put pressure on a bleeding wound and to call 911 again immediately if this person's condition deteriorated, or he lost consciousness. Again, Dorothy said "thank you."

At 11:05 she did call again, and was assured that they were almost there. She concluded that exchange with "OK. Thank you." At 11:09, when she called again, there were no more assurances that they had almost arrived because, in fact, they were parked near her house, waiting for the police. But Dorothy did not know this. Instead, the dispatcher sympathized with her impatience and asked her questions she had already answered—again, for example, to identify the gun—but she said, "I don't even know. He's gonna die if they don't get here." For the first time, she sounded frantic: "I don't give a damn about all these other questions. Just get the ambulance here." When he reassured her, she thanked him again.

At 11:14 when Dorothy phoned for the final time, she complained anxiously and accurately, and still sounding angry, that she had now waited twenty minutes for the ambulance. The dispatcher responded with,

"Ma'am, are you the wife of the man who shot himself?" She said, "Yes." The dispatcher explained to her then that they had to wait for the police to "secure the scene." "But he's dying," she said. When the dispatcher told her that they would follow the police as soon as they knew that the "scene is safe," she said "thank you" for the last time. The RCMP and the Calgary police entered Dorothy's home at 11:21 a.m.

I was surprised that someone—the lawyers or the psychiatrists—did not spend more time discussing this transcript, because it is a revelation of Dorothy's state of mind that morning. I'm sure that most people who need to phone the EMS are frightened, excited, anxious, confused. Still, Dorothy's responses, and the progression of her responses, must have been unusual even for the EMS operators. When she first spoke to them she said explicitly, accurately, using the first-person pronoun, "I have an emergency here." She told the dispatcher her address, how to get to her house. Then she retreated. She said, vaguely, in the passive voice, not telling the dispatcher who had fired the gun, "Well, somebody's been shot." When the dispatcher asked her to describe the weapon, she moved even further away, diminishing not just the instrument but the danger of it—"just a gun." We could hear Earl—the person she had tried to silence—swearing, demanding, pleading for her help. He was probably saying, with justification, "I'm dying," which someone might have argued is exactly what she had wanted him to do. Later, on the witness stand, she said that she could not remember hearing Earl shouting, and that she was surprised when a neighbour told her, after Dorothy returned from California, that her husband had heard Earl. This remark, which was not accepted as evidence, was a candid and spontaneous admission of her inability to remember what happened that morning.

But we could hear, now, the EMS operator on the other end of the telephone, speaking into her ear, addressing her directly, and she was beginning to realize that she must prevent Earl from dying, and also perhaps that she would be responsible if he did die. And she assumed, superficially at least, what Earl calls her "usual efficient self," in an effort to hurry up the ambulance, to come to his aid, to save him. Like some other women who have tried to murder their husbands, Dorothy also tried to save her husband's life. But Earl was luckier than most of these other husbands. Dorothy succeeded.

Most of us take for granted the advanced technology of our time because our lives are so suffused with it. I suspect that the people in that courtroom were so absorbed by what they heard on the EMS tape—what Dorothy said, how she said it, Earl's shouts and pleas for help in the background—that they did not realize, perhaps until they thought about it later, that a telephone and a recording machine were allowing us, all of us, to listen to what actually happened in the privacy of Dorothy Joudrie's home just a few minutes after she shot Earl on that Saturday morning fifteen months ago. Dorothy's facial expression as she strained to listen to her own voice was extremely pained and puzzled, as if she could hardly believe what she was hearing. If she felt again any of the rage, the intense anger that became apparent during her conversation with the EMS dispatcher, I could not see it. I wondered, also, if she noticed the number of times she said "thank you."

It wasn't until I read my notes of this tape that I realized the enormous complexity of the emotional turmoil Dorothy seemed to be experiencing and expressing during those twenty minutes. I wonder if Selinger realized as he listened to the tape, surely not for the first time, how helpful it was to O'Brien's defence of her. I wonder why O'Brien did not examine it very specifically to defend her. I wonder why the psychiatrists, when they explained a dissociative state, did not discuss it. This tape, it seems to me, is an aural miniature of Dorothy's state of mind during those crucial moments immediately after she shot her husband. Her reaction, as she listened to the tape in court, is equally important. All this was left, without analysis, for the jury to examine and deliberate.

When the police officers from Cochrane arrived at Country Club Lane, the Calgary police and EMS were there, on the street, waiting. Two policemen finally entered through the garage door which Dorothy had opened, and they found Earl lying near the steps leading to the house. One officer had gone into the house with Dorothy when the other saw a bullet wound in the middle of Earl's back, and more. He went directly into the house, knowing that this was not an accidental shooting. A police officer persuaded Dorothy, with some difficulty, he said, that they could not help Earl until she gave them the gun. Finally, she led him to the bottom drawer of the bedroom dresser and the black leather pouch which held the .25 calibre Beretta, the hammer of which was "still back." This officer "seized" the gun. Another put handcuffs on Dorothy, read her her rights, and arrested her for attempted murder. They took her away.

O'Brien, in his cross-examination of one of the police officers, asked some questions that might have been in the minds of the jury and some of the spectators, especially since they had now heard Earl's testimony. Was Earl conscious? Was he able to talk? Did he use swear words? "Yes" to all of these. Did he say, O'Brien asked, referring to police testimony at the preliminary hearing, "I got shot, asshole"? "I don't remember," said the officer. But when O'Brien asked him if Dorothy made any comments, this cautious, young man said that at 11:49 Dorothy said, "I can't believe I'm in this situation." He also told the court that along with the handgun, they found in the bedroom closet a shotgun and ammunition for it. The police officers from Cochrane and Calgary testified that when they tried to talk to Dorothy, she was alert and polite, but that she also seemed distraught and would not answer them directly. She said, "My husband and I discussed this and he told me not to talk about it." They also said that she wanted to go with Earl in the air ambulance to the hospital.

Earl testified that he did not tell Dorothy to say nothing to the police. O'Brien and the three psychiatrists, the experts who testified, put great emphasis on Dorothy's "massive denial" of the reality of her life, and there was ample evidence to justify their conclusion that this was a very serious problem for her, a problem that may have caused her and allowed her, finally, to shoot her husband. But no one ever discussed Earl's capacity for denial.

After the shooting, some of Earl's business acquaintances expressed shock at her actions, but they also said that they were surprised because they did not know about Earl's family problems. After Dorothy's testimony, and Earl's, I found it impossible to believe that at least some of these people did not know about the Joudries' troubled relationship and even about Earl's abuse of Dorothy. And I believe now that some people may have cooperated in Earl's silence, in his denial of the tragedy of his marriage. What is this power that Earl has, I wonder, that makes others who know him so reluctant to criticize him, or even to talk about him at all.

There are many examples of Earl's denial of the reality of his life. When, in 1971, Earl was diagnosed with Hodgkin's disease, a form of cancer of the lymph glands, and Dorothy and the children accompanied him to Stanford, California, so that he could receive the newest and still experimental treatment, he told Dorothy, she testified, to tell no one, even her parents. In 1989, when Earl moved out of their home to live in an apartment in downtown Calgary, Dorothy said that again he told her to tell no one, and they continued to appear in public as a couple. When Earl moved to Toronto in 1991, it was his secretary who told Dorothy that he no longer lived in Calgary. Earl began to spend time with Lynn Manning, in Toronto, and they went together to Florida for a vacation. Earl told Dorothy that he and Mrs. Manning had not taken a vacation together. Between January 21, 1995, and the trial, Earl allowed himself to be interviewed only once, at which time he referred, cryptically, to a "family tragedy," which he implied was Dorothy's violent act. During his testimony at the trial, when O'Brien questioned him about specific acts of his abuse of Dorothy, except for those few incidents which Earl cited himself, he tried to deny having committed other acts of abuse, or he claimed not to remember the incidents.

Dorothy's denial of her real life has caused her severe emotional, physical, and legal damage. But one of the things I realized during the trial was that Earl Joudrie not only caused her need to deny, he taught her to deny, and he was complicit in her denial. In a strange and perverse intertwining of control and dependence, they were partners in denial.

# Earl

... the reality of acute battering incidents is that they are
genuinely life-and-death situations, replete with all the
inherent terror that violence wreaks upon its victims. Rage,
fear and pain are unlimited and uncontrolled ...
> Lenore E. Walker, *Terrifying Love.*[39]

Passivity and denial of anger do not imply that the battered
woman is adjusted to or likes her situation. These are the last
desperate defenses against homicidal rage.
> Elaine Hilberman, "Overview:
> The 'Wife-Beater's Wife' Reconsidered."[40]

Earl Joudrie is well known in Canada's corporate world, but until
Dorothy was charged with attempting to murder him, the Joudries had
never attracted public attention. After the shooting, Earl's business associates, and the Joudries' acquaintances—people of a certain social class in
Calgary—seemed very reticent to speak out publicly about them. The few
candid comments to the media were expressions of surprise, and guarded
criticism of Dorothy. No one criticized Earl. But during the trial, the sad
and shocking details of their marriage were offered up daily in newspapers
all across Canada. If Dorothy and Earl read these news reports of her trial,
and I'm sure that they read at least some of them, they must know that
journalists are selective in what they see and hear. They cannot be anything else. Nevertheless, most of the reports were careful and accurate.

Editorials, opinion columns, and letters to the editors must have upset both Dorothy and Earl sometimes. But even the official transcripts of the trial are not an unbiased, truly accurate report of what happened there. The transcripts include only a record of what was said. They do not include a gasp, a sigh, tears, a smile, a look shared between two people. They cannot include the whole, long, complicated history of a marriage, and the true essence of the more than forty years during which Earl Joudrie was the centre of Dorothy's existence.

In Rob Reiner's film *When Harry Met Sally*, older couples, interspersed throughout the film, sit facing the camera, telling about how they met, how they knew that they wanted to marry each other, and how many years they have spent together. The spokesperson for most of the couples is the man and some of the women say nothing, but one woman anticipates every-thing her husband says. She begins to speak while he is speaking, adding details, nuances, and completing his statements. It is like a duet, the coun-terpoint and harmony and echoes filling out and finishing their story. In every case the two are joined together by some inexplicable force of famil-iarity, acceptance, and pleasure at the miracle of their having found each other. All this is fiction, of course. Nora Ephron, who wrote the screenplay, made it up. But what a stroke of genius it is in a romantic film about a cou-ple who know each other for twelve years before they marry.

The other day my husband and I went to see a movie in a shopping mall. I was pressing ahead through the mall in my usual compulsive way, anxious to get in line, to get a good seat, when I noticed that my husband was no longer beside me. He was looking at a sweater or a shirt in a shop along the way. I called to him, impatient, annoyed, telling him to hurry up. Neither of us was embarrassed by my behaviour, although some people would think that I should have been—it was not ladylike. I noticed a woman of about our age smiling at this public display of domestic irrita-tion. She was careful not to look directly at either of us, eager to appear to be minding her own business. If I had been with a friend, I would have walked back and waited, saying nothing, but my friend probably would not have stopped in the first place. My friends have not shared a bed with me for thousands of nights, or countless meals at home, in restaurants and hotels, as guests in the homes of others. They have not stayed at my side, encouraging me, as excited as I, when I gave birth to two babies; they have not bathed two little boys and read to them every night, long after the boys could read themselves; they have not come home, late, from summer school courses, evening classes, weekends in the badlands, to find me wild with frustration and worry about a snow storm and dangerous driving conditions, or a child with an earache and a high fever; they have not tolerated my complaints of a sore neck, or back, or head; they do not know that the flowers I love most are anemones, or that every night I bath in a tub filled recklessly, wastefully with water almost too hot to endure; they have not supported me confidently as I studied and struggled to write a thesis, and worked quietly in another part of the house, as I marked thousands of essays and exams and prepared lectures for my own students; they have not listened to me read aloud almost everything I have ever written, making careful, helpful comments; they have not listened to me talk, talk endlessly about novels, stories, poems, our children, students, and the people with whom I work; they have not argued with me about literature, movies, music, paintings, politics, putting on the storm windows and cleaning up the basement. My friends have not lived with me for thirty-five years.

A husband and wife may be friends, in which case they are lucky. But marriage is more complicated than friendship. Earl said, when O'Brien was questioning him, that he and Dorothy "may have loved each other, but we may never have found out how to be friends." His comment was sad. And I suspect that Dorothy did not miss the suggestion in it that he has found friendship in his present relationship with Lynn Manning. I'm not sure that a husband and wife decide to be friends, or learn how to be friends. I think it must be a bonus, a gift, something that just happens between two people, and perhaps this was what Earl meant.

When I read over this little sketch of my own marriage, my effort to show both how mundane and complex marriages are, I see first of all how inadequate, how incomplete it is. Then I see how romantic it is, how romantic I have made my marriage seem. Like Dorothy, I wanted, and expected, to have a traditional, romantic marriage, the kind of marriage I had read about, that other young women talked about, a fairy tale. All young women of our generation were taught to expect such a marriage. We were also taught, but it was easier not to think about this until after we were married, that it was up to us to make the fairy tale have a happy ending. Our husbands would be busy at the office, getting ahead with their lives, providing the means for this comfortable, happy, romantic life. If they were unhealthy, unhappy, or if they found someone else they preferred as a sexual partner, it was our fault. While we kept the house clean and tidy, cooked appetizing, nourishing meals, bore and cared for the requisite number of children, and provided clean underwear, and pairs of clean socks, and freshly starched, perfectly pressed, clean white shirts, we also wanted to be slender, pretty, exciting, good natured, and seductive. We didn't need to be told, as we were in any of the flood of women's magazines on the newsstand, that no husband wants to make love to an exhausted, overweight, stringy-haired, cranky woman, in a bedroom overflowing with laundry we had rescued from the line before an afternoon thunder storm—even two dozen sweet-smelling, carefully folded diapers. So there are many things I did not put in that list. One of the most important is that during the first few weeks of my marriage, I felt more alone than I ever have in my life.

Before I was married, I worked for several years at a job that was important and satisfying to me. I "went to the office." Every weekday morning, and often on weekends, I left my tidy, modest, but pleasant and uncluttered apartment, and met my colleagues with whom I shared skills, training, intelligence, challenges. When I came home, everything was just as I had left it, and if I was too tired to be hungry, for an hour or two I read, or lay down, or just sat, enjoying the peace, the quiet, the solitude. Of course I neither expected nor wanted to spend my whole life this way, alone. I wanted to marry my husband more than I wanted anything else in the world. But I did not spend one second thinking realistically about what being married would be like.

After our wedding, because my husband did not want me to work, it was only he who left every morning, taking the car to get to the high school where he taught, several miles away. Everyday I had eight hours that were entirely my own, and this sudden change was more dramatic than I could possibly have imagined. We were living in a charming little cottage on Georgian Bay; it was spring, and warm, and we had a beautiful, frisky, red and white border collie who kept me company and walked with me for miles every morning on the sunny beach. I read, listened to the CBC, wrote letters, and thank-you notes to friends who had given us gifts, and I prepared suppers—awkwardly, anxiously—that I hoped we would enjoy when my husband arrived home from work. Our evenings were pleasant, spent alone or with his friends whom I liked well enough, but didn't really know, because I hadn't lived here before we were married.

My husband had arranged this perfect, romantic life for me. But I felt lost. I couldn't find myself. I didn't know who I was. I had no friends nearby to provide an anchor to the life I had known before I married, and besides, I had been taught that when a woman marries, her husband is her whole life. How often since that time I have wished that I could relive those weeks and months; how much I would have appreciated them in the midst of my later, busy, chaotic existence. My husband says that he was very happy during that time, "idyllically happy," he says, and I'm glad and relieved to know that. But it was not easy for me to become a married woman, a wife. A few years later, but long after I thought I was comfortable in my role as a wife and mother, we attended a conference together where, when we arrived, someone tried to hand me a tag that said "Mrs. Doug Andrews." I was horrified, and could not take the tag in my hand. "But that is not my name!" I said desperately to the woman behind the table. "What is your name?" she asked kindly, prepared to look through the tags. I did not know what to say. This was the beginning of my realization that women do not have names of their own—that women are named for men. We are men's daughters, or men's wives, even if we are divorced, or our husbands are dead. When Dorothy and I were married it was almost unheard of for a woman to keep her "maiden name"—a label which, itself, defines our relationship to men. When I was married I had assumed, if I thought much about it at all, that I would be proud to take my husband's name. This was the custom, the tradition in our society. But when I was offered that name tag, it seemed to me that my very self was at stake.

It wasn't until I was thirty-eight, as I was making our bed one morning, and caught a glimpse of myself in the mirror, that suddenly, out of the blue, I realized that I did know who I am. I stopped and stared at myself. I remember this as a moment of enormous relief. Until that moment, except when I was with my husband and my family—safe in their embrace—I had been haunted by a suspicion that there was nothing unique about me that allowed me to feel confident and self-possessed with other people generally, and especially with those I wanted to know and with whom I wanted to be friends. But how long it had taken me to come to this realization of myself—eleven years of marriage, and twenty-seven years before that.

I suspect that in everyone's life there are only moments of such conscious completeness. By this time, I thought that I enjoyed my domestic days at home. I thought that I was content with the milky, sweet fecundity of rising bread, sewing projects, a thriving garden, jelly dripping, healthy, active, curious children, their father arriving home in the late afternoon, cheerful, optimistic, ready to take them off my hands while I prepared our supper. I knew, though, that soon, when both of the children were in school, my life would change.

Sometimes I woke during the night and got up and wandered through the dark, cool house. I loved the silence, the signs of the comfort and safety of our life together. But there was also a restive quality to my private nocturnal existence. Often on those nights, I curled up on the chesterfield with a blanket and the dog and one of the endless library books I borrowed, having been alerted to the new books that would interest me by the expert town librarian, who knew every book in the library and how frequently and when, exactly, they had last been borrowed. She learned very quickly that what I wanted to read was books by women, books about women. She ordered each new book by Margaret Laurence, Alice Munro, Mavis Gallant, Margaret Drabble, Doris Lessing, and biographies of women, autobiographies and memoirs by women, which did not exist in the numbers they do these days. I had an insatiable curiosity about how other women lived their lives. Sometimes I shared the new books during the two-week borrowing period with my friend who taught English at the high school, and talked with her about them. This woman was a wife and mother too, but her children were older than ours and she had moved on to the next phase in her life. I wondered what my life was to become.

After we had been married for more than twenty years, and I was working on my M.A. in English literature, I had a chance to go to Amherst College in Massachusetts to do some research. An opportunity to see and use the archives at Amherst thrilled me, but my first and typical reaction was that I could not manage to go: we could not afford it for one thing, but also I questioned my having the luxury simply to disappear and leave my husband with two teen-aged boys and a household to manage on his own. In all the time we had been married, neither of us had ever been away alone for more than three or four nights at a time. My husband, who is a generous man, and a man for whom everything is possible, was adamant: "You must go," he said. But what finally convinced me was my discovery that with my research grant from the university I could pay for this scholarly adventure myself. So I just took off—for two of the most satisfying weeks of my life. Trips such as this are almost insignificant to many women these days, but this was one of the most exciting experiences I have had. The letters and journals and papers were extremely important and useful, but more important was the great pleasure I took from the fact that I was on my own, doing exactly what I wanted to do and feeling quite capable of doing it. When I came home, I didn't admit this to some of my contemporaries, who would have been surprised at my naivete, my lack of sophistication and experience. But even now, after fifteen years, I think sometimes of the eight glorious hours I spent every day in the library, of my walks in the evenings around the campus and the town, of buying flowers and fruit at the town market, of working alone at night in my room in the inn, of sitting in comfort and solitude watching and listening to others as I ate meals someone else had prepared. There were some things I could not do without a male companion to accompany me, to protect me, especially during a long weekend I spent in Boston. The taxi driver who drove me to my hotel warned me not to go out alone after 6 p.m. The concierge at the hotel stopped me as I started out the door on foot the next morning, a map of Boston in my hand, anxious to see as much as possible in the short time I had. He suggested that I decide where I wanted to go before I left the hotel. He told me to put the map away, and act like a native. Tourists, especially women alone, attracted attention, he said, the wrong kind of attention. He helped me plan my route, mentioning certain streets I should avoid, and suggested that I take a taxi to the Gardner Museum and Harvard. My enthusiasm was dampened a little by his advice, which I thought was probably over-cautious, but I listened carefully to what he said, and as I set out across the Boston Common on my way to Beacon Hill my determination and excitement returned.

When Dorothy told, sadly, of travelling, "for the very first time by myself" in Southeast Asia, I couldn't help comparing her experience to mine. There was a purpose to my escape from my normal life; I felt confident that what I was doing was valid and important—not on a grand scale, of course—but in respect to a task I had undertaken and wanted to complete. She, on the other hand, was travelling to the other side of the world, taking a vacation she had planned all along to share one day with Earl. The fact that one of her sons accompanied her part of the time could not satisfy her dream of an exotic holiday with her husband.

As I think about the difference in our two experiences of travelling alone, I know that it is my good fortune to have a husband who encourages me to seek out adventures—with him, or on my own. Partly because he supports my need for independence, I can relish it, for what it gives me, and also for what it adds to my relationship with him. It took me longer than it should have, after we married, to realize that he did not want a wife who lived her life through him. He gave up his idea of my being a chatelaine sooner than I was ready to cast off his expectations and those I had learned by heart as I grew up. So we both learned, and not always at the same pace and the same time, that we would have to create our marriage as we went along, and adjust to our different prejudices and dreams. My husband has sometimes accused me of having what he considers, contemptuously, to be "middle-class" values or behaviour: he warned me early on that Sunday dinners in our home would not be roast beef, canned peas, and ice cream. He says he comes from the lower class because he was a farm boy. This infuriates me, and I remind him that he had steak for breakfast throughout his childhood, and proudly wore cashmere sweaters while he was in high school—both luxuries my family could not afford. I regale him with the facts of my parents' modest means, and remind him that even he falls prey to the myth many farmers believe, that city folk are always better off than they are. But we are both confusing middle class with middlebrow, and while the latter label, if it were attached to us, would be a bitter blow, we are middle class and we will never be anything else. Also, the truth is that we are both snobs, not about material possessions or money, but certainly about taste, and intellect, and knowledge—and other things we think we know are important for us and for society generally. We think we are not conservative in our politics, and in the way we live our lives.

Earl's and Dorothy's lives were quite different from ours. After they married, as they became caught up in a socio-economic class quite beyond anything they had experienced as children, they were not encouraged to cast off conservative and traditional values. On the contrary, they learned to embrace these values even more firmly. In many respects their lives were quite glamorous and exciting. They skied and swam and played golf at famous tourist resorts. They travelled to Florida, Mexico, Hawaii, London, Paris. They attended the Kentucky Derby, and were invited to receptions for important people. Dorothy became the chatelaine Earl expected her to be. She devoted herself to helping her husband further his career. I asked Dorothy, when I talked with her finally, if she thought sometimes, after her children were in school, of having her own career. She said that Earl did not want her to "work."[41] She submitted to his expectations of her, which were, I am sure, that she could not afford the time, the energy, and most important, risk threatening his reputation, his pride, his security, his control. He was her career. She accepted his demands of her, partly because this was what most corporate wives and women of her class did, and perhaps also because she did so well what he wanted. But there was something else. At the centre of their marriage there was a dark, secret poison that gradually seeped closer and closer to the surface. This was what really controlled Dorothy's life, and it seems to me that Dorothy spent much of her marriage treading water, or more accurately, perhaps, lying low[42]—waiting for Earl, surviving, trying to hold at bay her loneliness and pain and fear and the darkness she could not share with anyone else. Even taking a vacation on her own to the other side of the world was simply more of the same thing.

When Earl was asked to tell about the amount of time he spent away from home, away from Dorothy, often many thousands of miles away, he agreed that it was excessive, but he added that she was busy with the children and her social activities and responsibilities, and he ended this discussion asking, "So what is lonely?" This seemed to me to be a defensive and callous remark. Perhaps it was also a suggestion that he, too, for reasons of his own, was lonely.

As I listened to Dorothy and Earl talk about their marriage, and watched Dorothy's anguish as she saw the X-rays and photographs of the bullet wounds she made in Earl's body, and listened to her say that she loves Earl and will always love him, I could see the disturbing energy between them in what is still, apparently, a complex and powerful relationship. I could see, also, that they shared sometimes, in the past, as both of them said they did, an intense, positive attraction to each other. I am speculating now in my analysis of their marriage. I am creating my version from what I saw and heard, and from my own notes of the trial and official transcripts. My views are influenced, as well, by the experts who have worked with and written about abused wives. These experts are adamant that battered wives who stay with their husbands are not masochists. This is part of their argument against that of onlookers of situations like that of the Joudries, who cannot understand why an intelligent woman like Dorothy Joudrie would stay, for so many years, in an abusive relationship.

It is not unusual for many people, including many women, to be incapable, consciously, of identifying with an abused woman. So they reject her, and also blame her. Blaming the female victim of abuse, rape, or severe sexual harassment is not so prevalent as it was a few years ago, but it still exists with a vehemence that surprised me both during and after Dorothy's trial. One of the many reasons abused women stay with their husbands is that they fear they could not survive on their own; many observers were quick to point out that this could not be so in the Joudrie case. However reduced her financial means might be, and however deprived she might have become of her social status and privilege had she instigated a divorce from Earl, it is unlikely that Dorothy would have been destitute. Nevertheless, I'm quite sure that she had learned from the experience of other women in her socio-economic class that she might be rejected and blamed and, possibly, no longer welcome in the circles in which she belonged and felt comfortable. But there are other possible repercussions when abused women leave their husbands, one being that this is the time when the abuse becomes worse. It is the time when some men murder their wives. The competition that existed between Dorothy and Earl and the power struggle between them was intense. During the trial, Earl sat, safe, in the witness box and attacked Dorothy relentlessly. Anyone who listened to the evidence of Earl's abuse of Dorothy and also observed his temper, even in the courtroom, could not help but wonder what might have happened had Dorothy left Earl, especially during the early years of their marriage. I wondered how anyone in that courtroom could not imagine the terror Dorothy had lived with for years.

But Dorothy had also been thoroughly indoctrinated in the belief that it is up to women to make their marriages work, and there is ample evidence to indicate that throughout her marriage she did everything possible to show to the world outside her carefully secured doors a happy and normal marriage. The annual Christmas letters she sent to her friends for more than thirty years—two to three hundred of them each year—copies of which she had prepared to give to Earl on the morning she shot him, became a tangible symbol not only of the marriage and family life she wanted but didn't have, but also of the extent of her denial of the reality of her life. Dorothy knew before she married Earl that he could be jealous and hot-tempered and that he might act out against her if she incited his jealousy and disapproval. But I am sure that she believed, as most young women in her situation did, and still do, that after she married him, and he was secure in her commitment to him, he would no longer have cause to be jealous. She was wrong. Earl began to abuse her on their honeymoon.

Nevertheless, I thought I could see, even now, evidence to support Dorothy's saying that Earl has always come first in her life, and her children second. This is what Dorothy and I were taught was the correct way to behave and to feel in the days when we were learning how to be wives and mothers. In the 1950s young women were taught, still, to be "angels in the house," as Coventry Patmore named selfless, submissive, Victorian, ideal women. Many women have learned now that they are happiest when they put themselves first—and so, consequently, are their husbands and their children. Dorothy must have felt angered, threatened, and terrified (with good reason) by the fact that she could not stop Earl's physical and emotional power over her. But at the same time, there seems to be another part of her, still, that is willing to accept his authority. She seems to expect, or perhaps more accurately, to want him to cherish her, to protect her. This is how she behaved in public at least, how she behaved at the trial. She did not fawn and play a false role of submission. She may have been cautioned not to express overt antagonism toward him. Her lawyer knows that society generally—quite apart from judges and juries—does not sympathize with an angry woman, and especially an angry woman who tried to murder her husband. But I wonder if this issue ever arose in her discussions with O'Brien, because she has learned to repress her angry reactions to Earl, at least in public, so successfully. She appeared, even now, genuinely, to accept Earl. She acted as though she is quite confident that he is a gentleman. And she acted, as she has been taught to act, like a lady. She was obviously exasperated and very hurt by some of the things he said about her as he testified, and he caused her to weep quietly and to shake her head in shock and disbelief, but she did not lose control of herself.

Dorothy's lawyer, and the psychiatrists and psychologists who examined her, must have assured her that she did not cause Earl to abuse her. I think she wanted to believe this. But at the same time, I think there continued to be a part of her that blamed herself for Earl's treatment of her, and also for his abandoning her. In his testimony, Earl repeatedly and angrily told the court, and at the same time, implicitly, he seemed to be reminding Dorothy—as I'm sure he has many times—that she drove him to behave as he did. I thought that he made her feel ashamed. There were times when she appeared to be helpless, caught, torn apart by the group of people who were helping her on the one hand, and the man who had terrified her and violently abused her, but who was also her husband for almost forty years, on the other. She seemed to be incapable of assessing either herself or him clearly, realistically. Earl was the man who chose to marry her, and despite her private, angry accusations for years, and her final act, which appears not to be a part of her conscious mind at all, and despite the dramatic evidence to the contrary, she seemed almost incapable of acknowledging that he is now divorced from her.

During the months between Dorothy's preliminary hearing and her trial, I arranged to meet with several women who have been abused by their husbands. Sometimes I talked with them individually, sometimes in small groups. I asked them, among other things, to tell me about their anger. I will never forget the expressions on their faces, their body movements, the sound of their voices, as they described how they felt. I could not have imagined such intensity of emotion if I had not seen and heard it first-hand. Most of these women experienced their husbands' abuse many years ago, and in the years that followed others have helped them, in various ways, to live with the pain and damage in their lives. But they have not forgotten; they will never forget. What impressed me most dramatically was that these women know that their anger is justified.

During the trial, Dorothy's appearance was always appropriate. She varied four or five outfits throughout the two-and-a-half weeks and all of them were suitable and tasteful. But on the two days during which Earl testified, she paid special attention to her appearance. Her hair was freshly washed and set, and on the second day of his testimony she wore a light grey pantsuit, with a mandarin collar, and matching grey, very high-heeled open sandals. All of us who watched her carefully noticed this sudden change from her usual, less dramatic apparel. She may have wanted to show Earl that she still cares about her appearance as a woman—a perfectly valid gesture on her part. But it seemed to me that she was also attempting to attract his attention to her, in the oldest, most acceptable way our society knows. Her doing this revealed her feelings for him, and it was an open declaration of her vulnerability in her relationship to him. Of all the things she said and did during the trial, this was one of the saddest indications that her grasp on the reality of her situation—that her marriage was over—was extremely fragile. For the rest of us, including, I suspect, the judge and the jury, Earl was quite convincing when he said that for some time he had felt separate from Dorothy, that he had drawn away from her. We were not aware, at first, that he had not relinquished the power he knows he has over her still.

———————

When Selinger questioned Earl on the witness stand, he asked him to describe "any difficulties" in his relationship with Dorothy. What ensued revealed that Earl was prepared for the necessity of this discussion.

Earl: Yes, I assume you are speaking of fights and probably, in particular, those which would have led to and concluded with physical violence.

Selinger: Yes
Earl: So if that's the subject I will bore in on it a little bit.
Selinger: Thank you, go for it.

Earl said that there had been "three major incidents but there were two or three others of a less major—of a less major nature." There was "one exceptionally difficult occasion in Kentucky in 1978, I believe, which was quite violent in the sense that Dorothy was hurt. She was also hurt in Toronto. She was also hurt in Calgary." But Selinger wanted Earl to tell the jury about the incident in Kentucky in 1978.

> Earl: 1978, my recollection of it is that I came home from God knows where, I believe it was from overseas, and got in about midnight or 11:30 or something like that. And there was a quiet party of two or three tables, or one or two tables of bridge going on. And Dorothy was entertaining well, as usual. And nothing particularly was occurring. I am God damned if I can remember what the fight started on, but it progressed to the point where she was struck and her ribs were—I mean, proven later to be sore, I don't think they were broken, but she was certainly hurt. And those things were traumatic for both of us, not just for Dorothy.

> . . . . . . . . . . . . . . . . . . . . . . . . . . . . . . . . . . . . . . . . . . . . . . . .

> Following that event, which was really quite a terrible situation, physically as well as psychologically for—psychologically for both of us and obviously physically for Dorothy . . . I phoned Dorothy, or she phoned me, but maybe—I think I phoned Dorothy, but in any event, the gist of our discussion and conversation was that on her part that this could not be allowed to happen again. I also said that on my part it could not be allowed to happen again because I would leave.

> . . . . . . . . . . . . . . . . . . . . . . . . . . . . . . . . . . . . . . . . . . . . . . . .

Selinger: Was this 1978 incident a defining moment in your relationship?
Earl: It was for me, and I think it may have been for Dorothy, because several things happened after that and, in my view as a result of that.
    In that discussion I said that I couldn't expose myself to that kind of activity anymore, which is essentially what Dorothy said, maybe for somewhat different reasons. I agreed that I would not, you know, do that and Dorothy agreed that she would try somehow to be somewhat less provocative and back the hell off on occasion. And I think we stuck to that pretty well.

I looked over my travel schedules and came to the conclusion that—several conclusions. I had, in the last six months of 1978, averaged three nights per month at home. I had been in Europe 16 times and the Far East some other times.

. . . . . . . . . . . . . . . . . . . . . . . . . . . . . . . . . . . . . . . .

I was a very senior officer with a very large corporation. I was a senior vice-president and group operating officer of a big company. And I had been moved into significantly enhanced responsibilities and authorities and it came to my attention that if I stayed any longer they'd probably promote me, which would keep us there. That, coupled with the fact I was never home, the fact that we'd had this very, very difficult circumstance, and the fact that I wanted to spend more time with my family and I resigned . . . and we came back to Calgary by mutual desire, I think.

When Earl and Dorothy both attended marriage counselling during the mid-1980s, he began to think, he said, as he listened to Dorothy, that she didn't love him anymore, and he drew away from her. He did not explain what she said or did that caused him to think this. It wasn't until I had read my notes of the trial many times, and also the official transcripts of Earl's testimony, that I realized that Earl was probably right the first time. I think the incident in Kentucky in 1978 was, as Selinger called it, "a watershed event" for both of them. Earl injured Dorothy much more severely than he lets on during Selinger's questioning of him. Dorothy told about this incident, during her testimony, in a flat voice. Her description was more graphic. It was quite apparent that neither Earl nor Dorothy has forgotten that tragic evening in Kentucky. I could see that Earl was very frightened by his behaviour that night. Earl and Dorothy both told of talking together about this event. And they both take responsibility for saying that this could not happen again or "I" will leave. But despite what Selinger wanted the jury to believe, this was not the end of Earl's abuse of Dorothy.

Earl made it clear that leaving Kentucky was a sacrifice for him, that if he had stayed he would have advanced significantly in his position, in his corporate leadership. But, he said, he was willing to move to Calgary for the sake of their marriage.

Later, when O'Brien cross-examined Earl, he very cleverly incited Earl's anger, almost to the point of Earl losing control. Their sparring was bitter and swift and, on Earl's part, mean. But O'Brien remained cool and polite throughout.

O'Brien asked Earl to tell about what caused his fights with Dorothy.

Earl: . . . but on each of those occasions, and almost invariably when Dorothy and I were in an argument, it was not about something that Dorothy had done that I was angry about; it was something that I had or had not done which Dorothy was angry about.
O'Brien: This is your generalization?
Earl: It's a generalization which applies to most of these events because Dorothy would never leave anything alone. . . . She's—she's physically inclined, she wants to look straight in your eyes when she's discussing these matters and is not satisfied with leaving anything alone.

. . . . . . . . . . . . . . . . . . . . . . . . . . . . . . . . . . . . . . . . . . .

So, in any event, when you want to know what the fight was about, almost invariably the fight was about absolutely nothing. The striking was about my saying get away from me, you leave me alone.
O'Brien: You're saying—
Earl: Then I'd lash out. Trying to deal with Dorothy, it was a matter of frustration, exasperation and almost always for God's sake let's leave this alone, let's deal with it some other day, and that's the generalization I'm talking about.
O'Brien: So you—your assessment in this generalized way is that it was Dorothy's fault?
Earl: No, that's not at all what I said, that's not what I implied, and very specifically when one strikes someone that is the guy who strikes fault. There's no question it shouldn't happen, there's no question I shouldn't have done it, there's no question I did do it, there's no question I was wrong, and it was not Dorothy's fault. It was my fault.
O'Brien: Thank you.
Earl: Okay? But the occasion that caused this—caused these discussions to arise, it moved from conversation to angry voices, to pushing and shoving, to my striking her were for the most part inconsequential issues.
O'Brien: Let's just follow it up for a moment, inconsequential issues. Do you recall in . . . 1963 in a trip to the Kootenays where you struck Dorothy while she was pregnant with Carolyn; do you recall that?
Earl: Absolutely not.
O'Brien: Do you recall striking her in the stomach when she was pregnant on that trip?
Earl: Absolutely not.
O'Brien: And when you say absolutely not—
Earl: I recall Dorothy telling me several times that I had.

O'Brien: Yes.
Earl: And I didn't.
O'Brien: So you're say—
Earl: So my answer is no.
O'Brien: The answer is no, you did not do it or is the answer no, you don't recall it?
Earl: No, I did not do it.
O'Brien: Do you recall testifying under oath at the preliminary inquiry to this matter sir?
Earl: You bet.
O'Brien: In October of 1995?
Earl: Yeah.

O'Brien read Earl's testimony at the preliminary inquiry, that he cannot recollect striking Dorothy on a trip to the Kootenays. O'Brien asked Earl, "Would it be something that, if it occurred, you would be likely to forget or have you attempted somehow to forget some of these incidents?" Earl responded: "Could well be."

O'Brien: Do you recall giving that evidence?
Earl: Yes.
O'Brien: Today you say it's not a question of you not being able to recollect the incident. Today, sir, you say it did not in fact happen?
Earl: Today, sir, it's the manner of your questioning. I have said both I do not recollect it, and I didn't. Because, in my view, if I can't recollect it, I guess I didn't do it, and so that's—that's that.
O'Brien: So that's that. The thing that you don't recollect you didn't do?
Earl: You said that. I didn't say that.
O'Brien: You're saying now—
Earl: If you want to ask a question, ask a question.
O'Brien: Well, a few moments ago, sir, I asked you to make the distinction, did you not recollect it or did it not happen?
Earl: I said I didn't recollect it. I said I didn't recollect two things and in my view, they didn't happen.
O'Brien: Did you break Dorothy's nose?
Earl: I don't recollect doing that either. I know she got hit in the face one time with an elbow and tells me that her nose was broken.

Again O'Brien read aloud Earl's testimony at the preliminary inquiry, which ends:

O'Brien: And do you agree that you broke her nose?
Earl: I believe so, yes.

Earl became more vulnerable; he admitted to more, and more severe abuse than he had been prepared to discuss with Selinger. When he and O'Brien were discussing the episode in Kentucky, Earl said something interesting: "Okay, Dorothy blames and has blamed consistently—Dorothy has got a couple of neat things going for her." I can only imagine that what Dorothy has "going for her" is Earl's abuse of her, and her refusal to let him forget it, and also her realization and his that he could, if he really lost control of himself, injure her irreparably.

It was particularly revealing of Earl that on the witness stand, where he knew that he was protected, physically at least, he continued to fight with Dorothy, to try to control her, and to attack her. He said many things that he knew would hurt her and embarrass her, and possibly would be used to incriminate her—this was part of the accepted legal process and, perhaps, fair enough. But he also said some things that seemed to be unnecessary, and were very revealing of him. When he was discussing a gift he sent to Dorothy at Christmas 1993, five years after they had begun to live apart, he said, "I've been giving presents to Dorothy, for God sakes, for so long it's painful."

Despite the fact that Dorothy and Earl were formally separated in 1991 and had not lived together for more than a year before that, and that he has had a relationship with Lynn Manning for several years and has lived with her in Toronto since 1993, the birthday and Christmas cards he sent to Dorothy were warm, generous, and loving. O'Brien read aloud parts of one card and when he asked Earl to read one or two specific sentences from another, Earl insisted upon reading the entire text, including his signature, "Love, Earl." Apparently he is proud of these declarations of his appreciation of Dorothy, or perhaps he really believes that the letters would convince the jury of his essential good will toward her. I wondered how a man of his intelligence could underestimate so dramatically the common sense of other adults—the jury, the spectators. He knows Dorothy very well. Certainly he should know her well enough to anticipate how she would interpret what he said: that he thinks about her with affection and love. In fact, she showed these cards to one or two of her close friends as evidence of his continuing love for her. I agree with O'Brien that these cards were a means of allowing, or encouraging Dorothy to believe that her marriage was still alive, of exerting control over her. Perhaps what he was really doing was tormenting her.

I can imagine that when she was in her teens, Earl was attracted to Dorothy partly, at least, because she was intelligent, energetic, and full of fun. She moved easily among both acquaintances and strangers. She knew the social graces. Earl, who I suspect was less sure of how to act, and was a more quiet, withdrawn person, saw that she would complement his personality. Perhaps he also saw that she could help him to achieve his goals for the future, which I am sure were not insignificant, not modest. Society expected a bright, ambitious young man like Earl to marry a lady. Dorothy certainly knew how to be a lady, but I suspect that she was not always perfectly delicate or demure. She was too fun-loving and skittish to meet these standards all the time. She was also too clever. Choosing to marry Earl, despite her parents' concerns, was an act of independence. Earl must have admired this in her. I imagine that even as a very young man Earl was determined to prove that he could be a success, and that this was partly a private challenge, something he was driven to do for his own satisfaction as well as, and perhaps even more than, any public recognition. Marrying Dorothy was one of the first steps toward his future.

But despite my observations of him and my speculations about him, I have to admit that the Earl Joudrie who appeared at Dorothy's trial is, in some respects, an enigma. I suspect that this has been true of him during most of his life, and perhaps it is one of the things that attracted Dorothy to him in the first place. She said that he was "exciting," but she did not define, and she was not asked to define, what she meant by that. He was a brave kid, leaving home at the age of fourteen, defying his father who had treated him cruelly. But I suspect that he was always a loner, too smart to have much in common with most of his classmates and contempories; and an adventurer, too daring, too bold in a quiet, determined way, to suffer fools of any kind. That was what I saw as we were growing up and heard my friends who were his classmates say about him. His playing the violin and persevering with his music training to the point where he was hired to play with the Edmonton Symphony Orchestra is part of the mystery of his personality. When he told about Dorothy's moving out of the "ranch house" in Bearspaw, after he left her in 1989, he said sarcastically that she took all of the furniture, including a pool table she had given to him, but that she was "kind enough" to leave some of his books and paintings—"104 paintings," O'Brien noted. As I listened to him and watched him at the trial, he did not strike me as a man with any particular aesthetic sensitivity. His choosing to drive a white Cadillac while in Calgary is, for me, a sign of nouveau-riche vulgarity. I know that Cadillacs are different now, but in my mind, I see a white Cadillac of the 1950s, an enormous vehicle flanked by huge fins in the rear which guide and protect its commanding movement, and the inordinate space it requires as it swims silently among less ostentatious vehicles on the road. But it is quite possible that Earl behaves this way deliberately, knowingly, inviting the disapprobation of people like me. A man of his experience and intelligence is surely aware of good taste, and he provided evidence that he is quite confident that he is a man of taste. At both the preliminary hearing and the trial, when he told of arriving at Dorothy's house that Saturday morning in January 1995, he said he heard no response at first when he rang her doorbell. Even though he recognized her car parked outside the garage, he said he wondered if he was at the wrong house, because "these places all look alike." This was part of his story, this deprecating remark about Dorothy's house, and indirectly, her taste. Dorothy told of his very specific demands about the clothes she wore, and that he wore, and the food and drink she served at parties to entertain his friends, and that it had to be prepared by her, not caterers. One of O'Brien's examples of Earl's cruel treatment of Dorothy is of an occasion when she was invited to meet Earl for a social event at a downtown Calgary hotel. She took a clean shirt and a tuxedo for him. But the shirt and trousers were "wrong" and he stormed out of the hotel, leaving her there alone.

It seemed to me, during Earl's testimony, that he has cultivated the persona of a rube, which he uses, probably, only occasionally. I doubt that he did this as a young man, but I imagine that it serves him well now. In moments at work when his control and authority might be intimidating, he can reveal his working-class background, a man with rough edges who knows what it means to struggle, and therefore, paradoxically, a man who knows more than the others thought he did. He can say, as he did during the trial, "Dorothy ran the joint effectively as usual," or point out himself in a photograph taken after the shooting, "I'm somewhere between the garbage can and the door." But he misjudged his audience this time. Such remarks seemed rude and insensitive, rather than naive, funny, or in any way endearing. And when Noel O'Brien, during his cross-examination of Earl, incited his anger, to demonstrate an Earl Joudrie few people other than Dorothy and their children have ever seen, and Earl said such things as "She was going to stay the hell away from me, so I hit the wall . . . I knocked the god damn door down," we knew that he was not posing. This was part of the real Earl Joudrie. The real Earl Joudrie is, as Dorothy's psychiatrist Dr. Weston said, "a very tough person."

I have wondered how difficult it was for him to sit in the witness box, in front of his business acquaintances and colleagues who were present when he testified, knowing what they might discover about him during the next few hours. (Earl refused to sit during his testimony at the preliminary hearing. Perhaps Selinger advised him to sit in the witness box at the trial, enhancing his role as the victim.) Dorothy was on trial for attempting to murder him. He was the victim of her assault, and he obviously saw himself as the victim, and notwithstanding his treatment of her during more than forty years, I think that for some people, Earl was quite convincing as the victim. Earl would appear suddenly, with his pal and corporate lawyer, Len Sali, immediately before he began to testify, and during breaks and after his testimony was completed, he disappeared completely, accompanied by his brother, Keith. Keith Joudrie was there to support Earl, as were their two step-sisters. Keith is a large man, obviously strong physically, and it seemed to me that he acted like Earl's henchman, his bodyguard. The Court of Queen's Bench provides careful security for witnesses such as Earl, but it occurred to me that he may have felt endangered by Dorothy's presence. I wondered if she could measure what he was feeling. It was not easy for the rest of us. After all, appearing calm, cool, and in control is what he does for a living. It is part of his "job," as he would put it.

The first time Earl related his version of the sequence of events on the morning of the shooting, when Selinger was questioning him at the beginning of his testimony, Earl spoke clearly and calmly, and once or twice he wiped tears from his eyes. I was not sure then if he was weeping about the recollection of his last conversation with Dorothy, about the end of their marriage, or if these were tears of self-pity. But later, near the end of his testimony, when he and O'Brien were discussing the same sequence of events and particularly Dorothy's manner and tone of voice when she phoned for the ambulance, there were no tears. Earl's behaviour was completely different: very cool, very revealing, as he played on the words "efficient" and "execute."

Earl: Yes, she became her efficient self. She was also pretty efficient shooting the gun, too.

O'Brien: All right, all right.
Earl: That was all pretty efficient.
O'Brien: All right. At that particular point—
Earl: So the tone of voice might have been a little different, but the efficiency was the same.
O'Brien: All right.
Earl: Dorothy's ability to execute.
O'Brien: Would you mind answering the question, sir?
Earl: I'd love to answer the question.
O'Brien: All right, okay. Did she from your observations after that particular point, after she said those words, make a concerted effort . . . to contact an ambulance for you?
Earl: That's after—I had quite a long dialogue or monologue that said, "For God's sake, get an ambulance. I still may be able to make it if you can help me," and she after that said, "No, I can't do that" or "No, I wouldn't do that," or whatever and she finally agreed to do it. She didn't agree to do it, she did it.
O'Brien: She did it?
Earl: And when she did it, she was very effective, very Dorothy-like, very efficient.
O'Brien: Yes.
Earl: She phoned two or three times, and I'm screaming to phone again. And—and that was Dorothy's very effective, very efficient execution of getting an ambulance.

Earl seems to be surprisingly fit. He wore a dark suit, a white shirt and a tie, and I noticed that his hair appears to have been dyed since the last time I saw him, at the preliminary hearing. He is obviously proud, and concerned about his appearance. And apparently he is also concerned about his age. Lynn Manning, with whom he lives now, is about eight years younger than Dorothy. Dorothy's hair is white, and so is the hair of the men who know Earl, and who worked with him, and now had come to the trial to see him, and perhaps to support him.

The courtroom was full during Earl's testimony. Two new rows of benches had been added to accommodate the crowd of about sixty people. Shortly after Earl began to speak, there was a disturbance at the door of the courtroom. Some people who had arrived late were surprised to discover that there was no room to seat them. But Earl continued to speak, either unaware of or unperturbed by the disturbance. There was no break in the emotional pitch he and Selinger were creating in the room. The analogy of the courtroom as theatre occurred to me again momentarily as I watched this central character, so well prepared for his performance, so completely absorbed by it, that he was not distracted.

But O'Brien disturbed Earl's cool demeanour, and their performance as antagonists was fascinating. I wondered if all witnesses would get away with the impertinence Earl expressed in some of his responses to O'Brien's questions. O'Brien ignored this, letting Earl reveal himself, and Justice Lutz said nothing. I also wondered if the jury noticed something else that was happening. Early in his cross-examination of Earl, O'Brien asked him about his conversation with the police shortly after he arrived at the hospital. Earl said that he was more concerned with Dorothy's welfare than he was with his own, even as soon as ten minutes after she shot him.

> Earl: I mean, when the police officers came—I had been looking after Dorothy for 30 years or 40 years.
> O'Brien: Sorry?
> Earl: I had been looking after Dorothy. We had been together for a long, long time.
> O'Brien: Yes.

Apparently Earl was not aware of the ambiguous significance of his expression "looking after Dorothy," but O'Brien's response and the repetition of these words helped some of the rest of us. Also, this appeared to be the beginning, during the cross-examination, of Earl's growing awareness that he was no longer "looking after" Dorothy. Her psychiatrist, her psychologist, other people, and especially her lawyer are looking after her. It seemed to me that Earl's reaction to this realization caused a rekindling of the abusive nature of his assumed and exclusive right to control her.

Because no one else was present when Dorothy shot Earl, Jerry Selinger needed Earl to be a reliable witness. I doubt very much that Selinger could have anticipated what would happen when O'Brien cross-examined Earl. With practiced skill, O'Brien allowed Earl to reveal that he was not always reliable or trustworthy; that while he wants to control others, he is not always in perfect control of himself; and that he can be competitive, insensitive, a bully—and apparently, even now, jealous.

At the conclusion of his examination of Earl, Selinger asked him to describe Dorothy. Earl did "describe" Dorothy, but his description is also very revealing of himself, especially of the competition he experienced in his relationship with her, and also of his expectations of her—that despite his treatment of her, she ought to have been able to let things go, she ought to have been able to "back down."

> Earl: She was tremendously capable at whatever she undertook. She was a very popular person, made friends easily, and in a very real sense with just about everybody that she met. She was very positive about just about everything. Her putts always dropped for that reason. She beat me at golf. She beat me at gin rummy. She beat me at just about everything we undertook. And she was a winner and saw herself as such.
>
> She was also a very dominant powerful, positive personality, which is why she did things so well. Everything she did she did very well, very effectively and in a very organized way. At the same time, she could be—she could be pretty tough, pretty aggressive and peri- odically downright nasty . . . I guess the only point I am trying to make is that Dorothy is a very powerful individual on her own—in her own right, and at the same time in pursuing—she never let anything go. I mean, I loved everything about her except the fact that she would not back down. She would not let anything rest and she liked to be right. And so she had a bit of a streak of—she could be vindictive and vengeful at times.

Earl said all this in a quiet, polite, confident tone of voice.

During O'Brien's cross-examination, he antagonized Earl not only by pointing out the discrepancies between his answers at the trial and at the pre- liminary hearing, but also by allowing Earl to reveal the inconsistencies in his story, his increasingly cavalier attitude, and his skewed logic—for example, "I didn't beat Dorothy, I struck Dorothy." Earl interrupted O'Brien:

> Dorothy is aggressive. She can be vengeful. She is vengeful. She is vin- dictive and sometimes she can be vicious and sometimes she can be vio- lent. So this wasn't a one-way street this pushing and shoving going on.

I wondered if Selinger had neglected to warn Earl that the abusive husband always blames his wife, and that by speaking this way Earl was setting himself up as a classic abuser. In some people's minds he was mak- ing himself an object of pity, so tormented by his wife that he was forced to use his greater size and strength and power to stop her, to silence her. But O'Brien did not miss this cue.

O'Brien: And you have a severe temper I am going to suggest to you sir?
Earl: No, not particularly.

. . . . . . . . . . . . . . . . . . . . . . . . . . . . . . . . . . . . . . . .

Earl: We're not dealing with a shy, retiring violet here, Mr. O'Brien.
O'Brien: Right. You're saying a shy, retiring violet?
Earl: That's what I just said.
O'Brien: Did you ever go to the hospital?
Earl: I got chased around the house, I got chased down the hall, I got chased from room to room. I had to leave the place on several different occasions to get away from Dorothy because Dorothy would push. She would push and push and push.
O'Brien: I think you've made your—
Earl: She was never—well, I'm going to keep making it.
O'Brien: All right. Let me ask you this, sir, did you ever go to the hospital as a result of these altercations?
Earl: No, I didn't.
O'Brien: You're physically stronger than Dorothy?
Earl: I would think so.
O'Brien: No contest in a physical, violent altercation between the two of you?
Earl: I don't believe so.

Despite Earl's revelations of his physical and emotional abuse of Dorothy during O'Brien's cross-examination, Selinger ended Earl's appearance as a witness by citing three incidents of abuse: in 1963 when Earl struck Dorothy in the stomach when she was pregnant with Carolyn—"33 years ago"; in 1971 in Calgary—"25 years ago"; and in 1978 in Kentucky—"18 years ago." Some people left the trial at this point, assured that they had heard the most important witness and convinced that there were only three real episodes of abuse in the Joudrie's marriage, and that they occurred so long ago they are of little consequence now. Despite the fact that Earl had admitted to injuring Dorothy in Toronto, albeit in his strangely passive fashion—as if he were the observer of a phantom doing the damage—Selinger did not even mention Toronto in his conclusion. The jury would hear in a few days something of what happened in Toronto. But I am convinced that this little summary at the end of Earl's testimony affected public opinion quite dramatically. People who spoke both publicly and privately about the Joudries referred repeatedly to three or four incidents of abuse which ended about twenty years ago.

Ann Jones, a journalist who has studied and written extensively about spousal abuse, writes:

> domestic violence is *not* just a series of isolated blow ups, the result of anger or stress or too much to drink, though it often looks that way to the woman who is the target. Rather, domestic violence is *a process of deliberate intimidation intended to coerce the victim to do the will of the victimizer.*

Jones tells that Emerge, "a Boston counseling program for men who batter" uses the following as their working definition of violence:

> any act that causes the victim to do something she does not want to do, prevents her from doing something she wants to do, or causes her to be afraid . . . violence *need not involve physical contact with the victim* since intimidating acts like punching walls, verbal threats, and psychological abuse can achieve the same results.[43]

---

On the two days of Earl's testimony people began to line up at the door of the courtroom more than an hour before the sessions began. There were many couples in their sixties. As they waited, the men moved among the crowd, talking quietly, soberly, with other men they knew, while their wives kept their places in the line. The atmosphere was funereal. I don't know how many of these men know Earl personally, but obviously they all know about him. The men avoided people they didn't know. I think some of them did not want to be recognized, named. But I talked with some of their wives.

These women were cautious at first, but gradually they talked about Dorothy and about themselves. Several of them told of having spent their entire adult lives in the oil business. Some of them told of having moved all over the world with their husbands and children, living an isolated, artificial, very lonely existence—much like the military, one woman said. These women seemed not to want to talk about Earl. They expressed sympathy for Dorothy; they said how sad they felt for her. Some of their husbands have not reached the top of the corporate ladder, their lives have not been as luxurious, as affluent as the Joudries', but they seemed to understand what Dorothy has experienced. If their marriages have been difficult, they didn't say. But they were here at Dorothy's trial with their husbands, sitting with them comfortably, talking with them companionably. The women spoke to me with compassion and generosity. During breaks I saw Dorothy talking with some of these women, embracing some of them. Their meeting was sober, sometimes tearful, and Dorothy always thanked them for coming.

# Guy and Carolyn

Louie's lip trembled, "When I begin to get near home,
I begin to tremble all over—I don't know why, I never told
any one what it is like at home."
                    Christina Stead, *The Man Who Loved Children*[44]

But suppose I had gone into a store—perhaps a department
store. I see a place with the brisk atmosphere, the
straightforward displays, the old-fashioned modern look of the
fifties. Suppose a tall handsome woman, nicely turned out,
had come to wait on me, . . . I would have wanted to tell her
that I knew, I knew her story . . . I imagine myself trying to
tell her. (This is a dream now, I understand it as a dream.)
I imagine her listening, with a pleasant composure. But she
shakes her head. She smiles at me, and in her smile there is a
degree of mockery, a faint, self-assured malice. Weariness as
well. She is not surprised that I am telling her this, but she is
weary of it, of me, and my idea of her, my information, my
notion that I can know anything about her.
    Of course it's my mother I'm thinking of, . . . .
                    Alice Munro, "Friend of My Youth"[45]

During the trial I wished that I knew more about Dorothy's childhood,
about her relationships with her brother and her parents as she grew up,
about the effects on her family of her father's absence when he was in the
RCAF during the war and later while he attended the University of

Oregon. But there was no discussion of her childhood except very brief references to her parents and her recollection of their marriage as having been ideal, perfect. To demonstrate her parents' devotion to each other, Dorothy's psychiatrist, Dr. Weston, said that their deaths were separated by only six months. I was surprised at Dr. Weston's romantic interpretation of their love, their dependence on each other. But perhaps I should have been surprised at my resistance to his willingness to accept the proximity of their deaths as evidence of the nature of their relationship. Certainly on the basis of his evidence, I agreed with him when he said that it was natural for Dorothy to dream of a marriage like theirs. Dorothy told the court that her father was a well-educated man, who had earned a Ph.D., and who was very much respected and admired by his colleagues and friends. Dorothy spoke of her father with great admiration and love. She did not speak, directly, about her feelings for her mother. But what she did say about her was an important revelation of their relationship.

When Dorothy told of Earl's abuse of her in Kentucky while her parents were visiting, she seemed to believe that they were critical of her, and that what they saw on that occasion confirmed their worst possible fears about Earl—fears which, apparently, for more than twenty years she had assured them were unfounded. I have wondered what it was like for Dorothy all those years, defying her parents' concerns for her, refusing to admit that their doubts about her decision to marry Earl were justified. How could she possibly confide in them, or turn to them for the support she needed when she could not, or would not, admit that their opinion of Earl was reasonable after all, and when she believed that she had failed to make her marriage a success. Many of us marry people whom our parents do not like, or respect, or whom they would not have chosen for us had they the right to do so. Sometimes parents are wrong. If they are not wrong, families live with the young people's choice, as they must, accommodating to it with grace, or sadness, or recriminations, depending on the kind of people they are. But the life Dorothy chose with Earl was more dramatic, more dangerous than most. She was in danger physically and emotionally, and by not wanting her parents to know this she must have created an estrangement between herself and them, which surely was very difficult for her. Most of us believe in the emotional shelter our families can provide for us, even when we are adults. We need and want to believe that it exists, because to be criticized, rejected, unwelcomed, or abandoned by our kin is terrible.

One of the many surprising revelations young parents experience at the arrival of their first child is the weight of the responsibility that is suddenly theirs. It is they, now, who must create an emotional shelter for their child. This realization may come more slowly to new fathers who are not tied so physically as mothers are to the care of their helpless, newborn infants, but fathers are learning these days to share equally in the early care of their babies. When Dorothy and I had our babies, fathers were not expected to share this responsibility, and those who did were the exception. Grandmothers often visited, to help their daughters during the first days of being a mother. My parents visited us soon after the birth of our first child, but it was my father, not my mother, who helped me and, by example, showed my husband, and me, what to do. It was my father who took our new son into his arms when he was restless and we could not understand what was wrong. He held him gently, confidently, walking, talking, singing to him until he was quiet and comfortable. We learned from my father.

I have never believed in maternal instinct: that women, by virtue of their biological makeup universally and instinctively love their offspring. I think such an idea is another romantic myth. I have seen mothers who do not, and cannot love their babies, and perhaps for this reason I will never forget the inexpressible relief I experienced when my children were born and I knew without a shred of doubt that I loved them more than I could ever have imagined was possible. But this is a gift; I am sure of that. I remember the wonder of holding them close against me; of looking, long, into their eyes as they gazed into mine; of touching their tiny toes and fingers, the perfect shells of their ears; of laying my cheek and lips against their heads, feeling their satiny hair and skin, and of breathing that most delicate scent—the sweet scent of a baby. I wonder if Dorothy has similar memories of her babies.

But the truth is that not all parents can or do provide the loving shelter that we believe children deserve. Certainly not all parents can provide it all of the time. And many parents know that they, too, can be excluded from their families by their children. Literature is filled with examples of troubled families. Snow White must try to outwit her jealous stepmother; Hansel and Gretel are abandoned by their selfish stepmother and their weak father; Hamlet cannot bear his uncle's greed and what he believes is his mother's infidelity; Lear, in his old age, and rash, selfish, paternal authority, casts out the one daughter who truly loves him and is betrayed, utterly, by his other two daughters to whom he leaves his estate; Leontes, the jealous husband in *The Winter's Tale,* imprisons his innocent wife, Hermione, and banishes their daughter, Perdita, to the desert to perish. In the literature of this century, one of the most memorable and complex families is the Ramsays in Virginia Woolf's novel *To the Lighthouse.* In this novel, a woman must free herself from a powerful mother figure, despite how much she loves her.

Dorothy impresses me as a powerful mother. But I see her also as a dependent mother. And I think this was evident in the testimony her son, Guy, and her daughter, Carolyn, provided for the Crown. Some journalists made a point of observing that her children were not present at the trial, except Guy and Carolyn when they came to testify against her. These journalists sometimes mentioned that Colin lives and works in South America, and Neale in the United States. But none of us knows why at least the two children who were not witnesses were not in the courtroom regularly. Perhaps Dorothy or Earl asked them not to come. Perhaps they decided, as a group, that they would not or could not come.

I have tried to imagine what their home was like as these children grew up. Earl told of family holidays in British Columbia in the summers, skiing in the mountains in the winters, trips to Hawaii. One of Dorothy's character witnesses told of Dorothy's presence at the boys' baseball games, and her active participation as a "band parent" during their high school years. This witness described Dorothy up to her elbows in dishwater at three a.m., cheerfully cleaning up after a party for her children and their high school friends in their home.

O'Brien asked Earl at one point where the children were when Dorothy and he were fighting and Earl said he supposed that they were in bed. But we know from what their nanny, Elizabeth Griffiths, said that they were not always in bed. And if they were in bed, were they asleep? Could they not hear Dorothy and Earl when they argued and fought, when Earl hit Dorothy, or knocked her down, or slammed her against the wall, or broke furniture, or punched holes in the walls, or knocked down doors in their home? They must have looked forward to seeing their father because he was away so much of the time, but surely they must also have dreaded what inevitably happened when he came home. And when he was away, when they were in their teens, did they want to bring their friends home late in the day when they knew that Dorothy may have been drinking? I think of all this when I try to understand why two of their children were prepared to testify against their mother at her trial. I also wonder about a justice system that allows family members to testify against each other—especially parents and children. The two children's willingness to do this was more disturbing to many people than what they said, and it was quite apparent that seeing them in the witness box and listening to them was almost more than Dorothy could bear.

Guy, at twenty-six, is the youngest of Dorothy's children. On the day that he testified as a witness for the prosecution, he was neatly dressed in a blazer and grey trousers, a shirt and tie. There was nothing modest or hesitant in his presentation of himself, and in fact, his cavalier attitude was not to his advantage that morning. From what Dorothy said about Guy, it seems apparent that they saw him as their problem child, who was often the subject of their disagreements. He has not yet been as successful as his two older brothers, and unlike them, he has stayed close to home. I had seen Guy and listened to him testify at the preliminary hearing, and as I watched him enter the witness box at the trial, I felt sorry for him and for what he was about to do. His posture, the way he stands, is similar to Earl's, and it became evident as he talked, and later as Dorothy talked about him, that he aspires to be like his father. He described meeting his father and Lynn Manning in a downtown hotel for breakfast on the morning of the shooting, and then driving his father out to the "ranch house," the acreage, in the white Cadillac Earl had rented. Guy and his wife were living temporarily in the former family home, and perhaps they had borrowed the car on Friday evening after they and the other children had dinner with Earl and Lynn Manning. It appeared from what Guy said, and also from what Earl said about that morning, that their original plan may have been that Guy would accompany Earl to Dorothy's house for the arranged visit, but, as Guy said, it was late, and he had to go to work. So Earl visited Dorothy on his own.

Selinger moved quickly to the reason for Guy's appearance at the trial, asking him if, when he visited Dorothy in jail after the shooting, with his wife Michelle and his sister Carolyn and her husband Mark, Dorothy and he had had a conversation. "Yes," said Guy. "While discussing our terms of bailing her out, she confronted my wife and me with the statement that it was our fault she had shot my father." If Guy felt hurt by what Dorothy said that evening, it was not apparent. In fact, he seemed to be pleased to repeat his mother's remark. And if what he said during those first moments of his testimony was dramatic, the way he said it did not endear him to anyone. As he described his relationship with Dorothy, and later when Dorothy talked about Guy, I wondered why Guy and his wife had visited Dorothy that night at all. Everything he said about Dorothy, and especially his and Dorothy's description of their feelings about his recent wedding, suggest that his appearance at the jail with his wife would upset his mother. In that context, considering how confused and distraught Dorothy was, and especially considering Carolyn's version of what Dorothy said to Guy, Dorothy's accusation is not so insensitive as it appears to be initially.

Guy described his version of his parents' relationship: that whenever Earl came home, "on a monthly basis," they had "heated" confrontations, "yelling and screaming," which could begin over something as simple as a hand of cards and end by one or the other of them leaving—"usually father" because of his "not wanting it to go further." Dorothy, said Guy, is "not a person who likes to be ignored," so Earl's leaving would upset her. "We," he said, meaning, I assume, his brothers and Carolyn, "tried to avoid the area." The substance of what Guy said, and the way he said it led Selinger to suggest that he was a "bit of a bad boy," and that his relationship with Dorothy was the same as his father's. "My confrontations with mother were similar to father's," he said. Like his father, Guy punched holes in the walls of their home, and he said that he and Dorothy had "physical confrontations": they hit each other; Dorothy pulled Guy's hair. These violent confrontations ended, according to Guy, after Carolyn tried to stop a fight between Guy and their mother, and Guy "inadvertently" struck Carolyn. Dorothy insisted that Guy must leave the house. Earl spoke to Guy: "He was of the opinion, strongly of the opinion, that there was no way I should ever hit a female, or anyone else, especially my mother," said Guy. He seemed to be unaware of the irony in this remark about his father's high standards. Guy added that his father warned him that if he did not stop this behaviour he would have him to contend with. Guy and Selinger chuckled over the fact that such a confrontation with his father was definitely something Guy wanted to avoid.

Selinger asked Guy to talk about Dorothy's drinking. Guy said that his mother began to drink as early as eight or nine in the morning, would "nurse" drinks throughout the day, and drink more heavily during the evening. Was Dorothy drunk? "Daily . . . often . . . she drank seven days a week," Guy said. He told of one time when Dorothy woke in the morning not remembering that her car had slid into the ditch the night before. O'Brien, in his cross-examination of Guy, noted that because Guy had not lived with Dorothy since October 1990, he was not in a position to comment on her drinking during the past few years—daily, hourly, or, he implied, at all. O'Brien spoke to Guy in much the same manner that he had used with Earl. O'Brien never raised his voice, overtly he was courteous, but it seemed to me that every gesture, every look, and everything he said was infused with cool disdain and authority. O'Brien was also careful, and obviously aware of the ethical delicacy of questioning a son about his mother. He did not allow Guy to reveal himself as blatantly as he might have, and he did not incite reckless remarks that Guy might later regret.

Selinger left until the end of his examination of Guy his discussion of Guy's wedding on December 10, 1994. Guy explained proudly that he and his wife had organized their wedding at the Banff Springs Hotel themselves, and that they had invited "who we wanted—for example, Lynn Manning." Dorothy testified later that she was very upset that Lynn Manning and her daughters had been invited to Guy's wedding, and also that she was not included in any of her son's wedding plans. Guy said that his mother had no responsibility "in the wedding" except to introduce people during the reception. As he said this Dorothy shook her head, probably because she is still offended by his exclusion of her, but also I wondered if one of her responsibilities, which Guy neglected to mention, was that she helped to pay for his wedding. Guy said that Earl made a toast to "the family" which was "quite emotional" and called up "the siblings and mother" saying that they should be supportive of each other. "Mother was surprised, but she came up. . . . Later in the evening I saw her. She was intoxicated and upset, not belligerent, but upset."

In his cross-examination, O'Brien pointed out that the last time Guy struck Dorothy, he was five feet eleven inches tall and weighed 175 pounds, and explicitly, that he was full-grown. O'Brien also mentioned the salsa episode. Guy had said that once when Dorothy and Earl were playing cards and arguing, Earl had thrown a bowl of salsa against the ceiling, breaking it, and making a mess. O'Brien asked who had cleaned up this mess. "Mother and the siblings. Father left," said Guy, smiling. "Do you find this humorous?" O'Brien asked. "Yes," said Guy. Guy also told O'Brien and the court that he is closer to his father than to Dorothy, that his mother had never "verbalized" to him her distress about Earl's living with Lynn Manning, and that in late 1994, as Guy was preparing his wedding, she was "no more than usually stressed." All this was Guy's effort to enforce the seriousness of Dorothy's accusation.

There was an adjournment after Guy's testimony, and several of us heard Dorothy say, "I can't stand this!" to Noel O'Brien. She was very upset. I can't imagine what O'Brien could have said to Dorothy to comfort her.

Carolyn's testimony the next day was different from Guy's. The intervening testimony by police officers helped to separate Carolyn from Guy in the minds of the jury. Nevertheless, having heard one of Dorothy's children, observers were ready for the other. The fact that women in the gallery outnumbered men three to one, indicated the seriousness to women of a daughter's willingness to testify against her mother. Carolyn's manner suggested none of her brother's arrogance. But she appeared very cool, controlled, determined, and sometimes even contemptuous. Unlike many others who listened to her and watched her, I thought that Carolyn was courageous. I believe that this was something she had to do for herself, despite the pain she knew it would cause her mother—and herself. I wondered if she realized what lay ahead for her when at her mother's bail hearing, on the Monday after the shooting, she agreed, with her husband, to take Dorothy into their home, to take responsibility for her for what became not two, but three weeks, until she could attend the Betty Ford Center. Carolyn had offered her mother shelter, emotionally and physically. But now, she was pushing her away and, in a sense, abandoning her.

When Dorothy came into the courtroom on the morning of Carolyn's testimony, she had been weeping. She went directly to the prisoner's dock and sat, obviously disturbed and preoccupied by what was about to happen. Selinger seemed to be nervous about questioning Carolyn. Before Justice Lutz appeared, Selinger paced, and shrugged his shoulders, perhaps to relieve his tension. He may have been included in whatever it was, specifically, that distressed Dorothy.

Carolyn appears not to have her mother's flair for feminine charm, her style. During the trial, Dorothy became increasingly distraught, and this was quite evident in her appearance, particularly in her facial expressions and her body movements, which revealed the pain and tension she was experiencing. But her general appearance, especially during the first few days of the trial, continued to be neat and suitable and carefully calculated. Dorothy's hands are expressive, attractive. Her long, rather bony fingers are spatulate and throughout the trial she kept her fingernails short and painted with clear polish. All this expressed the importance to her of her outward appearance, expectations of herself as a woman which she has learned, and which are now, I suspect, almost unconscious. Carolyn was dressed quite appropriately, but there was nothing about her appearance that was outstanding, or that attracted attention—except that in this aspect of herself she was a contrast to her mother. Some might see her, perhaps, as being in her mother's shadow. But Carolyn seems to be a realist. It appears that she has looked honestly at her relationship with her mother and she feels anger and resentment and, as she admitted, a need to protect herself.

Carolyn identified herself—that she is thirty-two years old and the second oldest child in the family, and that she has been married since October 1993. Hers was the first of the three marriages of the children for which Dorothy asked Earl to postpone their divorce. Carolyn said that she moved out of her parents' home when she was twenty-five, but that despite the fact that she lived away from them she continued to act as an intermediary between Dorothy and Earl. When she was twenty-seven she realized that she was too involved with their lives and too identified with them, and particularly with her mother, and that if this continued she would have a nervous breakdown. She resolved to end this unnatural relationship. Then Carolyn used the pronouns "they" and "them" and I assume she was referring to Dorothy and Earl when she said, "I told them . . . they were angry . . . so for a while there was no contact . . . but eventually they settled down and accepted it."

But when she and Mark Murphy decided to marry, Carolyn could not withstand the pressure to do what her mother wanted. She said that Dorothy had looked forward to her daughter's marriage since Carolyn was born, and that she had her own opinions about Carolyn's wedding and that "it got to the point where it was easier to just do what she wanted." She said, for example, that she and Mark had chosen their own marriage vows, but that at the last minute, Dorothy insisted that they be changed to the traditional vows. She said that her wedding "was very stressful for all of us." She said that Dorothy interfered in Colin's wedding as well, but that "there was not much interference with Guy's wedding" because Dorothy did not like Guy's wife.

Dorothy had been watching Carolyn closely and listening with sadness and obvious compassion for Carolyn. But Carolyn's cool revelation of her mother's interference in her wedding caused Dorothy to stand up suddenly in the prisoner's dock, raise her hands above her head, and as she bent over, leaning her head on her hands, she let out a wail of protest and

pain. For a moment or two, as she sobbed, it appeared that she might collapse. Justice Lutz announced a recess. As O'Brien called for a woman
Dorothy knows to come to her aid, Dorothy began to recover her composure. She was very contrite, apologizing to O'Brien. She left the courtroom silently, but in the waiting area, a journalist told me, as she followed
behind Carolyn, Selinger, and an RCMP officer, she continued to protest
her daughter's ingratitude. She continued to speak—to Carolyn, and anyone else in her vicinity—"I can't believe this. . . . "

As I walked out into the waiting area, silently—everyone was silent—
I could not help thinking of myself at Carolyn's age, and my mother, who
was hurt by my behaviour and wanted me to feel guilty. She wanted others to know that the way I behaved and what I chose to do was beyond
her influence or control, and in getting the sympathy of others there was
a deliberate attempt to influence me, to manipulate me. This happened
not frequently, but certainly dramatically after I was grown up and had the
courage and self-possession not only to defy some of her cherished beliefs,
but to risk the loss of her approval, and even her love. My husband and I
decided to be married in Toronto in a private ceremony, in the presence
of only two witnesses, partly to avoid the interference—and the presence—of my mother. Fortunately my father understood my need to do
this, and I think my mother understood as well, and was very relieved that
we would not be married in Edmonton. But I doubt very much that she
admitted this to her friends, or even to herself.

My mother never visited me after I left her home without expressing,
usually indirectly, her disapproval of what I said, or the way I acted, or my
friends—our friends, after I married—or what I was doing—my studies,
my work, or the way I cared for my children. I cannot remember many
specific incidents now, which is probably a good thing. I had been aware
of this attitude towards me since I was a child, and I was used to it. But I
resented it, more than I realized. While my father was still alive, my mother seemed to be not quite so judgemental as she was later. Perhaps she
complained to him about what irked her, and he placated her, and that
was all she needed. She enjoyed our children; we always talked companionably; my husband indulged her and made her laugh. But there was
always something wrong. After my father died, my visits to her in
Edmonton were pleasant enough, but dutiful. Her visits to us, no matter
how much I tried to please her, were very difficult for me, and I was always
glad when it was time for her to go home. I was ashamed that as a grown

woman I felt anger and resentment toward my mother, but at the same time, I recognized that I did not want to give up these emotions, even if I could. It wasn't until I was in my late forties and my mother was more than eighty that suddenly all of that bitterness simply disappeared.

I was writing about a modern American poet, Louise Bogan, who had an extremely difficult relationship with her mother. Bogan said that she wrote out her relationship with her mother in her poems, but she also wrote about her mother in her journals and letters, and she said more than once that the details of their relationship were too terrible for her to tell anyone. I, of course, wanted to get to the bottom of this relationship in order to understand what Bogan was saying in her poems. While I was immersed in my search to understand Bogan's poetry, I had a long, complicated dream in which a friend, who looks very much like Louise Bogan, and whose name is Grace, confidently and sympathetically offered me my mother—as a gift. And my mother's heaviness, the great weight of her, which I felt that I had carried all those years, was suddenly gone. I have always seen my friend, Grace, as a wise and gentle woman, and it was as if she were explaining my mother to me. I woke from the dream amazed at the details, the complexity of it, but most important, completely free from the negative feelings I had kept for so long for my mother. Even now, as I remember that dream, I marvel at the mystery of the unconscious mind, and how sometimes it acts to protect us, and also to reveal to us what our conscious minds resist or cannot comprehend. This was an unusual experience for me because I seldom remember my dreams or take any interest in them at all. I had always been quick to dismiss, as false or hokey, tales others told of such experiences. I often did not believe them. But I have discovered that writers of theses or books, when they are quite absorbed with their subjects, do sometimes dream about them, often in a strange and mysterious intertwining with their own lives. Also, I have discovered that I am not the first woman who has had a dream similar to mine about her mother.

I think my mother was quite unaware of any change in me. I never told her about my dream. But I was fortunate: I was free to enjoy my relationship with her during the last years of her life. My mother continued to disapprove of me, of what I said or did, but it no longer bothered me.

As I am writing this, I remember a day about twenty-five years ago when I was visiting my mother in Edmonton and she asked me to help her to buy a new dress. In a shop she liked she chose two or three dresses and the sales woman took us to a pleasant fitting room, where I could sit comfortably. I remember that the room had a window and that it was a sunny, pleasant day. My mother took off the dress she was wearing and hung it up carefully. I admired her purposeful busyness, her plain but good and immaculate petticoat—for that was what she and I called a "slip"—and her trim, small body, different now that she had lost the extra weight of her middle age. The sales woman had brought a red dress first, which my mother slipped on quickly, efficiently, and without a second's hesitation she opened the door and walked out to the group of mirrors where she could see herself from all angles. She stood there, in the centre, patting and tweaking her hair a little, turning to one side and then the other, quite unconscious of anyone else, utterly absorbed and pleased with herself and her appearance. I realized then, not for the first time, that underneath her almost obsessive worrying and fretting and concern about what others might think, all characteristics of her which I disliked, she possessed a self-confidence—even an imperiousness—which I had seen, occasionally, since I was a child. But now, for the first time, I accepted this complexity in her nature, and even enjoyed it. This was a revelation to me. I think this helped, in an odd way, to cause the eventual change in my feelings about her.

Dorothy, I think, has a similar sense of herself, despite the discussion by O'Brien, and Carolyn, and Dorothy as well, of her low self-esteem. It is a healthy part of her, the part of her that embraces her anger. But like my mother, she has learned to deny this self-possession, even to repress it much of the time, because it is too threatening, not only to others, but to herself.

What happened during the break in Carolyn's testimony was a strange, hushed continuation of the drama we had just witnessed. Women in the gallery were deeply affected by what they had just seen and heard. All of us were daughters, and many of us were mothers as well. And as we left the courtroom we were absorbed by our own lives, suffused with memories of our own relationships with our mothers or our daughters. All over the waiting area women stood in small groups, talking quietly. Many of them expressed sympathy for Dorothy. But there was little analysis of Carolyn's behaviour, or Dorothy's. A much more compelling need, for everyone it seemed, was to tell something about themselves, as I have done now. In the group in which I stood, each woman revealed, almost involuntarily, and to perfect strangers, an intensely personal anecdote. One woman talked about her parents' difficult marriage and divorce, and how resentful she feels about her mother's behaviour. Another woman talked about the almost unendurable anxiety she has experienced since she and her husband were told that their newborn daughter was given a transfusion of what may have been tainted blood, immediately after her birth. Old memories, deeply buried injuries we thought we had forgotten, pushed suddenly to the surface and broke through our usual control and decorum. I can't imagine any more profound evidence of the compassion we felt for Dorothy and Carolyn than our need to add our stories to theirs.

When Selinger resumed his examination of Carolyn, there was no sign that Dorothy's outburst had affected Carolyn's composure, except perhaps that she was even more firmly resolved not to be deterred by Dorothy from saying what she obviously had decided to say. I think that Carolyn's testimony, and her willingness to testify at all, was fueled by anger and a need to assert her independence. Perhaps eventually Dorothy will understand that. At the time, Carolyn broke Dorothy's heart. But Dorothy too, was angry. She seemed to see Carolyn, and I think she wanted others to see her, as an ungrateful daughter. Carolyn was publicly demeaning Dorothy. More important, Carolyn was exposing Dorothy's dependence on her, her vulnerability, her fragility, and her inadequacies as a mother. And who of us would blame Dorothy, if she was deeply offended by that.

Selinger asked Carolyn to discuss Dorothy's drinking. Carolyn said she "believed" she saw it in Toronto, in Kentucky, and increasingly in Calgary. She said that when Dorothy consulted "a couple of psychologists and psychiatrists," Dorothy reported that tests showed that she was not an alcoholic. Carolyn said that she thought that her mother did have a drinking problem. She said that she preferred to talk with Dorothy on the telephone in the mornings because by late afternoon, although Dorothy was coherent, the conversations were not satisfactory because she seemed forgetful and would repeat herself.

Carolyn told about visiting Dorothy in jail on the evening of the shooting. She said that as she and her husband arrived, Noel O'Brien was leaving and he told them not to discuss the shooting incident with Dorothy or to ask questions about it. She said that Dorothy had been crying and wanted to talk about it, but when Carolyn and Mark said no, she "refrained." She said that the next day when she and Mark visited, Dorothy wanted to be sure that she would be able to play bridge as usual and attend the other engagements on her social calendar that week. This upset Carolyn "greatly"—Dorothy's behaving "as if life would just carry

on as usual." Guy and Michelle were present also, and Carolyn said that
while she and Mark were explaining to her the conditions of her bail,
Dorothy interrupted, saying that Guy and Michelle were responsible for
upsetting her. Carolyn said, "I told her she must never make such comments again or she could not stay with us."

Selinger led Carolyn through a series of questions to support his theory that Dorothy's directing Earl to enter her house through the garage that
Saturday morning was unusual. Carolyn said that she, herself, always used
the front door to enter Dorothy's house, and also that the fact that her
mother's car was parked in the driveway to the garage entrance that morning was "very unusual." Selinger would use this as evidence of motive, that
Dorothy planned to kill Earl that morning, and had deliberately emptied
the garage. But what interested me about this exchange between Selinger
and Carolyn was what Carolyn said about the garage. She said that
Dorothy always parked her car in the garage and that Carolyn, too, wants
an attached garage. She said, "This is my own need for security, and also
from my mom." Everything else Carolyn had said in defiance of her mother fell away suddenly, and although I could not see Dorothy's face at that
moment, I wondered if she heard "my mom" as I did.

O'Brien's cross-examination of Carolyn was gentle, but pointed, and
in the end helpful to his defence of Dorothy. Carolyn said that when she
talked with her mother on Friday, the day before the shooting, Dorothy
told her that she planned to get her hair done the next morning, and to
have dinner, Saturday evening, with a friend. She said that Dorothy's
behaviour on the day of the shooting, when she saw her, in jail, in the
evening, was "different," "surreal," and that Dorothy seemed like a "different person." She agreed that her conversation with Dorothy the second
time she visited her, on Sunday, revealed "almost denial" that anything
unusual had happened. She said that Dorothy and Guy had never got
along. Carolyn agreed with O'Brien that since Dorothy returned from the
Betty Ford Clinic she has not resided with her, and that Carolyn has
"stepped back" from a relationship with her mother and that Dorothy has
"pretty much respected that." Carolyn also agreed that when the four children were teenagers their mother was very involved with their school and
other activities. O'Brien listed Dorothy's various and many social responsibilities and volunteer work and suggested to Carolyn that Dorothy is a
"very exceptional person." I thought Carolyn's tone of voice when she
echoed O'Brien's "very exceptional" was bitter, and that this was a jarring

note in the cross-examination. But O'Brien brought her back to his side, and Dorothy's, very quickly. O'Brien said that the Christmas letters which Dorothy has sent out for more than thirty years and has collected in albums for the children and for Earl painted a picture of a happy, perfect home, which simply did not exist. Carolyn agreed.

O'Brien asked Carolyn if Dorothy talked with her about Earl's abuse of her. Carolyn said, "not much—sometimes." O'Brien sympathized with the "uncomfortable, intermediary role" required from Carolyn and sought her agreement, and got it, that both Dorothy and Earl "used" her to make contact with each other. O'Brien asked Carolyn about the effects on Dorothy of Earl's cards to her during the past years, since their separation. Carolyn said that they made her mother very emotional, they caused her to weep, and to wonder about Earl's intentions. O'Brien asked her about Dorothy's self-esteem. Carolyn said, "She has very little self-esteem. I see that people who are very gregarious have low self-esteem. This is true of mother." She agreed that both Dorothy and Earl strive for perfection; that Dorothy had always hoped that she and Earl could retire and travel together; that Guy's wedding plans were very distressing for Dorothy because of his wanting to invite Lynn Manning; and that Dorothy's family and her home are very important to her, and implicitly that this was why Carolyn's wedding was so important to Dorothy. O'Brien ended this dialogue by referring to Carolyn's wedding "in 1963" and both he and Carolyn laughed at his mistaken date. He suggested that it is not uncommon for mothers and daughters to disagree over marriages. Carolyn responded: "Yes. It is very common." So again, O'Brien defused intense emotion, but not without impressing the jury with his side of the argument.

We broke for lunch then. Carolyn disappeared quickly, but as Dorothy went out the door six or eight women gathered around her, patting her gently on the back, hugging her, supporting her. Later that afternoon, during a break, Dorothy stayed in the prisoner's dock. I, also, stayed in my chair. Dorothy was preoccupied and unaware of anyone watching her. She seemed very tense still, sighing, trying to relax her shoulders and neck. Suddenly she slipped off her shoes and put her stockinged feet up on the edge of the dock. She leaned forward, diverted for a moment looking thoughtfully at her toenails which were painted red.

# The Nanny

A man beats up a woman not because there is something
wrong with her (though he says so) or even because there is
something wrong with him (though women say so) but
because he *can*. He can because nobody stops him.
            Ann Jones, *Next Time, She'll Be Dead*[46]

At the preliminary hearing when O'Brien asked Earl to tell about the
number of incidents when he had physically assaulted Dorothy, Earl was
gripping the front edge of the witness box. His hands were together. As
Earl said, "Two or three—but maybe four—or five—," he looked down
at his hands and moved them apart until they spanned the full length of
the front of the box. I remember this image of him vividly, and I have
wondered about it many times. The movement of his hands seemed to be
an involuntary expression of the extent of his abuse of Dorothy. It may
have revealed his resignation to the fact that he could not escape a discussion of his abuse of Dorothy, directed not by the lawyer for the Crown,
who would try to diminish the extent of it, but by the lawyer defending
Dorothy. Certainly spreading open his hands in this gesture made him
seem more vulnerable than he ever was again on the witness stand.

   I wonder how anyone who attended the trial and listened to Earl as
O'Brien cross-examinationed him could come away believing, as Selinger
proposed to the jury, that Earl Joudrie abused his wife on only three occasions. Thinking of this makes me realize the depth of Dorothy's exasperation

when she was in the witness box herself and Selinger was pressing her, bait-ing her, and suddenly she exclaimed, "Mister Selinger!"

During the fifteen months between the shooting and her trial, Dorothy learned many things about herself. She learned, she said, that she is an alcoholic. She heard the words "abuse" and "divorce" until she was able to use them in relation to herself. If she could not accept the full emo-tional impact of these words, she was reminded repeatedly by psycholo-gists, psychiatrists, and her lawyer that accepting the fact that she was abused by her husband and that he was now in the process of divorcing her must be keys not only to her defence but to her mental health. She could not continue to exist in a romantic dream. With her own hand, if not with conscious intention, she had ended that dream. But how had she felt, I wondered, when after the shooting she received Elizabeth Griffiths' letter saying, "Dorothy, if you need me, this is where I am."

When Noel O'Brien saw Ms. Griffiths' letter, he must have consid-ered it the greatest good fortune imaginable. I am sure that Dorothy felt grateful for this offer to help her, but I suspect that her feelings were more complex than gratitude and solace. She had not seen this woman since she was the Joudries' live-in nanny in Toronto from 1973 until 1975. Dorothy knew that Elizabeth Griffiths had witnessed some of Earl's most severe abuse of her. There could be no denying what she knew about Dorothy and Earl. Dorothy may have wondered if she was ready to face this woman and her knowledge of her marriage. And, in fact, Dorothy did not see Elizabeth Griffiths until the morning she appeared on the witness stand.

It was during the second week of the trial, in the middle of O'Brien's defence. Dorothy had testified, as had one of the expert witnesses, Dr. Roy O'Shaughnessy. Suddenly O'Brien presented a witness no one had expect-ed. When she worked for Dorothy in Toronto, Elizabeth Griffiths had recently arrived from Britain. She was then in her early twenties. Now, a teachers' assistant, in her mid-forties, quiet-spoken, modest but self-possessed, obviously intelligent and compassionate, she was a dramatic presence in the courtroom. She seemed nervous, but also assured, and per-fectly articulate.

When O'Brien asked her to tell about her observations of violence in the Joudries' home while she lived with them, she said, "I saw Earl Joudrie hitting Dorothy Joudrie on numerous occasions. Do you want me to describe one?" With O'Brien's permission, she proceeded to describe a scene at suppertime one evening when Earl suddenly pushed back his chair, walked up past the children, grabbed Dorothy by the hair and dragged her into the livingroom, hitting her. She described the children's reactions: "Neale just stood in shock. Colin closed his eyes really tight and screamed and screamed. . . . I can't quite place Carolyn. I can't remember where she was seated." Ms. Griffiths carried Guy into the kitchen, where she telephoned the police.

"I was afraid he would kill her," Elizabeth Griffiths said about Earl. But when the police arrived a few minutes later, Earl was gone, and "Dorothy would not lay charges. I couldn't believe it," Elizabeth Griffiths said. Women were more reluctant in the 1970s than they are now to charge their husbands with assault. The police then rarely supported them or encouraged them to take legal action against their husbands. Even today some women fear their husband's retaliation. Some believe that taking this step would be a betrayal of their husbands. Some women want simply to deny what happened, hoping that they can cope with the problem themselves. Dorothy, probably, knows all of these emotions.

Elizabeth Griffiths wept while she described another incident when she saw Earl beating Dorothy and kicking her, injuring her so severely that he had to take her to the hospital. She said that Earl was usually calm, but that suddenly he could be very violent. He was always "so sorry" afterwards, she said. "He was like a baby; he was so sorry."

The first time Ms. Griffiths saw Earl being violent to Dorothy, he pushed her over a kitchen chair, saying "Damn you Dorothy!" But Elizabeth Griffiths said about Dorothy, "she had a way of pulling herself together," of "regaining her decorum." She said that on a few occasions Dorothy left their home and went to a hotel, or sometimes to friends' homes. She also said that because she had weekends off there were many things she did not see, but that she would know when there had been incidents because when she came back Dorothy would have bruises, black eyes, which she tried to cover with make-up. Ms. Griffiths said that Dorothy always tried very hard to cover up any signs of the violence.

As Elizabeth Griffiths stepped down from the witness box, the jury and the people in the gallery sat perfectly still, silenced by their emotional response to what they had just heard. Here was credible evidence of Earl's abuse of Dorothy from a person outside the family. Ms. Griffiths' description of the children's reactions to their father's behaviour affected everyone who listened to her, and Dorothy especially, and it added a new dimension to the violence in the Joudrie family.

Dorothy seemed physically weakened by the intensity of her emotions during Elizabeth Griffiths' testimony. She seemed to draw into herself as she listened to this evidence. Before Ms. Griffiths appeared, before the court was in session, in a brief conversation between Dorothy and O'Brien, he appeared to be placating her. Dorothy was objecting, quietly, but at the conclusion of their talk she was not agitated. She seemed ready for what was to come. I wondered what they were talking about, what Dorothy was thinking. I did not know what was about to happen. It was apparent that she and Elizabeth Griffiths had had a good relationship while she worked in Dorothy's home, but not necessarily that Dorothy had confided in her about her marital problems. If Dorothy felt vindicated, or even relieved by Elizabeth Griffiths' testimony, she showed no overt signs of this. She seemed to be numb.

In his very brief cross-examination of Elizabeth Griffiths, Jerry Selinger made no attempt to challenge her account of Earl's violence.

When I arrived in the vestibule of the courthouse during the lunch break, Dorothy was waiting with Elizabeth Griffiths and her husband for a taxi. Dorothy was taking them to lunch. Her face was drawn and pale. She appeared to be immune to the activity around her, jarred and buffeted by it, but at the same time separate from it and almost unaware of the journalists crowding, pressing against each other in their efforts to ask further questions of this former nanny who had witnessed the violence in Dorothy's life. Dorothy was standing next to a newspaper columnist, and as I approached them, hoping to get through the crowd to the doors, Dorothy turned to the columnist, and looking at her carefully, composing herself suddenly, she said, "I love your outfit."

---

Lorna Wendt, former wife of General Electric Capital CEO, Gary Wendt, "raised a big ruckus" when she demanded, in their divorce settlement, half of the $100 million she believed he was worth. Wendt said that much of her life as a corporate wife "was a command performance." "You were always to have a smile on. You always acted as if you wanted to be there, liked everyone you came in contact with . . . Acting as if. I spent my whole life acting as if."[47]

# Dorothy

And that's what it was like at the trial, I was there in the box
of the dock but I might as well have been made of cloth, and
stuffed, with a china head; and I was shut up inside that doll
of myself, and my true voice could not get out.

I said that I remembered some of the things I did. But
there are other things they said I did, which I said I could
not remember at all.

· · · · · · · · · · · · · · · · · · · · · · · · · · · · · · · · · · · · · · · · · · · ·

Did he say, You are a good girl?
He might have said that. Or I might have been asleep.

· · · · · · · · · · · · · · · · · · · · · · · · · · · · · · · · · · · · · · · · · · · ·

Did I push him away? Did he say I will soon make you think
better of me? Did he say I will tell you a secret if you promise
to keep it? And if you do not, your life will not be worth a
straw.

It might have happened.
Margaret Atwood, *Alias Grace*[48]

She could only stare at this absence in herself for a few
minutes at a time. It was like looking at the sun.
Carol Shields, *The Stone Diaries*[49]

# Dorothy I

On the wall above my work table, where I hung it almost fifteen years ago, is a large framed poster, a notice of a show of Milton Avery's work at the Whitney Museum of American Art in New York in 1982. Avery called the painting reproduced on this poster *Conversation*. Two women, seated side by side, look directly at each other as they talk together. They are smiling, perhaps laughing. One of the women is holding a small book, and her finger marks a place in it. The colors of their clothing are light, delicate, soft—blue, lilac, mauve. The chesterfield on which they are sitting is dark—navy; the wall behind them is dark—grey. One woman has bright pink hair, and her complexion is dark. The other woman's hair is black, and her complexion is light, ivory-coloured. *Conversation* conveys a delicate and subtle depth, and at the same time an open liveliness that, together, are very inviting. I love this poster. It defines this small space that is mine. It reminds me of women who have been my friends, and with whom I have talked and laughed. It reminds me of women who have listened to me, comforted me, confirmed me. I have looked at it for years as I sit here at my table, working, thinking. As I look at it now, I wonder what Dorothy Joudrie could tell me, if we were to have such a conversation.

When Dorothy's trial began in April 1996, I did not want to approach her for a few seconds of conversation. When Noel O'Brien requested a publication ban after Dorothy's arrest in January 1995, I had no idea then that the trial would be so far in the future, but I was disappointed that I could not talk with Dorothy. I suppose I must simply have assumed that she would agree to talk with me if it were possible, and my presumption astonishes me as I think of it now. I was very naive. I had not even begun to understand the chaos of Dorothy's life.

In the beginning, during those early months, my justification for wanting to talk with Dorothy was that I thought I could tell her story. Gradually, without talking with her at all, Dorothy Joudrie became a part of my life. At the same time, however, as I went about my research, I realized, finally, that the only person who can tell her story is Dorothy herself. Even if I were to talk with her for hours, for hundreds of hours, what I wrote about her would be my version of her story. It could not be anything else.

Still, at the trial, while the immediacy of what was happening was very important to me, I continued to hope that if I did talk with Dorothy, it would be a private, quiet conversation when I could ask her the many questions that had been on my mind for some time, and the new questions which had occurred to me during the trial. On the second day of the trial, during the lunch break, I discovered suddenly that we were standing next to each other in the line in the cafeteria. I introduced myself and reminded her that we had been classmates in elementary school in Edmonton. She responded pleasantly, and asked my birth name, my "maiden name," but she admitted finally that she could not remember me. And she added, to reassure me, "But this is not surprising, because I have difficulty these days remembering even my own name!" She laughed gently as she said this. She was unaware, I am quite sure, of the poignancy of her remark. It took my breath away for a second. Dorothy's name, and her memory, were central issues in this legal drama. But what struck me most about our brief encounter was how animated and engaging she was, despite the emotional strain she was experiencing. I had watched her during the preliminary hearing and now, again, as she sat in the prisoner's dock, but this view from a distance did not do her justice. As we talked, she looked me directly in the eye, and gave me her full attention. We parted casually, each going to join our companions. We did not speak again during the trial.

The next time we talked, it was on the telephone, after the trial, while Dorothy was in the provincial mental hospital. She was responding to a letter I had written to her. She assured me then that she did remember who I was; she was straightforward, open, and accepting of me and my interest in her; what she said was articulate and relevant. We spoke quickly, easily, at first. But I began to be concerned, perhaps unnecessarily, that her telephone calls from the hospital might be monitored, and I ended our conversation more abruptly than she expected. I could tell that she was rather surprised that I did not encourage her to elaborate about what she was telling me. I was frustrated by this conversation and I even felt that I was betraying her to some extent by not responding as she seemed to expect I would. But I did not want to allow her to say too much, to vent her anger and frustration and fear to the point that she might risk jeopardizing her position in the appeal Noel O'Brien was preparing for her release from the hospital. Nevertheless, again, as I talked with her, she engaged me completely. Dorothy has an irrepressible energy, and an essential honesty, that she conveys in her face, her body movements, her good manners. And she also conveys it in her voice—in her voice alone, which has a low register, and a tone of confidence. Her energetic candour makes what she says compelling.

I suspect that it was partly because of this open and candid presentation of herself that Noel O'Brien wanted Dorothy to testify at her own trial. He probably thought that the jury would believe her, and I think that they did. But despite my belief, and apparently Noel O'Brien's as well, that Dorothy ought to be allowed to testify, that people ought to listen to her, that this is essential in the process of judging her, as she spoke from the witness stand I could not help wondering if her testimony would be as helpful to her as O'Brien had hoped. The reasons for this are complex.

---

As the trial progressed, even in the four days prior to Dorothy's testimony, days which were long and difficult, Dorothy became increasingly distraught. Her costumes continued to be immaculate and carefully chosen, but her hair was sometimes dishevelled, as if she had forgotten, or simply neglected to look at herself in the mirror when she arrived at the courthouse. Her face often seemed puffy, from tears or lack of sleep perhaps, or from some other physical effects from the emotional upheaval she was experiencing. It was her facial expression that was most startling—revealing strain, anxiety, vulnerability. Yet there were also times when her expression was inscrutable. I realized how important her earlier composure had been, how dramatically it had affected people's impression of her—my impression of her—and without our realizing it, how effectively it had kept us at a distance from her. Now she seemed not to be contained, not to be in perfect control of herself. She was affecting the people who watched her in a way that they could not define exactly, but which made them uncomfortable.

For some people attending the trial, seeing and listening to Dorothy Joudrie, who everyone knew now was an abused wife charged with attempting to murder her husband, was too gritty, too close to the bone. Murder is a terrible thing, but most people can think about it, and even be entertained by stories of murder because they have so little conscious emotional investment in it. They are fortunate enough to be able to put it in a safe compartment, separate from themselves. The jurors and the spectators read murder mysteries and see films and television dramas about murder. Journalists and the people in law enforcement and the judicial system are much more familiar than the average person is with the emotional costs of dealing with real cases of murder and attempted murder. Most of us, if we were honest, would admit that the thought of murdering someone has occurred to us momentarily, if not really seriously, at least once in our lives. But we did not, and we believe that we would not actually commit murder. People came to this trial believing that the concern was that Dorothy Joudrie had been charged with attempting to murder her husband, and they believed, from the reports in the media, and now from evidence at the trial, that the charge was justified. This fact made Dorothy Joudrie different from the rest of us. Everyday, people who sympathized with Dorothy, and those who did not, ended their discussions about her with the remark, "but you can't just go around shooting people."

But Dorothy was also charged with aggravated assault[50]—the intent to wound, maim, disfigure, or endanger the life of another person—and this charge, which initially had seemed redundant, had taken on a new importance, because what we had heard in this courtroom, and listened to again as Dorothy testified, was evidence that someone else—her husband—had assaulted Dorothy, endangering her life physically and emotionally, not once, not three times as the prosecution insisted, but many times, over a period of forty years. Earl Joudrie had never been charged with committing a criminal act.

The most disturbing revelation at Dorothy Joudrie's trial was that society, generally, is not yet properly educated about the plight of the abused wife. During the past ten years most people have heard and seen in the media shocking cases of abused women. Many people remember Joel Steinberg, his abuse of Hedda Nussbaum and their daughter, Lisa, whom he tortured and murdered.[51] Everyone knows about O.J. Simpson and his abused and murdered wife, Nicole. They know that cities have shelters to protect abused women. They know that police departments in some cities are making dramatic changes to help these women. Nevertheless, and despite increasing public awareness, some people seem to continue to want women who are beaten up by their husbands to be invisible, and when they are not invisible, the attitude is often that "there are two sides to these situations, you know"; "she made her bed"; "why didn't she leave?" Joel Steinberg is known to have told Hedda Nussbaum, after beating her viciously, "Just look at what you've done to yourself!"[52] And during Joel Steinberg's trial, shocked by the sight of Hedda Nussbaum's horribly battered body and psyche, observers said about her: "Just look at what she let him do to her. Look at what she let him do to her *child*."[53] Wife abuse is still considered by some people to be private, "domestic," outside the law. More enlightened people understand that this is a social and a political problem. Still, people seem to be more comfortable when such a problem is "out there," like murder; something that they believe they can consider rationally and logically; something not so infused with outrage, anger, pity, despair, judgement, fear, and even—for some—personal experience. As we watched and listened to Dorothy's painful and tentative attempts to face the reality of her life, and sometimes her inability to do so, the discomfort of some of the people in the courtroom was manifest. What had become clear during Earl's testimony was even more evident as the trial progressed: Dorothy Joudrie's capacity to embrace the intricacies of denial was not peculiar to her.

An example of this problem appeared on the front page of the "City and Life" section of the *Calgary Herald* on May 2, 1996, the day after the Joudries' nanny in Toronto, Elizabeth Griffiths, testified. In a two-column article on the right-hand side of the page, under heavy black headlines, Bob Beaty, who reported regularly on the trial—and whose reports were careful and accurate—described Elizabeth Griffiths' testimony, and quoted her saying, about Earl attacking Dorothy on one occasion, "I was afraid he was going to kill her."[54] Parallel to this report, in the centre of the page, was a comment on the trial by *Herald* columnist Don Braid. This columnist did not attend the trial regularly; he had other work to do. But now he was defending Earl Joudrie: "Few victims of a major crime—he was shot six times, after all—have ever had their names so thoroughly dragged through the media and the mud . . . some days you would almost get the impression that Earl Joudrie is a criminal, not a victim."[55]

Noel O'Brien's defence of Dorothy was that an abusive husband and the effects on her of living with this abuse were so terrible that finally she surrendered her voluntary judgement and behaviour, allowing her to act out in what psychiatrists call a dissociative state. O'Brien called Dorothy's mental state on that Saturday morning by its legal term, automatism. I do not know if Dorothy was defending herself physically on January 21, 1995. But everyone who sat in the courtroom and listened carefully to Dorothy and Earl and Elizabeth Griffiths knows that Earl Joudrie, in angry, violent attacks, and with powerful emotional control, had threatened Dorothy's life and her safety for years. If she was frightened, if she felt lost and abandoned, if she wanted to end the fear and pain she has experienced for forty years, should we be surprised that she acted to defend herself? She may have been defending her integrity, her self-respect, and an identity she could barely recognize. But this is not enough, under Canadian law, to ensure a justification of her actions as self-defence. How can we separate, I wonder, the visceral terror a woman has experienced from these more abstract but crucial elements of herself?

Dorothy had tried various means of coping with her unhappy and abusive marriage, and the most dramatic was denial. She was devastated by her husband's betrayal of her. She believed that she loved him, and perhaps she still believes this. But her coping mechanisms were failing. Because of his relationship with Lynn Manning, Earl was keeping Dorothy at arm's length, but still, often in a cruel and perverse fashion, under his control. We saw this control and heard it during his testimony. Dorothy's alcoholism—a symptom of her denial of the reality of her life—was affecting her dramatically. Her children were objecting to her lack of stability, her dependence on them, her demands of them. Because of her attempts to hide, to cover up Earl's abuse of her, Dorothy had lived for many years in an emotional state of isolation from her parents while they were alive, and from many of her friends, unable to share with them what was happening to her, unable even to use the word "abuse," she said. But she did share this secret—a dark and terrifying secret—with her husband. This intimacy, this strange interdependence, however perverse and unacceptable, was a bond between them, and this bond was so strong that at times it was apparent in the courtroom, when we saw the two of them together, and even when Earl was absent and Dorothy was alone. At one point, during Selinger's cross-examination of her, he suggested that when Earl did not respond to her demands for his attention, she would become increasingly exasperated and confrontational. Dorothy responded:

I can't remember all the things. I can't remember the arguments, and I can't remember the escalation of them either. I can't—I mean this is years and years of living with somebody. I can't remember all of them.
Selinger: Can you give me one? Take, for instance, the one that you described to your counsel [on Friday]. Isn't that a fair comment of what happened with your—
Dorothy: But we didn't get into a fight that night.
Selinger: Ah.
Dorothy: Okay.
Selinger: What happened? Did he leave the house?
Dorothy: No, we went to bed.

Dorothy did not challenge Earl's story of their quiet, sad conversation as they drank coffee together at her kitchen table on the morning of January 21, 1995. But her telling about it was hesitant, tentative. And Dorothy says that she can remember nothing of what happened after Earl got up to leave. But she can remember her relationship with the man she married, the man she has known since she was fifteen, the man she knows better than anyone else does. Nevertheless, and despite inconsistencies in Earl's story that everyone heard at the trial—and not just about their final meeting, but about their relationship generally—when most people talk or write about the Joudrie case, Earl's version of what happened is repeated as fact. This was true of some television and newspaper journalists, and consequently of the people who relied on their reports. It was true of many of the people who phoned in to CBC's "Cross-Country Check-up" on May 26, 1996, when it asked the question, "Was Justice Served in the Joudrie Verdict?" It was also true of the host of this program, Rex Murphy. Murphy's opinions usually delight me, because I agree with them and I enjoy his sharp wit and good sense. But that Sunday afternoon I was very disappointed. Murphy accepted as fact Earl Joudrie's version not only of what happened on the day of the shooting, but his version of the history of abuse in the Joudrie's marriage. Murphy said more than once that Earl's abuse of Dorothy ended in the "late 1970s."

---

I had thought endlessly about the sequence of events on that morning in January 1995, as Earl told them, trying to imagine every possible and reasonable variation. One day I remembered something Guy said during the preliminary hearing in October 1995. I had not read my notes of the hearing for months because I was concentrating on the trial, and specifically on what the jury saw and heard. It was during Selinger's examination of Guy, and a discussion of what happened that morning before Earl left the "ranch house" to visit Dorothy. Guy said about his father that the "only unusual thing was that he asked me to go with him to visit Mom." Guy said that he did not accompany his father because he had to go to work. Selinger did not ask Guy to elaborate about Earl's "unusual" behaviour, nor did he pursue this with Earl. But why, I wondered, had Guy's comment disappeared during the trial. I knew that Earl had signed final papers for their divorce on Friday, January 20, the day before the shooting. I had seen these documents at the Court of Queen's Bench. Was Earl fearful about Dorothy's reaction if he were to tell her what he had done—worried that there might be a scene, a confrontation? During Dorothy's testimony, when she was telling O'Brien about her preparation for Earl's arrival that morning, after he telephoned her to say that he would be there "shortly," Dorothy said that she poured herself a drink.

> O'Brien: Why did you pour yourself a drink?
> Dorothy: Well, because—whenever I'm—I guess when I've been with Earl in the last—well, I'm pretty nervous, and I—not that I [don't] know now that [it] isn't probably a very smart thing to pour a drink, but that's what I did then.

Both Selinger and O'Brien, during Earl's testimony and his cross-examination, discussed phone calls Dorothy made to Earl for a period of time after Earl moved to Toronto in 1991. Earl said that he recalled "occasion, after occasion, after occasion" when Dorothy phoned him during "the middle of the night" or at the office during the day. He also said that during "several" of these calls she had told him, "I'd rather you were dead than leave me. I would rather you were dead than have a divorce."

O'Brien said, "Not something that you would have forgotten?"

Earl responded, "No, I didn't forget that."

O'Brien asked Earl if he recalled a sworn statement he made to RCMP Constable Lowe, in the hospital, on January 28, 1995. Earl said that he did. O'Brien read aloud part of this statement, when Corporal Morrison asked Earl if Dorothy, prior to the incident on January 21, had "ever made any mention to you . . . that she was out to get you some way, if in fact you went ahead with the divorce?"

Earl replied:

No. No, not at all. I mean, she—she made a comment one time, I guess, this is how it is. I—you know, I was really ill earlier, you know in my career. Actually I was very fortunate to survive some problems I had and she had at one point in time she said, well, I would rather have you die than [*sic*] have a divorce. I don't think she meant I would rather kill you than have a divorce. I don't think that it was in the context of—at least I thought it was in the context of—it was in the context of well, we survived this one terrible thing, and I could have been a widow, and you know, you could have died of this terrible disease and this is better. That would have been better than losing you to a divorce. But, you know, this I think—I have never seen her as a person, and I mean, you know, on and off for 40 years I guess, got married in '57, and we knew each other before that, as cold and indifferent and just like stark cold. [Earl is describing Dorothy as she was shooting him.]

O'Brien: Do you remember giving that statement to the police?
Earl: You bet.
O'Brien: All right, and you never indicated to the police officer at that time that you had received any phone calls in 199—
Earl: I thought the police officer was asking me if I—
O'Brien: Can I just finish the question, sir?
Earl:—was being—if I had been threatened, and that's the question I was answering.
O'Brien: Can I just finish the question?
Earl: And I also had no—I had, you know, frankly no expectation or anticipation or thought that those kinds of statements over me—to me over the telephone meant that somebody was going to kill me.
O'Brien: All right, all right. So you never took any of those particular conversations as threatening then?
Earl: No, I didn't.
O'Brien: All right.
Earl: If I had thought they were threatening, I sure as hell wouldn't have been out at the house.
O'Brien: Well, you sure wouldn't probably send her Christmas cards and the like either, would you?
Earl: No, I guess not.

Earl's statement to the police was ambiguous and contradictory, but his inclusion at this time of his description of Dorothy's stark, cold, indifferent demeanour as she was shooting him, and his referring, in a slip of the tongue, as O'Brien continued his cross-examination, to her statements "over me," give the impression, without his saying so directly, that he may have thought that she had, indeed, threatened him. What is apparent here also was Earl's inability to appreciate what Dorothy was telling him: her sense of the humiliation and shame and betrayal of divorce as opposed to the unavoidable loss if he were to die.

During the trial Earl was not consistent in stating what he believed Dorothy knew about the divorce proceedings before January 21, and what, exactly, he told Dorothy about the divorce that morning. Near the beginning of his testimony, while Selinger was examining him, Earl said that he told Dorothy that he had been in the "lawyer's office the other day" and that he had signed papers, which, along with her signature, would allow them to apply for a duplicate certificate of title to the "ranch house" because they thought they had lost the original certificate.

> And she asked me if I'd signed any other papers and I said, Yes, I'd signed some affidavits which I think had the effect of saying, yes, there was a divorce in process and, yes, the assets had been divided. Some document of that nature.

Later, during this examination, Selinger asked Earl again about Dorothy's knowledge prior to January 21 of what Earl had done to finalize the divorce.

> Selinger: To your knowledge, Mr. Joudrie, was the accused aware that the divorce was continuing on between December and January? Was she aware—
> Earl: I—yeah, I'm quite sure. Her attorney certainly did. I mean, we were discussing why we needed the duplicate certificate of title so that we could move the assets and stuff.
> Selinger: So this wasn't, in your mind, a surprise then when you discussed this on the morning of January 21st?
> Earl: No. For reasons that absolutely escape me I can say maybe that Dorothy didn't know exactly when this was going to happen, because she seemed to be puzzled on that day that this was going on. I mean—

I wondered what, exactly, Earl was saying. His new, hesitant response could support the argument that Dorothy's dissociative state on January 21 may have been "triggered," as the defence argued, by her realization that morning that now the divorce was inevitable. On the other hand, what he had said could also support the Crown's argument that Dorothy knew that a divorce was imminent, whenever the final papers were signed, and that she had planned to shoot Earl when he visited her that morning.

But at the preliminary hearing Earl was not hesitant about what happened. He said that on January 21 he told Dorothy that he had signed affidavits for the divorce and that now she must sign the papers regarding their property. He said that he told her that she could get the settlement arrangements from her attorney. Earl testified at both the preliminary hearing and at the trial that Dorothy said that the divorce would be easier for him because he was not alone. She was alone. He also testified, on both occasions, that after Dorothy shot him the first time, as he went down the steps into the garage, she stood in the doorway, holding the gun, and said, "I told you I wouldn't let you get away with this."

At both the preliminary hearing and the trial, Earl wept as he talked about Dorothy shooting him. At the preliminary hearing, during these traumatic moments, Selinger offered him a glass of water, which he declined, abruptly. At the trial, Selinger tried to interrupt him, "If I might . . . " But Earl's sense of drama seemed to be more astute than Selinger's and he was undeterred. He continued, ignoring Selinger's comment. Earl, apparently, wanted to tell his story without interruption. Months after the trial, as I read my notes and the official transcripts, it occurred to me that while Dorothy wept many times during the trial, her tears never appeared to be those of self-pity. It seemed to me that she wept in outrage at what her former husband said about her as he testified; she wept in despair over what she had done, as she saw Dr. Joyce Wong's slides of the bullet wounds in Earl's body; she wept in concern and anger at what her children said; she wept out of overwhelming sadness, betrayal, and shame. But Earl's tears seemed to be for himself.

At the preliminary hearing, Selinger asked Earl if he was looking at Dorothy "when the gun was going off." Earl said that yes, when he was lying on the garage floor, she seemed like a person he didn't know—"calm," "detached." But at the trial, Earl omitted this observation. It was not until O'Brien cross-examined Earl, reminding him what he had said at the preliminary hearing, that we heard both words "calm" and "detached" again. O'Brien would use Dorothy's appearing calm and detached, as he would use Earl's statement to the police that he had never seen Dorothy "as cold and indifferent and just like stark cold," as evidence of her state of automatism. How deliberate, I wondered, were these discrepencies in Earl's testimony.

Also, Earl added details at the trial which he had not mentioned at the preliminary hearing. Selinger gathered, from Earl's testimony, a list of five comments Earl said that Dorothy made as she was shooting him, during what he described as their "weird conversation." The first was Dorothy's saying, "I told you I wouldn't let you get away with this." The second was after Earl told Dorothy that he thought he was dying, and he suggested, "why don't you sit down over here and talk to me. . . . " According to Earl, Dorothy asked, "Well, how long is it going to take you to die?" The third comment was, "You haven't changed your will so I'll get everything." The fourth comment was "We'll just have to load you up in this car and get you out of here and dump you off in a ditch some place." The fifth was Earl's saying about Dorothy, "I heard a new voice say, in a rather plaintive way, 'Oh, my God, what have I done? I wish I hadn't done that,' or something like that." During his cross-examination of Earl, O'Brien elicited from him the fact that he had never mentioned, during his statement to the police or at the preliminary inquiry, Dorothy's saying that she would have to dump him off in the ditch, or her question, "How long is it going to take you to die?" Earl said that he gave this information to Jerry Selinger and Constable Derwin Lowe on "Saturday . . . Saturday three days ago"—two days before the trial began, and fifteen months after the shooting.

Another puzzle was that while Earl, at the trial, agreed with his statement to the police that Dorothy had acted in a stark, cold, indifferent manner when she shot him—and his list of the comments she made while she was continuing to shoot him seemed to indicate such a state of mind—Selinger, during his examination of Earl, did not support Earl's account of what happened and use it to enhance the case for the prosecution by asking Earl about the possible presence of the gun in the kitchen during their conversation. When I asked Selinger why he did not ask Earl any questions about the gun, he said that this was because Earl did not see the gun until Dorothy shot him the first time.[56] But Selinger might have asked Earl if Dorothy had left the kitchen at any point during their conversation, when she could have got the gun from the dresser drawer in the bedroom. He might have asked Earl if Dorothy was wearing clothing in which she could have concealed the gun. He might have asked if Earl noticed her opening a cupboard in the kitchen or the utility room to pick up the gun from where she might have placed it before Earl arrived. Also, we must assume that the RCMP did not, apparently, make any attempt to pursue the story of the gun. Specific information about the gun, along with a definite assertion from Earl, or from Dorothy's divorce lawyers, that Dorothy knew before the Saturday morning that Earl had signed the divorce documents, might have provided motive, and perhaps even intent, on Dorothy's part, to kill Earl. With respect to these crucial facts, the police, and Selinger, and Earl all failed to produce convincing evidence for either motive or intent.

But also, the fact remains that despite the number of times she shot him, Dorothy Joudrie did not kill her husband. And, ironically, she was responsible for saving his life. She might have behaved quite differently, refusing to call the police and an ambulance when, according to both Earl and Dorothy, he directed her to do so. She might have used the last bullet in the gun to shoot Earl one more time. She might have resisted arrest and not cooperated with the police when they insisted that she must give them the gun before they could attend to Earl's injuries. She might have been belligerent, or in a state of mental collapse, prolonging the interval before she gave them the gun and thus allowed the medical crew to treat Earl and the police to arrest her and take her to jail. All of the police officers who were present that morning testified that although she appeared to be confused and upset—she was "distraught," "almost disoriented"—she was polite and cooperative, except that she insisted that Earl had told her not to discuss what had happened. All of us who attended the trial regularly knew that this direction from Earl to Dorothy, "do not tell," had occurred repeatedly throughout their marriage. Earl denies that he said this, but it is quite reasonable that he might have, knowing that for her sake, and no doubt for his as well, she should talk only with a lawyer. Finally, Dorothy wanted to accompany Earl, in the air ambulance, to the hospital.

Both of the two central characters in this drama were sometimes prompted by their emotions to improvise, unconsciously, in their hesitations, and contradictions, and slips of the tongue. The unhappy truth of their lives spilled over into the superficially tidy theatre of the courtroom. I think they were unaware when it happened, but the rest of us caught some of these accidental revelations, and they stayed in our minds.

# Dorothy II

Noel O'Brien's presentation of his defence of Dorothy was quiet, confident, pithy. He spoke directly to the jury, explaining that in all criminal cases there must be criminal intention and a criminal act. He said that it is a fundamental principle of law that the criminal act must be voluntary and conscious. He explained that when a person acts in a state of automatism, they have acted without volition. When automatism exists, he said, the person must be found not guilty. He said that it is the Crown's duty to prove that Dorothy Joudrie was not in a state of automatism when she shot her husband. O'Brien said that two psychiatrists would testify that Dorothy's mind was normal, but also and why, at the critical time, she was in a state of automatism. "It is my intention to show you," he said, "that the mental state of Dorothy at the critical time of the shooting cannot be understood unless you look at it in the context of years of abuse, physical and emotional, of a volatile relationship, all of the underlying stresses that she was feeling at the time." O'Brien said that he would call other witnesses and that Dorothy Joudrie would be the first.

The courtroom was full as O'Brien spoke, and the spectators and the jury listened carefully. Dorothy seemed to be very nervous. Her sighs, which I had interpreted as a sign of her nervousness, but which were sometimes also, perhaps, a sign of irritation and impatience, were not evident this morning. On Friday, April 26, the fifth day of her trial, as Dorothy walked towards the witness box, all of us could see her struggle to maintain her increasingly precarious composure.

Dorothy began, as she was asked to do, by identifying herself. She is sixty-one, born in Camrose, Alberta, on March 16, 1935. She attended Edmonton schools and the University of Alberta, from which she graduated in 1957 with a Bachelor of Education degree—with a major in home economics and minors in English and history. She taught school from 1957 until 1961.

As she spoke, I was surprised that she was using a tone of voice and manner that appeared to be both girlish and innocent, and at the same time, rather condescending. Here, suddenly, was a false note. The jury had not heard her speak formally until now, and they listened to her and watched her carefully, with little visible reaction. But I suspect that they were not flattered by the way she was speaking to them—as if they were students in a classroom.

O'Brien ignored her tone of voice and manner, and proceeded to try to help her to feel at ease as he continued to ask questions of her and to prompt her when necessary. He asked her to tell about her life after January 21, 1995. Dorothy agreed that her life changed "substantially" after that day. She spent "a day or two in jail"; she attended the Betty Ford Center in California, which was "the best experience I had in my entire life." At the Betty Ford Center, for twenty-eight days, she was able to look at herself, and she realized that she needed help and she got it. O'Brien asked Dorothy what things she learned there about herself. She said she learned that she had "low self-esteem," that she was a "caretaker of other people and, I guess, I didn't take care of my own self." She learned that she is an alcoholic, and now, she is "dealing with that daily, one day at a time." Dorothy was tearful as she said this. After waiting a few seconds, O'Brien urged her to take her time, and to take a break if she would like to.

> Dorothy: . . . And I realized that I hadn't dealt with the things that—I guess I had been storing them up, but I wasn't aware of it. I looked at my life and I never felt that my life was a bad life. I felt that I had a good life, and I remembered all the good things about my life with my husband. And that was what I was remembering. And that's why I couldn't let go. I just—and I couldn't let go of him. . . .

Dorothy's "first step" at the Betty Ford Center, she said, was to write about herself. She presented forty pages to her counsellor, who looked at what she had written and said, "Would you please take Earl out of this?" Dorothy thought this would be impossible, because Earl had been part of her life for forty-five years. But she did as she was asked, and she was left with twenty pages, which she gave to the other women for a critique. "I just got rid of Earl," Dorothy said proudly.

O'Brien apparently decided that it was safe, now, in the light of what she had just said, to ask Dorothy how she felt when she signed her divorce documents in June 1995. "I was amazed," she said, "because I could never even say the word 'divorce.'"

O'Brien, apparently trying to help Dorothy to think and speak realistically, asked her to tell what she had learned from her examination by Dr. Lenore Walker during the few days she spent with her in Denver, Colorado. Lenore Walker is the executive director of the Domestic Violence Institute, adjunct professor of psychology at the University of Denver, and president of the Psychology of Women Division of the American Psychological Association. Dr. Walker is known internationally as an expert witness in trials of battered women who kill in self-defence. But neither O'Brien nor Dorothy explained who Dr. Walker is. I do not know why Lenore Walker was not asked to testify at the trial.

Dorothy said that she spent a whole day with Dr. Walker, answering many questions. During the days she was there, she also did tests.

> Dorothy: . . . I did these multiple tests of all kinds and I ended up in something like the 94 percentile. I also did an I.Q. test and I have a fairly high I.Q. So I'm not—that was good for my self-esteem, I guess, that I learned that I wasn't a stupid person.
> O'Brien: Okay.
> Dorothy: What else? Well, I learned a lot about—well, this Dr. Walker has written a book about abuse. I could never say that word about myself. I really didn't feel that I was ever abused. I felt that in every marriage you have problems, when you're living with somebody you have problems, and I thought I was doing that. And I had a good life. I cannot say that I didn't. I did a lot of things that—had a lot of neat things, a lot of beautiful places to live. I got to travel. I got to meet interesting people. I had four healthy children and I had a very talented and exciting husband.

O'Brien changed the subject. He asked her about Dr. Alan Weston, a forensic psychiatrist at the General Hospital in Calgary to whom Dorothy was referred after she was arrested. Dorothy said that she sees him still. She said that she has been examined also by Dr. Roy O'Shaughnessy, a forensic psychiatrist from Vancouver, and for the Crown by Dr. Julio Arboleda-Flores, a forensic psychiatrist in Calgary, and by Dr. Patrick Bailey, Dr. Arboleda-Flores' associate psychologist in Calgary. She said that she attends weekly meetings of Alcoholics Anonymous in Calgary.

And these people that are there that are alcoholics, as I am, are marvelous people. They're marvelous people. They've had troubles in their life, as I have in mine, and they have been a great help to me, a great help.
O'Brien: You've learned a lot about yourself, Dorothy, in the last year and a half or so?
Dorothy: Yes, this last year and a half has been an unbelievable year and a half. I didn't think at the age of 61 that I would have that much to learn.
O'Brien: When you came back from the Betty Ford Center, you were on your own?
Dorothy: Yes . . .

. . . . . . . . . . . . . . . . . . . . . . . . . . . . . . . . . . . . . . . . . . . . . . . . . . . .

And the hardest thing I had to do actually, when I got back was to go to the grocery store to buy some food . . . And that was the hardest thing that I did when I came back. And, also, I came back with people knowing who I was.

This comment may have seemed trivial to some people in the courtroom, but I was not surprised to hear it. I wondered if the jury appreciated how revealing it was of Dorothy's position, now, among her neighbours, and among her circle of friends and acquaintances, and of her sensitivity to their reaction, and to society's reaction to her behaviour. She made several comments like this which Noel O'Brien did not pursue. Perhaps he thought that her brief comments were enough and he did not want to prolong the tears, the discomfort they caused her. Again, he changed the subject, this time to a more positive reflection.

O'Brien: Do you have many good supportive friends, Dorothy?
Dorothy: Yes, I'm a very fortunate person. I have some absolutely unbelievable friends.

O'Brien asked her about her four children. She named the children and began to tell about each of them. She said that Neale, who is a graduate of Arizona University, and who lives in Los Angeles, is "the movie person in my family," and that he is working "right now" on a movie in Calgary. O'Brien asked her if she sees Neale.

"Yes, I see him." Dorothy began to cry. "And Neale—actually I should say, at the Betty Ford Center they have a family thing at the last week where someone of your family comes and goes through therapy with you and goes through a whole week with you, and Neale came down for me."

O'Brien asked about Colin, the third child. He did not ask Dorothy to tell about her second child and only daughter, Carolyn. Dorothy seemed pleased to tell that Colin graduated with an honours degree in geology from Queen's University, and that he works and lives in Santiago, Chile. O'Brien asked Dorothy if she keeps in touch with Colin and if he is supportive of her. Dorothy may have realized that O'Brien was inviting her to tell about the two children the jury had not seen. But she wanted to speak about the children "generally."

> Dorothy: Okay. The children have been supportive but we've had to draw apart because this has been a very, very—difficult for me and difficult for them and they have to heal in their own way, you know. Like, I can't help them any more. I helped them. I brought them up. I'm very proud of all of them. They're very—they're beautiful children but they have to deal with this themselves, and I can't help them because, guess what, I have to help myself right now.

This was a courageous statement, particularly in the light of some people's belief that the "drawing apart" of Dorothy and her children was at the instigation of the children and not Dorothy. She said it with some difficulty. What she said was also sad, after Guy's and Carolyn's testimony for the Crown, and the absence of all of her children in the courtroom—except that, according to one journalist, Neale appeared in the courtroom, unnoticed, on at least one day. Dorothy's expression "guess what?", which she used two or three times during the beginning of her testimony, was startling. It may have been part of the role she assumed, initially, on the witness stand, but it may also have been a quite honest expression of a new realization of herself that was not yet entirely convincing to her.

O'Brien revealed his protective attitude with Dorothy when he asked her then, to divert her, if she was a busy lady.

"Yes," she said, "I was . . . I love people."

Now O'Brien asked her about the early years with Earl. Dorothy told, as Earl had, that they met when she was fifteen, "went steady" in high school, were engaged to be married on Christmas Eve, 1954, and that they married in August 1957. She said that she lived at home until she was married. She named her parents, said that her father had a Ph.D., her mother had a "teaching degree," and also that her relationship with her father was "extremely special." She said proudly and affectionately, "He was an idealist . . . and an educator." I wondered, not for the first time, why the male authority figures in this courtroom—Dr. Joyce Wong, who testified about Earl's bullet wounds, was the only female authority figure—focused, and allowed Dorothy to focus, on her relationship with her father, and to say almost nothing about her relationship with her mother. Perhaps they did not realize the importance of Dorothy's relationship with her mother, of any woman's relationship with her mother. Perhaps they thought it unusual for a daughter to be so close to her father. They may have been suggesting that she expected Earl to be for her and their children what her father apparently was to his family. I wondered if it occurred to them that Dorothy's father may have been, as many good fathers were in those days, a benevolent patriarch, a kind man, who, nevertheless, did not expect his wife or daughter to be on an equal footing with himself. O'Brien was telling the jury, I suppose, that Dorothy's parents were stable, middle-class, good citizens, who provided a safe and loving home for Dorothy and a model of a happy marriage.

O'Brien asked Dorothy to explain her role since her marriage. True to the expectations of all women of her age, she said that first, she was the wife of her husband; second, she was the mother of her children. She said, "My family is the most important thing in my life." She told about her pleasure at the arrival of their adopted son, Neale, in the fall of 1961. She did not explain why she and Earl decided to adopt their first child. "At first it was—first my husband thought he'd like to have a daughter first and then I was very pleased when he decided—I thought it would be good to have a son being the oldest in the family. And so we decided we would have a son. And it's kind of nice when you're adopting somebody you've got the choice, and so that's what we chose to do." She told how on the day Neale was officially theirs, her principal came into her high school classroom in Calgary and announced to everyone that she was a mother. She stopped teaching that day. She sighed with the memory of the joy she felt then. From that day on, she stayed at home. Their other three children, who were not adopted, were born in Calgary.

At O'Brien's request, Dorothy told about the diagnosis of Earl's Hodgkin's disease in May 1971, and that because Earl was working for an American company, they found a doctor at Stanford University in California who wanted people for an experiment in a new program of treatment. She said that Earl had surgery and then he was the first person to have fifty-nine "lineal reactor treatments" without a break. She also said, "My husband didn't want anyone to know why he was down there. He wouldn't let me tell my parents why we were down there. So it was kind of difficult in a way, but, at any rate, we managed. . . . " Dorothy did not explain why Earl demanded this secrecy, but I assumed that it was his concern about his work, and his not wanting anyone to know that he might be a risk because of his health. She said that she and the four children stayed in a motel for two weeks, then in a rented house, and after she brought the children back to Calgary when school began in September, she and Earl rented an apartment, and she commuted between Calgary and Stanford. O'Brien asked her if there was much stress in her relationship with Earl at that time. She said, "I . . . hardly remember what I did down there." O'Brien prompted her, and she said that when Earl came home from the hospital, she was expected to look after him, and "I'm not a nurse!"

O'Brien asked Dorothy to tell about Earl's career and their relationship after they moved to Toronto in 1972. By this time Dorothy had lost some of the artificiality which had startled me at the beginning of her testimony. It may be that her initial manner and tone of voice were a result of her having told her story so many times to so many people that the effort to do it again, even at this crucial time, was difficult, and artificial somehow. Or perhaps she was simply terrified. She said that it was Earl, as head of an oil company in Calgary, who initiated the move of the head office from Calgary to Toronto. She said that Earl was away from home a lot. "I was home all week and Earl came home on the weekend, and even if he was home during the week he worked late hours."

> O'Brien: And the four children? Whose responsibility to the—did that fall upon?
> Dorothy: Well, the children were my responsibility. I'm not saying that Earl didn't do anything with them. He did, but, basically, I was the one that had to deal with the daily things that happened with the children . . .

Dorothy explained that moving from California to Calgary to Toronto, after "this dreadful thing in California," was very difficult.

> So it was very stressful. I mean, it was stressful. But, you know, we got so we really got—we really learned and profited by living in Toronto.

This comment is one of the many indications of Dorothy's denial of the reality of her life, of her ability to look on the good side of everything, of her determination to "manage," no matter what.

O'Brien asked her who disciplined the children. She said, "I did."

O'Brien: Were there ever any conflicts over the discipline of the children?
Dorothy: Yes.
O'Brien: Can you explain some of those?
Dorothy: Okay. It seemed that every Friday the children were being
more difficult, and I would be trying—I wanted everything perfect
when my husband came home so that we could have a nice time together. And it would seem that he would walk in the door—and I'm not
going to say I didn't scream. I did scream. I did, you know, I mean, I'm
just a person. But he would walk in the door and I'd be having an argu-
ment with Neale or one of the children and, then, the next thing I knew
I was having an argument with him. He never said—he didn't support
me in discipline particularly with Guy, the youngest.
O'Brien: Guy being the lad who testified the other day, of course?
Dorothy: Ummumm.
O'Brien: Have you had a bit of a strained relationship with your son
Guy?
Dorothy: Yes.
O'Brien: Can you explain that to the jury?
Dorothy: Well, yes, [Dorothy paused for a few seconds] I guess, I can.
My first three children I thought I was the perfect mother cause they
were so perfect and then I had Guy and I realized that it had nothing to
do with the mother.

Dorothy continued to explain that she and Earl have different blood
types: she is RH negative and Earl is RH positive. Consequently, when
Guy was born he had to stay in the hospital for a month. She said that
although he had "a slight problem" he was "full of energy" and she thinks
the nurses played with him in the hospital during the night. When she
brought him home, he'd wake in the night and want her to play with him.
"I'd give him his juice and stuff, but he didn't want to go back to sleep. . . .
I put him down and he would scream. He could scream and scream for
hours. So that was difficult, but that was just to start with."

The eleven women and one man on the jury watched Dorothy closely.
Some women in the gallery looked down at the floor, at their hands in their
laps, avoiding the eyes of their female companions as they recalled, perhaps,
their own experiences with an infant they could not comfort no matter how
hard they tried. Some other women watched her carefully, compassionately,

not disturbed by her honesty. Dorothy seemed to be unaware of any reaction to what she had just said, and she continued to explain.

> But then Guy did not like discipline of any kind and I found that he and I had problems because of it 'cause, let's face it, you can't run a household with four children and not have some discipline. And I was the disciplinarian.
> O'Brien: And was this an ongoing thing?
> Dorothy: Yes, it was ongoing.
> O'Brien: And in the teenage years did it continue on?
> Dorothy: Yes.
> O'Brien: And did it get to situations where it ultimately led to violence?
> Dorothy: Yes.
> O'Brien: Can you just explain that to the jury?
> Dorothy: Well, one particular incident or more?

O'Brien suggested that she select an incident that she thought would be appropriate. Dorothy told about an incident after Guy had finished high school, but was still living at home. She said, "I thought Guy was going to throw me out through the window in our family room. And I was fighting him back. I was. Anyway, it ended." When Earl came home she said, "This child has to leave this house. I will not have him stay here any longer." She said that they helped him find a basement apartment in Calgary and get settled in, because he had little money.

Dorothy told about several incidents as Guy was growing up, when she and Earl differed about what was best for Guy. She told about her efforts to get Guy into a college. While he attended a college in Scottsdale, Arizona, where she lived for part of each year, she and Guy lived in separate apartments. I suspect that O'Brien was trying to show that there was some real substance to the antagonism between Guy and Dorothy, and also that Earl and Dorothy could neither agree about Guy's problems nor resolve them. These were not minor and insignificant issues, as Earl had suggested, and also the difficult relationship between Guy and Dorothy was not new—it did not appear because of her verbal attack on Guy after she shot Earl. But, for various reasons, and especially I suppose, the difficult relationships between many parents and their children, these were uncomfortable moments for almost everyone during Dorothy's testimony. I wondered if it is possible that for years Dorothy has displaced some of her anger towards Earl onto Guy, that Guy has been a scapegoat, and that Guy, perhaps unwittingly, has invited this role in his desire to be his father's son, in his identification with Earl. But O'Brien did not examine overtly this complex and dangerous relationship in the Joudrie family. He moved on.

O'Brien asked Dorothy to tell about her "courtship years" with Earl. Dorothy said, as we knew, that while he was in high school Earl had left home and was living with another family. She did not explain why this had happened. She said, "Earl was an exciting person. He was very talented. He was a violinist. And he and I—I really cared for him. I really—anyway, we did have what you would call a volatile relationship even in those days. But it was exciting. I didn't think there was anything bad about it. And we did have arguments. And he—and, I guess, the problem. . . . " Dorothy paused, wondering if she should go on. O'Brien asked her to tell of any incident that caused her "concern and distress" before they were married.

Dorothy said, "Oh, yes. There were lots of incidents."

She said they would have arguments on the telephone. She said, "I waited a lot." She said that one time while she was waiting for Earl at the library, she talked briefly with another student, "some guy, I don't even know who it was." Earl arrived, and as they walked home, "all of a sudden he was furious at me and we were having an argument and he threw my books in the snow and walked off."

O'Brien: Was that type of incident, jealousy, was that a common occurrence throughout your courtship?
Dorothy: Yes, I honestly describe Earl as a very jealous person.

O'Brien asked Dorothy if Earl's jealousy continued after their marriage. "Yes," she said.

O'Brien wanted to know how Earl would "exhibit that degree of jealousy" in her company.

Dorothy said that they would go to the Oilmen's annual social events, which alternate between Banff and Jasper. She said, "It's all very social. And I was very social. I loved to dance and I loved to party. And, of course, I danced with other people, too. Earl and I danced really well together. But we never went to the Oilmen's once, not once, in all the years, that we didn't have an argument."

"Over what?" O'Brien wanted to know.

"Over anything," Dorothy said. "Like, me dancing, well, with somebody, or me having too much fun, I guess."

O'Brien asked Dorothy to tell about the first time she could recall Earl being violent towards her. Dorothy said that during the second year of their marriage, while they were living in an apartment in Calgary, Earl, "in the kitchen . . . slammed me against the wall and I was shocked. And I picked up a beautiful cookie jar that I owned, and I don't—I love dishes, and I don't like breaking things. And I threw it at him. I missed and it broke. And that's when the argument ended that particular time." But during that same year, "he did the same thing again. And I remember sliding down from the wall and I had high heel spike shoes on, and I took them off and there was a hallway and he ran down the hall, and I ran down the hall, and he closed the bedroom door and I threw the shoes and they hung in the door. And I was just horrified." The other people in the apartment building learned about the shoes in the door, "but nobody ever knew what happened before the shoes hung on the door."

O'Brien: What happened before the shoes hung on the door?
Dorothy: Earl had hit me.
O'Brien: Did you tell anybody about this?
Dorothy: No.
O'Brien: And in the subsequent years of acts of of violence did you tell people about it?
Dorothy: No.
O'Brien: Did you tell your friends about it?
Dorothy: No.
O'Brien: Did you tell the police about it?
Dorothy: No.
O'Brien: And do you know why you hid it from everybody?
Dorothy: Because I thought it was my fault.
O'Brien: All right.
Dorothy: In my family, we never had anybody throw things or anybody hit anybody, so I must have been doing something wrong.
O'Brien: Do you believe that now?
Dorothy: No, I don't believe that now.

O'Brien asked Dorothy to tell about Earl's first major assault. Dorothy explained that this happened while they were on holiday, driving through the Kootenays. Dorothy was pregnant with Carolyn, "and my husband was angry at me for something and all of a sudden he just reached across and hit me in my stomach. And I was petrified cause I thought something might have happened to the baby. That's the first one that was major." She remembered Neale, who was in the car, crying. She told about this incident in a flat voice, with no embellishment, but it caused a quiet flurry as jurors wrote in their note books, and an emotional reaction in some women in the gallery. During a recess, a few minutes later, some of these women spoke to Dorothy, expressing sympathy and support. O'Brien asked Dorothy if she told her mother about this incident.

> Dorothy: No.
> O'Brien: Why did you not confide in your parents with respect to these things that were happening?
> Dorothy: Because I didn't want Earl to look bad.
> O'Brien: All right.
> Dorothy: He thought a lot of my parents.
> O'Brien: Did your parents want you to marry Earl?
> Dorothy: No, I don't think they did. They didn't want me to marry Earl particularly.
>
> In fact, the night before our wedding, which was a wedding of about 250 people, my mother talked to me and she said, now, if you don't want to do this it doesn't matter that we've got all these arrangements made. It doesn't matter. And at that time she talked to me and she told me, you know, that marriage was a big commitment, and you had to work at it. You had to make it work. And, therefore, I never wanted them to know that it wasn't always working out.

Certainly not all mothers would be prepared to cancel their daughter's wedding at the last minute. Dorothy's mother seems to have possessed an unusually independent spirit. But I suspect, from what Dorothy said, that this was not the first discussion in the Jonason family about the wisdom of Dorothy's decision to marry Earl Joudrie. Earl and Dorothy had been engaged for almost three years, and it is very likely that her parents, one way or another, had helped Dorothy to decide that she should complete her university degree before she married. During those post-war years the one important goal for all women was to marry. Many young women, in the heat of passion and romance and the promise of living happily ever after, and particularly in the face of intense social pressure to help their men get ahead, abandoned their own education in order to support their new, young husbands as they pursued theirs. Dorothy's decision, or her agreement to wait, was probably very difficult for her, partly because there is little doubt that her parents hoped that as she waited, she would change her mind. The fact that neither she nor Earl changed their minds, is evidence of the intensity of their attraction to each other, and their determination to be together, and probably other crucial factors, including Earl's influence on her. Despite the fact that both of them testified in court that there were good things about their relationship, especially in the beginning, Dorothy knew even before they were married about Earl's competitive nature, his jealousy, his need to control her. And her parents knew Earl well. So it is quite possible that on the eve of Dorothy's wedding, her mother wanted to tell her that she was seriously, perhaps even desperately, concerned about her future. I think Dorothy suggests this, indirectly. And what appears initially to be a generous gesture from her mother, and I think it was that, begins to seem, as well, almost a threat. If Dorothy was determined to marry Earl, despite her parents' disapproval, it would be up to her to make the marriage work. She no longer would be her parents' responsibility. She would be on her own, with the man she had promised to love, honour, and obey. And Dorothy never forgot that. No wonder she did not want her parents to know that her marriage "wasn't always working out." No wonder she believed it was her fault that Earl abused her.

But Dorothy was not asked to comment on her conversation with her mother, and O'Brien continued. He asked Dorothy to tell briefly about her relationship with Earl during the 1960s. Dorothy said that it was "up and down," that they were either "really happy" or "things were very sad." She said that Earl was very critical—of her clothes, of what she bought, of her menus for dinner parties. She said that because Earl's career was on the rise, they had many social obligations, and that she could entertain "up to one hundred people for dinner." But on one occasion, when she was pregnant with Guy, they arranged to have a dinner catered. The night before the dinner, Earl cancelled the caterers. "I managed," she said. O'Brien asked her about an incident, in Calgary in 1971, when Earl struck her in the face and broke her nose. She said that she did not go to a doctor until the next year when she had difficulty breathing. She was hospitalized then and had surgery on her nose. Earl visited her "daily," she said. O'Brien asked about "the marks on her face" after Earl struck her. Dorothy said "I had black eyes," and that she went to Merle Norman, a beauty salon in Calgary, where they would apply make-up to cover the bruises. "I would go on a Friday and they would make my face up. It cost me five dollars to have my face made up and I'd keep the make-up on for two days, for Friday and Saturday. And I thought that was extravagant."

"You went to parties then with Earl?" O'Brien asked. "Yes."

What about while they lived in Toronto, as Earl's career was rising, during the 1970s, O'Brien wanted to know. Dorothy said that this was the time of "most arguments and the most violence." Did the police ever come? Dorothy remembered that once, when the police arrived, she would not press charges. It was Liz Griffiths, Dorothy's nanny, who had called the police. Dorothy's mind seemed to wander away a little, into these memories. O'Brien brought her back to what he considered the issue at hand, asking her to tell about another violent incident. "Yes, one night my husband called me from a restaurant in Toronto . . . and he was being nice. A bunch of them were down there and he called me to join them." But when Dorothy arrived, she discovered that they had been drinking "for quite a while . . . they drank that frozen stuff you know." Dorothy did not want to stay, so she said that she had to go to the ladies' room and she left and went home. "And needless to say that wasn't the smart thing to do . . . he came home and he beat me up."

> O'Brien: Do you recall what happened to you on that occasion?
> Dorothy: I was just bruised on my body.
> O'Brien: Were the police called on that occasion?
> Dorothy: No.
> O'Brien: Do you recall if the nanny was home at that time.
> Dorothy: Yes, she was.

Dorothy said that she didn't discuss this incident with Elizabeth Griffiths, but it is interesting to compare Dorothy's report of it to Ms. Griffiths' recollection of the extent of the violence that night, and that Earl took Dorothy to the hospital.

Did Dorothy ever stay in a hotel, O'Brien wanted to know, in the Inn On The Park?

"Yes, numerous [times]."

> O'Brien: Why?
> Dorothy: Well, I decided if I could—I mean, the children were being looked after. The nanny was there. And when I thought that the situation was getting out of hand I went to the hotel some nights and stayed

there. Didn't work for very long though because my husband found that was where I went.

O'Brien asked Dorothy if she recalled an incident at the York Downs Golf and Country Club. She said she did not recall the whole incident, but she remembered that it was a "really nice party" and that she was having a "nice time," dancing with members of the club she didn't know well, but at their request. She said that after dinner, when she came out of the ladies' room, "Earl was waiting for me and he slammed me against the wall in the lobby. And I ran and got away from him. I don't know—remember where I ran. I know I eventually ended up in the ladies' locker room and I was huddled in the corner crying when my friends found me." Her friends took her home with them and intervened with Earl, but because "he wanted me to come home," she went.

O'Brien asked Dorothy if she "would take steps" to try to avoid any violent episodes, and what would she do.

"Well," she said, "I tried to do—to avoid—. You mean, if I knew one was coming or just try and avoid it? I was—I tried to do everything. I wanted everything so there wouldn't be anything to fight about. I tried to make everything pleasant." She said that when Earl was in town, they would spend five nights a week with business friends, often in their home. Dorothy did not say, but it was hardly necessary now, that she was, therefore, always on display, never sure what would happen, never sure what her husband would say or do, never safe, never secure.

The Joudries moved to Kentucky in 1977. Earl was senior vice-president of his company. O'Brien asked Dorothy to describe the most violent incident in Kentucky. We had heard about this incident from Earl during his testimony. It was one of "the three incidents of abuse" during the Joudries' marriage, according to Selinger. But Dorothy's telling about it, despite her flat tone, and the exclusion of details of the assault, cast a new light on what happened that night. She began by saying, "My parents were visiting us from Edmonton and they had been with us in Florida for Christmas." There had been a rare snow storm in Ashland, the schools were closed, and because the Joudrie children had skis, sleighs, and toboggans, their friends had come to play on the hill below their house. There was a "glassed-in" room in the house from which the other children's parents and Dorothy and her parents could see the snow, the hill, the children. During the evening the adults played bridge. Dorothy and her father, who was "clinically blind" by then, were "sort of partners." Dorothy's mother had baked cinnamon buns; they made hot chocolate. Late in the evening, Earl appeared, unannounced, from Europe. "And I was sitting where I could see him come in the door. He came in the door and I saw this look on his face and it was a black look is all I can say." He visited with the guests before they left, and with Dorothy's parents, who then retired—"and Earl and I got into a fight, and he beat me up." Dorothy told, as Earl had, that Earl tried to get a doctor, who lived near by, but he would not come. Dorothy said that her chest and legs were injured so severely she had to spend the night on the chesterfield because she could not walk up the stairs. "And my parents—I saw them looking down at me."

> And, then, my husband organized for them to leave on a company plane the next day. They wanted to leave. And my husband took me to the hospital and I—just to find out if anything was broken. My legs and my back and my ribs were injured and there was nothing broken. They gave me some pills, pills for the hurt and I came home.
> O'Brien: What did your husband strike you with on that occasion?
> Dorothy: Well, as far as I know, he struck me with his fists and his arms and everything.

Dorothy said that she does not remember ever discussing this incident with her parents. She saw them next during the following summer when she and the children visited them in Edmonton. O'Brien urged her to explain why she had not discussed this incident with her parents. She said, "It was my choice to stay with my husband."

By this time in Dorothy's testimony, we knew that some of the Joudries' friends in Toronto knew about Earl's abuse of her: they took Dorothy into their homes and they helped her to hide from him. When Dorothy visited the Merle Norman beauty salon, in Calgary, to have her black eyes and bruises disguised by make-up, they, too, knew about the abuse. Some of her friends then, in Calgary, probably knew also, because while make-up can cover some discoloured skin, it cannot hide injuries completely, and certainly not the swelling of black eyes, or any severe injury to the flesh or bones. Dorothy was treated by doctors who must surely have known the cause of her injuries. The refusal of the doctor in Kentucky to come to their house to treat Dorothy suggests that he knew what had happened and did not want to be involved. Now her parents had witnessed the most serious assault by her husband, and they wanted to return to Edmonton, leaving Dorothy in Kentucky with Earl. Of all of these people, Elizabeth Griffiths was the only person who acted to protect Dorothy. But because Dorothy did not want to lay charges, legally, against her husband, and because, until recently and with rare exceptions, our laws were such that this responsibility was hers, the police left Dorothy alone to solve the problem of a husband who had just assaulted her, causing visible bodily harm, and whose assault on her had been witnessed by the person who reported it. But we had not yet heard the whole story.

O'Brien asked Dorothy to tell about incidents that were not physical. He prompted her by suggesting that she begin by telling about an incident that occurred in Glacier National Park as they drove home from their honeymoon. She told about how Earl had frightened her to the point of hysteria—"he was going to cure me of my fear of heights so he drove as close to the edge of the road as he could and I ended up sitting on the floor screaming and crying."

O'Brien: Did he stop?
Dorothy: Did what stop?
O'Brien: Did he stop driving in that manner?
Dorothy: Not for quite a long time, no.

She told about Earl, in a fit of anger, pulling their car engine apart. She told about Earl deserting her at a downtown Calgary hotel after she brought him the "wrong" shirt and trousers. She told about Earl's fiftieth birthday party: she had invited people from all over Canada—"110 people for dinner." When Earl arrived home, he "yelled and swore and locked himself in the bedroom. The guests arrived. Earl came out and was charming." She told about a trip to Hawaii with Earl and three of the children when Earl told her on the plane that he had to return home the next day, leaving her there with the children on a holiday she had thought she would be sharing with her husband. Dorothy told about a series of events between 1988 and December 1994—parties, receptions, conferences, Colin's graduation from Queen's University, a cruise she and Earl took together, after their separation, at her suggestion and expense, and the children's weddings. On all of these occasions, Earl appeared publicly with her as her husband, but they rarely shared a room when they travelled. She could not anticipate his behaviour. She was often humiliated, and always demeaned by his rejection of her.

Earl moved into his own apartment in Calgary in 1989. During the preliminary hearing Earl said that Dorothy "invited" him to leave their home. Dorothy said that in July 1991 Earl arranged a meeting to talk with her. He said he had "three scenarios" to propose. One, he could quit work, and travel, and play golf, and "just enjoy life." But he didn't like playing golf with Dorothy, and he was tired of travelling. Two, they could sell their big house, find an apartment in Calgary, and a less demanding job for him, and try to start over again. Three, he could accept a "new, fantastic" job as chairman of the board of Algoma Steel, which would be exciting and a challenge for him. Dorothy knew that it was the third choice that he wanted. "I said to him, 'Well, if you take that scenario do you have any room in your life for me?' And he said 'No.'" On August 21, 1991, Earl's secretary phoned Dorothy to tell her that Earl had moved to Toronto to live. This information stands out in the minds of those who heard it as one of Earl Joudrie's most invidious and cowardly acts. Most of the journalists writing about the trial included it in their reports. Earl had said, during his testimony, that Dorothy was "very angry about the fact that I appeared to have left her. Somehow that seemed to mean something." This remark about Dorothy, his attempt to be ingenuous, and in fact, his dishonesty, did not enhance the portrait Earl Joudrie attempted to paint of himself. Now Dorothy had told us why she believed that Earl "appeared" to have left her. "And so," said Dorothy, "I phoned my lawyer and I said I want to go for a legal separation." She said that it was very difficult for her to do this because "I felt I was a failure in my marriage and with my family."

O'Brien continued, asking Dorothy to tell, generally, about her relationship with Earl in the eighties. Dorothy said that they discussed the incident in Kentucky, and now that "I was back in my home, my own country," she told Earl she "would leave him if he did that ever again." She said that he did not hit her again, but "we had arguments and fights and throwing of things and holes in the wall and taking lamps and throwing them across the rooms . . . I really feel that at that time I was sort of walking on eggs all the time because I was never sure what was going to happen with Earl when he came home. I never knew whether he was—I never knew whether he was going to be great or it wasn't going to be great." So O'Brien asked her to tell about the good side of their marriage. She said that Earl had given her nice gifts, that they had travelled to many places, attended the Kentucky Derby, for example. "We'd have some really good times together," she said, with no enthusiasm.

O'Brien asked Dorothy to discuss her use of alcohol. She said that she and Earl did not drink at home during the early years of their marriage. In Toronto, her social drinking increased. In Kentucky, she did not "overdrink" socially, but it was then that she began to drink alone. "If Earl phoned and said he wasn't coming home for dinner, . . . I would pour myself a drink."

> And, then, when he left—when he moved out. He didn't leave me. He just moved out. He said—
> O'Brien: Are you quoting somebody there?
> Dorothy: Pardon?
> O'Brien: Are you quoting somebody with that?
> Dorothy: Yes, Earl—I'll quote Earl. When he left in '89, he told me he was not leaving me he was just moving out.
> And, then, when I was alone from '89 right up to '95 I definitely was misusing alcohol and I was pouring drinks by myself at home.

Dorothy said that during this period there were many "golden handshakes," functions at which Earl would be praised and given gifts as he retired from companies. She was often asked to choose the gifts because she would know, they thought, what he would like. But living out this pretence of intimacy must have been very sad, and combined with Earl's treatment of her in public, almost unendurable for Dorothy. She said that at one party Earl "got up and he made a big speech and he never mentioned my name." After Earl was finished, "somebody from the company got up and gave me a gift and thanked me for the things that I had done." Then the other man who was retiring called up his wife to stand beside him as he spoke, and he thanked her. Dorothy was "devastated" that night, she said. O'Brien asked her what year she was speaking about specifically. She had become very upset as she told about the retirement parties, and she was rather confused, and wasn't sure about the date. She asked O'Brien, "It was probably '88. Was that about the time?" And then they had an interesting exchange.

> O'Brien: All right. Just relax for a second.
> Dorothy: Okay.
> O'Brien: Are you all right?
> Dorothy: Yes, I just can't remember the year.

This was a quiet exchange, and no one seemed to pay much attention to what O'Brien and Dorothy were saying. It was not the first time O'Brien had encouraged her, kindly, to relax.

I have assumed, from my own experience with him, that Noel O'Brien does not always or necessarily defer to women. I remember the first time I spoke to him on the telephone. I had left a message the day before, and he called me at 7:45 the next morning. Before I could begin to tell him why I wanted to speak with him, he said quite aggressively that he was a busy man and did not have time to talk to journalists who were fishing for information while a publication ban was in place—or words to that effect. I was angry. I wanted to tell him that I, too, was a busy person, that I was on my way out the door to meet a student before my first class of the day at the university, that I had important things on my mind, and that this telephone call, at an inconvenient time for me, would mean that I would be late. But I did not tell him that. I deferred to him. As I think of it now, I am not sure if my behaviour that morning was traditionally feminine and passive, or simply expedient, because I did not want to risk losing the opportunity to speak with him. But I have forgotten neither my anger nor my frantic attempt to gather together the questions that were on my mind, and to ask them as quickly and cogently as possible, while at the same time, I reached awkwardly for my purse and my briefcase, to find my glasses and a pen. O'Brien never spoke to me like that again, and perhaps because he came to recognize me as an ally, my few conversations with him during and since the trial have been agreeable and helpful.

Many people have noted that Dorothy is very fortunate to be able to afford the services of a lawyer like Noel O'Brien. Her trial caused heated discussions about the fact that the justice system is unfair to people who cannot afford the best and most expensive legal assistance. Nevertheless, while justice is expensive, and it is wrong that some people are unable to pay for it, at the same time, Dorothy Joudrie should not have been denied the best defence she could get. But Dorothy has been most fortunate to have a lawyer who seems to be protective, compassionate, respectful, and competent. I saw no signs at any time that O'Brien patronized her, demeaned her, or asserted his authority and power inappropriately in relation to her. I suspect that O'Brien's manner with Dorothy was calculated, utilitarian, designed carefully to help him to win. But I also suspect that some other lawyers, expensive lawyers, both men and women, would not have met the demands on them with O'Brien's grace, and kindness, and exactly what I was observing now—his reassurance, and careful observation of her emotional stability during her testimony.

O'Brien's defence of Dorothy rested on his theory that she had been damaged emotionally by years of violent mistreatment by her husband. This is not a popular defence among some advocates for abused women in Dorothy's position. These advocates believe that society in general, and the legal and medical professions in particular, are much too quick to ignore the reasonable and justifiable actions of such women and, instead, to embrace the idea that there is something wrong with them, that they are sick, or that they have been rendered incompetent or dangerous because of the abuse they have experienced. Such advocates want society to realize that the problem is not the woman, but the abusive man. But despite the *Lavallee* decision in 1990,[57] the justice system in Canada has changed very little in keeping with these enlightened views. It seemed to be quite apparent that O'Brien understood who was the problem in the Joudrie family. Nevertheless, when witnesses testified to the abuse Earl Joudrie inflicted on his wife, and Dorothy's shooting her abusive husband, O'Brien referred to, and showed convincing evidence of Dorothy's "massive denial of the reality of her life" and during and immediately after the shooting, her state of "automatism." At the same time, he also seemed to recognize Dorothy's inclination, her having learned, to submit to the authority of a man. But O'Brien showed no signs that he took unfair advantage of this. It seemed apparent that during the months he had worked with Dorothy, he had won her confidence. Now, he needed the jury's sympathy and support. So I do not know if this quiet exchange between a lawyer and his client was for the benefit of Dorothy, or the jury, or both. But I was impressed by it. And I was not surprised when, at the end of the trial, Dorothy said that she thinks of Noel O'Brien as her friend. It is to her credit, and to his, that she did not say that she thinks of Noel O'Brien as someone who would take care of her.

Dorothy recovered her composure quickly, and O'Brien asked her about the marriage counselling the Joudries sought during the late 1980s. Earl had said, during his testimony, that "in '86, I believe," he discussed their marital problems and Dorothy's drinking with his physician in Calgary, who advised counselling. Earl also said that he told the doctor about "the physical harm that was done to Dorothy" and that he wondered if her drinking "had to do with that kind of trauma." At the preliminary hearing Earl said that his doctor assured him that alcoholism is a disease, and that experts agree that it is not related to such things as marital problems and, implicitly, abuse. Many experts would disagree with

Earl's doctor. One expert notes that "battering accounts for half of all cases of alcoholism in women."[58] Dorothy said very little about the counselling apart from the fact that she decided to lose weight—"for myself"—as she was told she should, "but I thought it might have other side effects." Between May and October of 1989 she lost forty pounds. She added, wryly, that Earl left home to live alone in October 1989.

When Dorothy returned to the witness stand after the lunch break on this first day of her testimony, O'Brien directed her to begin by discussing her relationship with Lynn Manning, the woman with whom Earl now lives in Toronto. Dorothy said that Lynn Manning is her second cousin; she is "about eight years younger than I am" and "I was her friend." She said that she and Earl "used to babysit her." Later, Lynn stayed with Earl and Dorothy when she visited Calgary. Lynn Manning's oldest daughter is the same age as Guy. When the Joudries lived in Toronto, and Lynn lived there also, Dorothy and Lynn visited each other, with their children. Dorothy said, "When she got divorced . . . I visited her a number of times in Edmonton, because she was alone with three children." Dorothy advised her about her second relationship. "Unfortunately, he died, and I helped her with that." Lynn took a job in Toronto, and while Dorothy was visiting Toronto she took Lynn out for dinner "a number of times and introduced her to some of my friends." Lynn also stayed at Dorothy's house in Phoenix, for a holiday, after her friend died. Dorothy told all this in an offhand manner, which made it easy for listeners to diminish her assistance to Lynn Manning. But when I talked, both before and after the trial, with other women who knew Dorothy, a quality about her which several of them mentioned was her generosity. One woman who knew Dorothy during the 1980s said, "Dorothy Joudrie was the most generous person I've ever known."

What about Earl and Lynn? O'Brien asked. Dorothy said that in 1991 Carolyn went to Toronto to visit Earl and told her mother when she returned that she had gone out with Earl and Lynn. Dorothy also learned that Earl and Lynn had vacationed together in Florida. Dorothy asked Earl if he had gone to Florida with Lynn. Earl said "No." Dorothy telephoned Lynn, who told Dorothy that she and Earl "had a lovely time in Florida." Before Carolyn's wedding in 1993, when Earl was in Calgary, he telephoned Dorothy to tell her "Lynn's moving in with me." It is not surprising if Dorothy felt violated and betrayed on two fronts, and very angry. But again, O'Brien did not try to analyze Dorothy's feelings, or remark about Earl's treatment of her, and now Lynn Manning's as well. He let her words and her tone of voice—flat, bitter, resigned—convey her emotions. She told Earl not to come to the parties before Carolyn's wedding. Earl and Lynn travelled together in Europe while "I was getting this wedding put together," Dorothy said. And O'Brien directed Dorothy as she continued with her story.

Dorothy moved out of the "big house" in 1990, and in 1991 she bought a condominium across the street from the one she had rented during the previous year in Calgary. Her purchase of the house probably followed the financial settlement with Earl at the time of their legal separation. O'Brien asked Dorothy if there were disagreements about money during the separation. Dorothy said that she was given half of everything, which Selinger told the court, more than once, was $1.9 million. (This amount of money was a subject of discussion among spectators throughout the trial.) But Dorothy thought Earl should give her "something monthly" as well. "The lawyer said no," Dorothy said, "$2000 a month for four years, before tax. That's $1000 a month, and I accepted it." O'Brien asked Dorothy if she ever mentioned Earl's abuse of her to her lawyers during the separation and divorce proceedings. She said "No, I didn't mention at all to my lawyer that there had been abuse."

O'Brien and Dorothy discussed the Christmas card and gift that Earl sent Dorothy in 1991—Dorothy "had asked Earl if he wanted to join us" that Christmas; the birthday card he sent her in April 1993; and his card to her at Christmas in 1993. During Earl's cross-examination he read aloud the Christmas card he sent in 1991 in which he described the gift as a "statue" of two children, which he thought was "quite unique." Dorothy sighed and wept as she told about opening the gift, in 1991, alone in her bedroom, before she showed it to "the kids." She said that it made her feel very sad; it "made me think maybe he did want to come back." She said that the birthday card in April 1993 was meaningful to her because birthdays "are very special for me . . . and I thought . . . he still cares. I think I showed it to a couple of my close friends." While O'Brien was cross-examining Earl, he had suggested to him that his sending the gift and the cards was an expression of his continuing "control" over Dorothy, and, implicitly, he seemed to suggest that Earl's refusal to relinquish his power over her and his ownership of her was a cruel game. Earl turned this discussion into a play on the words "sensitive" and "insensitive" in an apparent effort to diminish O'Brien, and indirectly to diminish the importance of the gift and the cards. I saw this as one example of Earl's continuing abuse of Dorothy even as he testified at her trial, and also as an example of his jealousy—that he believes it is he who knows/owns Dorothy, and not this lawyer who presumes to understand and defend his former wife. But O'Brien had made his point, and it was confirmed now by Dorothy's tears as she recalled her reaction when she received the gift and the cards.

Because she had spent Christmas of 1992 alone, for Christmas the following year, Dorothy invited her family to accompany her on a trip to Austria. Colin and his girlfriend, Carolyn and her husband, and Neale accepted. "Guy didn't accept," she said, "so I assumed that—that he was having Christmas with Earl and it was so." Dorothy sent with Guy a present for Earl, a sweater.

By discussing the gifts and cards, O'Brien was trying to call to the attention of the jury, as he had earlier in his cross-examination of Earl, the fact that Earl had continued to allow Dorothy to hope that there might be a reconciliation. I suspect he was pointing out Dorothy's romantic expectations of traditional holidays and family celebrations. And, no doubt, he was also showing the jury that Dorothy's elaborate travel plans for herself and her family in 1993 were an indication that she was making an effort to carry on without Earl. Her apparent acceptance of Guy's plans to spend Christmas with his father (although according to Carolyn, Dorothy did not invite Guy and his girlfriend on this trip to Austria) was another indication of her determination and independence, and also, of family discord.

--------

O'Brien had devoted two thirds of his examination of Dorothy to preparing the jury for a discussion of January 21, 1995. He began now, cautiously, with what I suspect he hoped was a relatively objective fact that she must clarify. When the police entered Dorothy's home that day, they found two guns: a shotgun with ammunition for it, and a handgun. O'Brien asked her to explain the presence of the shotgun.

"Well," Dorothy said "it was actually my father's. He gave it to Earl, and when I moved out of the house, I took it with me . . . I had it in my closet in my bedroom."

> O'Brien: Had you ever shot that firearm?
> Dorothy: Only when I was with Earl, when we went hunting many years before. . . .

Suddenly I was simply overwhelmed with the complexity of this family tragedy—with the abuse, and betrayal, and misplaced trust, and now a vision of Earl and Dorothy hunting together with a rifle her father had given to Earl. I turned in my chair to look out the window. The city had the shabby look of early spring, before the usual clean-up and the annual signs of new life. The roofs of the buildings nearby were dusty, dirty, scattered with dregs from the wind and recently melted snow. The trees and tiny patches of grass had not yet begun to show any green. I could see cars parked in a lot, and a few solitary people going about their business, their daily lives. I watched them, needing to take hold of a reality outside this room. Would other lives, if someone were to tell them selectively like this, be so entangled with irony?

"  . . . a small handgun." O'Brien was saying. Dorothy explained that in 1991, the year she had agreed to a legal separation from Earl, about ten blocks away from her house in Phoenix there was a shooting—"and when I was down there now I was by myself most of the time." She was frightened by this incident. There were other incidents. As she was driving back to Calgary, she stopped in Salt Lake City to have her car repaired. When she was ready to leave and she was putting her umbrella in the trunk of her car, a man approached her suddenly, asking her for money. She explained that she did not have any money. She just had credit cards. She got into her car quickly, locked the door, and left. Another time she was followed by a man in a truck, who would pass her and then slow down and cut her off, "and I was really very frightened because there's a lot of things that happen in—in the Phoenix area with cars and people." So she went to Mandall's Shooting Supplies, a store in Scottsdale, where she talked to a gentleman who thought it would be a good idea for her to have a gun. She got the required "card," verifying that she owns property in Phoenix, and the identification card required by the gun salesman, and when she returned to the store he suggested that she buy the .25 calibre semi-automatic Beretta. On November 25, 1992, Dorothy bought what she called "this gun."

"They have a thing down in the basement there where you—they show you how to shoot these things . . . I was—I'm very nervous with guns, so anyway, I went down and—so anyway, when I finished doing that, I said to him, 'I guess we better unload this,' and he said, well—he said, well, 'there's not much—there's not much sense having a gun unless it's loaded, because you can't just take a gun out and start loading it if there's somebody doing something to you.' So he convinced me to buy up this black fanny pack thing to keep the gun in, which I did, and I stored it in my house in Phoenix."

Friends in Tucson told Dorothy about dangerous incidents on the highway between Houston and Phoenix, so she decided, when she was driving to Desert Hot Springs to visit friends, to put the gun under the front seat of her car. "I mean I didn't take the gun out or anything. I just put it underneath the front seat when I drove to Desert Hot Springs." When it was time to return to Canada, because she was nervous about driving, she arranged to drive, in tandem, with friends. She had forgotten completely about the gun—"I didn't even think about it at all"—until, when she was back in Calgary, she was selling her car. This was in May 1994.

"And I was unhappy with this car. It was a Jaguar, and it was just like waving a red flag in front of people. They just don't like people—a lot of people don't like people, particularly a lady like me—owning a Jaguar. So I was really unhappy with this car . . . and I had another car as well, a Mazda. So I decided to sell them both and get myself a Lincoln. . . . And I was—I had to get all my stuff out of the car, like, to—so he [the new owner] could take the car, and I found the gun and I realized it was illegal to have the gun here in Canada.

"Anyway, I took it out of the car, and I put it in the lower drawer in my bedroom dresser, and I intended to take it back to Phoenix."

But Dorothy did not take the gun back to Phoenix because the next time she went to Phoenix she flew, and she knew that she could not take the gun on a plane. So it stayed in her bedroom dresser in Calgary. O'Brien asked her if, during 1992, 1993, and until May 1994, when she brought it to Calgary, the gun remained, except during her trip to Desert Hot Springs, in her dresser drawer in Phoenix. At first Dorothy said "Yes." And then she said, "Well, yes. I never took it out except—well, I did, I must say. When I go down, I—I went one or so times again just to go into this Mandall's place [where she bought the gun] just to see how you operate—how you could use this gun, because I just—I guess I maybe went once or twice down there. You know, when I go down for the first time in March." O'Brien did not help Dorothy with this explanation, which became a kind of apology for her need to learn how to use the gun. For those of us who believe that people should not own guns, her explanation became almost as disconcerting for us as it was for her, and we did not listen sympathetically to this woman whose world had recently collapsed, who was telling us that she had been frightened, that she had wondered who would be the next person to violate her, to "do something" to her.

O'Brien asked Dorothy about the location of the gun since she discovered that she had brought it to Canada.

> O'Brien: Had you ever taken it out before January 21st? Had you ever taken it out of that bag?
> Dorothy: No.

O'Brien asked his next question: "Could you direct your attention, Mrs. Joudrie, to the month of December of 1994? . . . " What has happened, I wondered. This was the first time during his examination of Dorothy, and even during his introduction, that Noel O'Brien had called her "Mrs. Joudrie." O'Brien's reactions are as quick as lightning. Was he surprised by her confession of practising using the gun in Phoenix? Was he nervous about the discussion that would follow, about the day of the shooting in January 1995? Had someone suggested to him during the lunch break that he should move back from Dorothy slightly, that he should be more formal? Dorothy seemed not to be concerned about this change, this sudden, subtle, cool air of distance. So I wondered if during their conversation at lunch, O'Brien and Dorothy had discussed his mode of addressing her. She seemed quite comfortable with the fact that O'Brien did not call her Dorothy again during her testimony.

O'Brien asked Dorothy if there were "some issues" during December 1994 which caused her "some strain."

"Yes, there were," she said. She offered to do for Guy's wedding what she had done for Colin's. She offered to have a reception for Guy and Michelle either in Calgary or Banff. They didn't want it. She offered to make the wedding cake. They didn't want it. "They invited me over for dinner . . . and they handed me the guest list, and they had already sent out all the invitations. . . . And both of my other children did not invite Lynn [Manning] to their weddings, but Guy and Michele invited Lynn and her girls to my wedding—to their wedding. . . . And so I—I was upset. I was really upset, and I went back home after that and I—well, I guess I said, 'well, if she comes, I guess I won't be at your wedding.'"

Dorothy phoned Earl and told him, "'I don't think I'll come to the wedding if she comes, and he is my son' . . . I just left it at that."

Dorothy did go to the wedding; it was never perfectly clear during Dorothy's testimony if Lynn Manning was also present. But the wedding was not easy for Dorothy. One thing that upset her particularly was that Earl "made a speech" and called up Dorothy, but to stand below him, not beside him. He wanted her to stand with the children. Dorothy was very insulted, "So I went up—I walked up and I stood up on the podium with my husband, and he was very upset that I did that."

O'Brien asked where the children were for Christmas. Dorothy told a long story about a disagreement she had had with the children about her drinking, that she and they were not speaking, but that she delivered their presents to their homes, the children attended her annual "Open House," and that at the last minute they all, including Guy and Michelle, seemed to resolve their differences, temporarily at least, and Christmas "was on." Dorothy said, "Everybody really tried really hard to make it nice, and it turned out fine."

"Mrs. Joudrie," O'Brien asked, "how were your spirits then in January of 1995?"

"Well, the weddings were all over, and I had told—told Earl that I—you know, I agreed to divorce him. He asked me at Guy's wedding."

Earl could not find the deed to the "big house," and Dorothy said that she would look to see if she could find it for him. "And so, in January—January, I—I was doing that, and I was feeling really good in January."

As she was tidying up the house, she said that she found the photo albums of her wedding, and of Earl as a child, and the Christmas letters. O'Brien asked her to explain the purpose of these annual Christmas letters—from 1961 to 1994. Dorothy said that she sent out two to three hundred of these letters every year, telling friends and relatives the latest news about her family. She said, proudly, "I made these letters up—or wrote these letters."

Dorothy's expressions and slips of the tongue were sometimes quite poignant. She did make these letters up. Every year she told her version of the lives of her family and herself as if it were freshly washed laundry pinned neatly to an old-fashioned clothes line—the soil and stains washed clean, purged and softened by the sun and a gentle breeze.

O'Brien asked if she had also found the deed to the house.

"Yes," she said.

"So, in January 1995, in terms of your stress levels, were you happy? Were you sad? What was your situation, were you peaceful?" O'Brien asked.

"I thought I was—I thought I was doing really well, and a number of my friends did, too, because I finally got over these weddings, and I thought I was doing okay."

"Did you harbour any feelings of animosity towards Earl at this time?"

"No, I didn't. I—I love Earl. I loved Earl. I still—I'll never—I mean, I'll never stop loving him in some ways, and I wanted—I basically wanted him to have something that—the memories of our life together, because it was—we'd been—we'd been together since I was fifteen, and it wasn't animosity. It was—it was that I cared for him." Why, I wondered, had Dorothy immediately associated O'Brien's "feelings of animosity" with the Christmas letters she had collected for Earl.

Finally, now, O'Brien introduced a discussion of January 21. Dorothy said that Earl had told her that he was coming to Calgary "around the 18th," and would get the things she had for him. "I believe I called the hotel and left a message, and I believe I called Gulf Canada and left a message for him to call me, which he did," she said. Earl telephoned her on Friday and said that he could not come to see her on Friday as he planned originally, but that he could come on Saturday. But Dorothy had a hair appointment in the morning and plans to go out to dinner with a friend that evening. "So call me . . . so I don't have to wait around all day," she told him.

Dorothy went to her hair appointment at nine o'clock, and when she got home at about ten minutes to ten she still had not heard from Earl. Dorothy said that she was going to give her old freezer to "the girl who cleans for me," and she decided to "transfer stuff from one freezer to the other." The freezers were in the garage, and because it was a nice day, she left her car out of the garage and the garage door open when she arrived home. She had not yet begun to move things from one freezer to another when the phone rang. It was Earl. He said he could come over shortly. Dorothy said, "Fine. I'll put the coffee on." O'Brien verified for the jury, the presence of two freezers in the garage from photographs in evidence.

O'Brien: Tell us what happened, from there.
Dorothy: I believe I closed the garage door. I—I went and I poured myself a drink.
O'Brien: How would you normally pour a drink?
Dorothy: I fill up a glass, like a glass, [she showed with her hand the size of about a three-and-a-half inch tumbler] and I fill it with ice, and then I pour the drink on top of it.
O'Brien: Do you know how much you poured in?
Dorothy: I never—no, I didn't measure.
O'Brien: All right. Why did you pour yourself a drink?

Dorothy explained that when she is with Earl, she is "pretty nervous."

> O'Brien: Did you consume some of the alcohol then?
> Dorothy: Yes, I did, and then I—
> O'Brien: Just go from there.
> Dorothy: And then I made the coffee.
> O'Brien: Yes, what happens.
> Dorothy: And then I—I—I was—I was doing something in the utility room, which is right off the kitchen, and I believe I was either—I could—I mean, you know, I really can't exactly remember what I was doing in the utility room. I could have been putting the wash in the dryer or anything, but I was in the utility room anyway.

As Dorothy said this she put her hands on the edge of the witness box. She was leaning forward, looking down, and she seemed to be straining to remember. She remembered that before she was in the utility room, she had opened the front door and locked the outer, glass security door.

> O'Brien: Sorry to interrupt you. Is there a security system in your home?
> Dorothy: Oh, yes. I have—I'm the one that put security systems in all the houses.

The panel for the security system in Dorothy's house is located in the utility room, next to the garage. For that reason, so she does not have to run through the house to turn off the alarm, which is set on a timer, she uses the garage door to enter and leave the house. She keeps a small garage door-opener in her purse. She said that sometimes her friends come in the front door, but "lots of times my friends come in the garage door." This extended discussion of the security system in Dorothy's house in relation to Earl's arrival and his presence that Saturday morning, diverted the listeners' attention from the extraordinary irony of the pains Dorothy had taken, for years, to lock in the danger—not only to lock it into her house, but to lock it into herself.

When Earl arrived, he rang the front doorbell. Dorothy called to him "from the utility room" to come through the garage, that she would open the garage door. So he entered the house through the garage. They went into the kitchen, where they sat at the table, drinking coffee.

"And then I had the stuff that I had gathered together, I had it sitting on the counter right by the—where the wall—there's a counter there, and I had brought it and set it there . . . the deed to the house, the—his album

of his childhood pictures, the wedding picture album, the—the—the
book with all the—with all the Christmas letters, and then there was
copies of these appraisals . . . of all of the stuff that we had owned.

"We started to talk, and we sort of were talking about the children and
the fact now that they were all married and—and a little bit about the
weddings, and then we were discussing Guy, because Guy was—and his
wife were living up at the big house and Earl was trying to sell it, and Guy
didn't have a very good job. I mean it was a good job. I don't mean that,
but it wasn't a high-paying job to have to support a wife with, and so we
were discussing that.

"And then we—we talked about the items and Earl—Earl looked
through them. He didn't read them or anything. He just glanced through
them." This was an intense moment in Dorothy's testimony, and I wondered why O'Brien did not ask her how she reacted when Earl "just
glanced" through her carefully prepared history of their life together.

"And then I said to him, 'Do you still want the divorce?' And he said,
'Yes.' He said—he said, 'The proceedings are going forward and your
lawyer should have the things.' And I said to him, I said, 'Well, you know,'
I said, 'You know, it's—it's gonna be easier for you than it is for me,
because you've got somebody, and I'm all alone.' And I—I just—I just
felt—I was so sad. I was just really, really sad, and I was really feeling lonely and very forlorn and lonely.

"And the next thing I saw was Earl's face, and it was terrible. It was
just—it was awful. Had a terrible expression on it. It was really ashen
looking and wrinkled and everything.

"Then the next thing that happened is I heard him calling me. He was
calling me for help. It sounded like it was far away, but he was calling me.
And I sort of came to, and I saw him lying on the garage floor, and then I
believe what I heard was, he said, 'That's a horrible thing you've
done' . . . and he said I'd shot him. And I was standing there in the middle
of the garage, and I didn't know whether I said it out loud or what, I just
thought—I thought, what have I done? I'm going to go to jail."

O'Brien: Do you have anything in your hands at that time?
Dorothy: No, I didn't have anything in my hands. I had nothing. I was
just standing there.
O'Brien: Do you have any recollection of obtaining a firearm from the
bottom of that dresser drawer?

Dorothy: I haven't any recollection, no.

O'Brien: Do you have any recollection of putting the firearm in that drawer afterwards?

Dorothy: No, I don't—I don't remember doing that either.

O'Brien: Do you have any recollection with respect to anything regarding the documents or the wedding albums or anything of that nature that may have fallen on the garage floor?

Dorothy: Well, I—I don't have any recollections, no. Not particularly, no.

Dorothy was very upset and tearful as she told all of this. She spoke hesitantly, quietly, supporting herself as she leaned forward against the front of the witness box. There seemed to be nothing artificial in her effort to remember, and to tell her story. But most listeners must have wondered what Dorothy was doing in the utility room before Earl arrived. The police found an empty glass in the cupboard in the utility room. They also found a glass, with lipstick on it, containing alcohol and ice, between the kitchen and the utility room. And why did O'Brien ask her if she had any recollection of the documents and albums that *may have fallen on the garage floor?* We had seen the police photograph of the binder of Christmas letters and the photo albums on the kitchen table. This photograph was taken by the police when they were in Dorothy's house after the shooting. Is it possible that Earl did not take these mementoes with him when he began to leave her house? Earl claimed during his testimony, when he was shown this photograph that the "boxes" on the kitchen table "might be the articles" Dorothy gave him. But when Selinger asked him if he had left these articles on the table, Earl said, "as I recall it I was packing them out of the garage with me" and that later they were on the garage floor with his glasses. The police would not pick them up and return them to the kitchen table. Did Dorothy do this before the police arrived, or had they never been taken from the kitchen table at all? Why did Dorothy hesitate, and say "not particularly" when she said she had no recollection of these things on the garage floor?

O'Brien asked her if she had "any recollection with respect to bullets or casings on the floor?" Dorothy said "No." And she had no recollection of picking anything up off the floor.

O'Brien: Did you make any phone calls to your recollection?

Dorothy: Well, he—I—Earl has—you know, he was talking to me and he was asking me to help him. He was asking me to help him, and he—he asked me to call 911, and I think I said I can't. And then I can't recall—I can't recall all the exact words and stuff, you know, that were said and—but what he generally said to me was, he said, I love you. I've always loved you. He said, The thing about Lynn isn't what you think, and he said, If you help me, I'll try to help you. And he asked—so I went, and I started calling 911.

Dorothy said that when she heard the EMS tape at the preliminary hearing she realized for the first time how many times she had called 911. She said that she did not know where Earl was shot. She also said that she did not recall what she did with the drink that she had poured while she was waiting for Earl, "but I suspect that I probably poured myself another drink when I was running back and forth between the garage and the phone and the front door." That is, she was having another drink while she waited for the police to arrive. She could not explain how "a drink" got into the cupboard in the utility room.

O'Brien asked her if, as she called the police, she could hear Earl yelling in the garage. Dorothy said, "No. I didn't hear Earl." She began to tell that she found out about Earl's yelling after she got back from "Betty Ford's" and talked with a neighbour who said that her husband could hear Earl, but Dorothy was stopped by Justice Lutz. Such second-hand reports are not allowed.

O'Brien: Have you or had you at any time prior to January 21st had any feeling that you wanted to hurt Earl or cause him injury?
Dorothy: No.
O'Brien: Did you ever express to him or to anybody that you wished to hurt him or cause him injury?
Dorothy: No, I didn't say that to anybody. I—I think I did say one thing, though, to some people.
O'Brien: What did you say?
Dorothy: Well, a number of my friends' husbands have been dying, and I said—I think I said at sometime that would be easier for me if Earl died than if he left me, because it was devastating to be left. I didn't want to—and I'd been facing with Earl all these years the possibility he might die. I didn't want him to die, no, never.
O'Brien: When he came over to your—to your house that morning, did you have any intention of picking up a gun and shooting him?
Dorothy: No, no.
O'Brien: And was the conversation that you had with Earl that particular morning a friendly one?

Dorothy: Yes, it was. It was—there was no yelling and no arguing and nothing like that. It wasn't—it was a nice conversation.

The court was adjourned until Monday morning at ten o'clock.

---

It is very common for people, and especially abused women like Dorothy Joudrie, who act out suddenly and violently in a manner quite contrary to their natures, not to be able to remember what they have done. O'Brien's questions were carefully designed to show that Dorothy stopped remembering what happened that morning after Earl told her that the divorce was going forward and that her lawyer would have the final papers. She was very persuasive as she told about feeling sad, forlorn, and lonely, that she could not remember shooting Earl, and that she did not plan to shoot him. O'Brien made no attempt to analyze Dorothy's state of mind, or to do anything more than name and describe very briefly, in his opening statement, his defence of automatism, which is more complex, and certainly more contentious, than simple loss of memory. He was leaving that, apparently, to the psychiatric experts. Nevertheless, he must have realized, and wanted the jury to realize, that in the light of everything else Dorothy had said, her recollection of a "nice conversation" with Earl was not convincing.

Dorothy's preparations for this meeting, and her anticipation of it, must have been extraordinarily stressful. It was she who had initiated the meeting, even before Earl left Toronto. After he arrived in Calgary, she left telephone messages for him twice, reminding him of it. Then he postponed the meeting from Friday to Saturday. On Saturday morning, when she went to have her hair done, she still did not know when he would come to her house, and she had to wait, as she had waited throughout her marriage, for his call.

Earl agreed to the meeting, possibly because he thought that it would serve as a confirmation of the end of their marriage. Earl said, when O'Brien cross-examined him, that while he and Dorothy were talking, "I think I had the impression that we both sensed that, you know, this was—might be the last time we'd meet." O'Brien asked Earl to repeat this comment, so the jury could hear clearly Earl's impression of the finality of this meeting. Even if Earl was planning to marry Lynn Manning, why would he think that he would never "meet" the mother of his four children again, that this "might be the last time we'd meet"?

Why Earl had asked Guy to accompany him on this visit is also a mystery. But Guy had testified that he could not go with his father, and, from what both Earl and Dorothy said, Earl came to her house alone. Also, Dorothy said that at Guy's wedding Earl had told her that he would proceed, now, with the divorce. Earl said that he was visiting Dorothy to get the deed to the "big house." They thought that they had lost this document, but Dorothy had found it. The lawyers needed to put it with the final divorce papers. But Earl had discovered that if it was lost it could be replaced, and he could have told Dorothy this over the telephone, or her lawyer could have told her.

For Dorothy, the purpose of this visit seemed to be her need to hear a formal acknowledgement from Earl that their marriage was over, that he had, finally, "left" her. Also, she may have considered this her last opportunity to tell him that she was devastated by his abandonment of her. Dorothy wanted Earl to have the mementoes, which she had collected for him, and which she believed represented the history of their life together. Her motive in doing this may have been ambiguous—both sentimental and punishing. But there is little doubt that this gesture was very important to her; she wanted to give these things to him herself. It seemed not to have occurred to her that she could have mailed him this "stuff" as she referred to it, paradoxically, in the courtroom. And when she did give him these things that Saturday morning, he was dismissive of the pictures and letters, just glancing at them, and not really reading them or even looking at them carefully. In his testimony, Earl referred to an album "loaded" with Christmas letters, and the "collection of things" Dorothy had prepared to give him. He said, "I did not look at them at the time other than to say yeah, I know what that is and that is. I didn't read anything nor did I look at anything." Fifteen months later, at the trial, he still had not read Dorothy's collection of Christmas letters, because he was unaware of the December 1994 letter that she had sent to her family and friends the month before the shooting. The police photograph suggests that when Earl got up to leave, he left behind the photo albums and the binder containing the letters, and perhaps also that this is why Dorothy has a clear memory of them in the kitchen.

Dorothy said that when she had been with Earl during this period she was "pretty nervous," which suggests that their recent meetings had been difficult, and actually or potentially volatile. Dorothy's report of Earl's treatment of her at Guy's wedding the previous month is a verification of this. Certainly from what both Earl and Dorothy had said about their relationship, it is quite possible that at some point during Earl's visit that morning she was hurt and angry and frightened—for her safety, and perhaps for her life.

A key line in the drama—the mystery—as both of them told it, may be Earl's saying, "If you help me, I'll try to help you." Earl said this when he thought that he was dying. Like many other things he said, it is very revealing of him, even if we were not to include Dorothy's recollection of his affirmation at that moment of his continuing love for her. Dorothy had helped Earl for more than forty years, and he had abused her and discarded her. Now, as he lay on the garage floor suffering the effects of the six bullets she had shot into his body, she helped him again. She called the police and the EMS and continued to call them until they arrived—to save Earl's life, and to arrest her for attempted murder. I wondered how Earl met his side of that bargain.

# Dorothy III

Noel O'Brien's examination of Dorothy ended the first week of her trial. During the weekend she could only wait, nervously anticipating Jerry Selinger's cross-examination on Monday. I wondered if Selinger's weekend, for different reasons, was also fraught with anxiety. For one thing, he was playing opposite a lawyer who is very adept in the courtroom, and taking centre stage after O'Brien's almost flawless performance during the first week of the trial was a hard act to follow. Selinger might also have been anxious because the public was watching him very closely. For months, gossips had insisted that Earl would use his power and privilege to prevent the criminal justice system from treating Dorothy too harshly—for her sake, but also for his. And I wondered about the reliability of this rumour. Gossips were also the source of the earlier rumour that there would be no trial. Both Jerry Selinger and Earl Joudrie had worked very hard to diminish the extent of Earl's abuse of Dorothy. But Selinger had allowed Earl free rein in his attacks on Dorothy during his testimony, his perception of her difficult behaviour during their marriage, and her aggressive and "weird" remarks while she was shooting him. Elizabeth Griffiths had not yet testified, and it was she who would give irrefutable evidence of the seriousness of Earl's assaults on Dorothy while the Joudries lived in Toronto, and that was only part of the history of Earl's abuse of Dorothy. Incredibly, even after Elizabeth Griffith's testimony, Selinger would insist that there had been only three incidents of abuse and all of these incidents, he would assure the jury, had occurred long ago, years ago, and therefore, implicitly, they were of little consequence in January 1995. It was difficult to know what, if anything, was going on, or had been going on, behind the scenes, or who, exactly, might be directing this hypothetical behind-the-scenes activity.

I talked with several people who were quite frank about the fact that they were attending the trial regularly to see if the justice system treats people of wealth and privilege in the same way it would treat ordinary people. There were moments during the trial when I found the naivete, the generosity, the willingness of these people to set aside their cynicism quite astonishing. They were counting on Selinger to represent the people. But, from their point of view, was Earl Joudrie the people? Hardly. Was he the victim? Well, yes, legally; in the minds of most people, he was. But it was increasingly difficult to sympathize with this victim, and for people with real knowledge about wife abuse, it was almost impossible. So this trial had become much more complex than most observers, especially those who are not familiar with the criminal justice system, had thought it would be in the beginning.

When I talked with Jerry Selinger on the telephone, about a year after the trial, he was polite, pleasant, quite willing to allow me to ask some questions.[59] I asked him how he had got this job. Had he wanted to be the prosecutor in this case? Had the job been assigned to him? Was he just the next person on the roster? "This is an internal thing, in the Crown Prosecutor's office," he said, and he could not discuss how it happened that he was the one. He was quoted in the *Calgary Herald*, at the time of the trial, saying, "I'm more of a law and order bent. I think it's important that justice be served."[60] As the Crown Prosecutor, he could hardly go wrong with that comment. My interpretation of this comment was that he is conservative, a traditionalist, and also that he was declaring, indirectly, his position with respect to Dorothy Joudrie—that she had committed a crime and that she should be punished for it. Perhaps because it is not in Selinger's nature to be pugnacious, he often appeared to be nervous and agitated, overplaying his role when he cross-examined witnesses, tapping his knuckle against his podium, flipping noisily through his notebook, pacing, barking out his "suggestions" without waiting for the witness to answer fully, and not appearing to listen carefully to what they said. This sound and fury diverted listeners' attention from his sometimes quite astute questions. While he was questioning the experience and authority of one of the expert witnesses, prolonging the exercise beyond what was necessary, I sketched his face in my notebook—brows furrowed, cheeks puffed out. I was thinking of La Fontaine's fable, "The North Wind and the Sun." Jerry Selinger was the North Wind, blowing, furiously, with all his might, but to no avail, opposite Noel O'Brien's assured, quiet, and strong Sun.

The newspapers during the weekend featured stories and comments about Dorothy and Earl and the trial. Some people discussed the Joudries with their friends and neighbours and families, speculating, questioning, criticizing, sympathizing. Others continued their silence, out of loyalty to their business associates and their circle of friends, and, perhaps, the Joudries, or because they found the spectacle too scandalous, too vulgar, or too disturbing to contemplate.

After the lunch break on Friday, the first day of Dorothy's testimony, there was a very long line of people waiting outside the courtroom—mostly women—well-dressed women—who talked quietly together as they waited. Several of these women knew each other, and they met others, who, in some cases, they had not seen for years. One woman with whom I talked, a bright, attractive, professional woman who is now in her early seventies, was married for fifteen years to an oil man during the fifties and sixties. They had five children. She said that as the oil business developed, her husband became busier, with more responsibility at work, and that she was left increasingly alone. She enjoyed some of the perks at first—the extra car, the larger more elegant house, the holidays. When she discovered that one of the perks her husband enjoyed, but without her, was a key to a downtown hotel room, she took the children and left. She used her professional skills to support herself and her children, and eventually she married again. Her second husband was with her at the trial. She said how sad she felt for Dorothy. After the cross-examination on Monday, she expressed alarm at Selinger's aggressive attack. She was protective of Dorothy. This woman is exceptional. Her sense of herself, her identity, her integrity may have been won at considerable cost earlier in her life. But for many years now she has been comfortable and confident about herself, and she is both generous and compassionate in her attitude toward other women.

# Dorothy IV

On Monday morning I noticed a few men and several women I had not seen at the trial before, including the society columnist for the *Calgary Herald*. Why had these people waited until this moment to appear? Could they no longer resist the gathering momentum of this saga? Did they want to see the Crown prosecutor challenge Dorothy Joudrie? It was easy, now, to separate the visitors from the regulars. An esprit de corps had developed among those of us who had attended the trial since the beginning. Despite our various expectations of what should happen at this trial, we were comfortable with each other, interested to know what others thought about the latest developments, no longer self-conscious about our presence here. Our discussions were serious, intense. There was little jollity anywhere near the courtroom, but the seasoned observers privately, quietly, exchanged an occasional quick moment or two of humour in the elevators, or the washrooms, or the cafeteria. Very occasionally, there was real laughter. One day a journalist and I were talking in an empty stairway. Something one of us said caused us to laugh. We knew we must be quiet, but we were overcome with wild, helpless, not quite silent laughter, leaving us weak with its blessed relief. We sat on the stairs for a few moments to recover. I thought of Toni Morrison's comment in her novel *Jazz*, that "laughter is serious. More complicated, more serious than tears."[61] The occasional visitors were noticeable partly because of their slight, or more than slight discomfort, in a place that was not familiar to them; their mixed emotions when they saw other people they knew; their surprise at the extent of their own curiosity and their need to see for themselves the details of this tragic story.

As soon as Justice Lutz appeared on Monday morning, Dorothy was directed to go to the witness box, where she stood, rather breathless. She

173

had seen Jerry Selinger perform, his style, and she was obviously steeling herself for whatever might occur. I am sure that O'Brien's presence in the room reassured her, but at the same time, she was on her own now. She avoided looking at the gallery, the many people there whom she knew. Dorothy was wearing a soft-blue pantsuit with a striped blouse— of pastel, spring-like colors. Her costume made her seem feminine, fragile, vulnerable.

Jerry Selinger looked very strained. He began by telling Dorothy, but without looking at her because he was pacing back and forth in front of the witness box, to listen carefully, to respond clearly and loudly. He said that if he raised his own voice, it was not because he was trying to "harass or badger" her. Thus, it seemed to me that Selinger put himself on the defensive before he even began his cross-examination. Then he said, "The objective here today is to find the truth, right?"

At the word "truth" part of my attention slipped away to a novel I had taught recently, *Before and After,* by Rosellen Brown, about the family of a teenaged boy who murdered his girlfriend. Carolyn, the boy's mother, a pediatrician, a scientist, a moralist, keeps insisting that she wants to tell the truth. She asks her son's lawyer, "What about the truth of what happened? Don't you ever ask?" Her daughter knows that "Her mother couldn't lie, it was one of her weaknesses." At her son's pre-trial hearing, not wanting to be silenced by the lawyer's "courtroom strategies," Carolyn speaks to the court, acting on her own initiative. When she comes out of the courtroom, she says, "I did it. In there. It's done. The tale is told." Her son's lawyer is furious:

> Carolyn, screw what really happened! What's it going to take for you to get this? "The truth" in a courtroom is just a construction of effects. It's theatre. There is no such thing as simple truth, as long as its presentation can be shaped, or perverted, or invented, even. Not the facts, mind you. I'm talking presentation. Either side can skew the way things appear, and how they appear is all that matters.[62]

For Carolyn the facts are the truth, and she cannot embrace the "theatre" of the courtroom.

How many of us, I wondered, could differentiate the truth from the theatre in this trial. Could the jury? Who knows the facts, what really happened on that Saturday morning in question? And what is the truth, when whole lives and a long, complex, tragic marriage have determined it?

So Selinger began. And his cross-examination was very aggressive. He suggested that there were "thirteen indications" since 1989 that the Joudries' marriage was over, and that Dorothy Joudrie had plenty of time to plan and prepare to take revenge on the man who was deserting her and depriving her of her social position.

Selinger reminded Dorothy that she testified on Friday that there was a period of the morning of January 21, 1995, that she "didn't recall." Dorothy said, "Well, I recalled our conversation. . . . But I didn't recall the rest of the time, no." She said that she recalled saying that a divorce would be easier for Earl than for her because he had someone, and she would be alone. Her next recollection was seeing Earl on the floor. "I saw his face. I saw his face. It was awful," she said. Then, Selinger said, she testified that after Earl spoke some words to her, she called 911. She agreed.

Selinger said that subsequent to the shooting incident, she was referred to the psychiatrists Dr. Weston and Dr. O'Shaughnessy for counselling and assessment respectively, and Selinger implied that on the basis of this psychiatric evaluation, her lawyer has "characterized this period of non-recollection as a dissociative state, right? . . . And that being the case, that this dissociative state came from a combination of things, correct?"

Dorothy: Well, I—see I don't understand about all that; okay? I just know that that's what I've been told.
Selinger: All right, and you were told that this extends from some physical and emotional abuse from Mr. Joudrie.
Dorothy: Yes.
Selinger: You were told that?
Dorothy: Yes.
Selinger: And that your—it came upon, upon your realization that the divorce was inevitable, it was going to come through at any moment, right? That was another thing that had added to your stress at that point, right? That's what you were told? Yes or no?
Dorothy: Yes, I guess that's right.
Selinger: Okay, and that, combined with your love of Mr. Joudrie and some alcohol consumption, that triggered it, too: is that a fair comment?
Dorothy: Well, I—guess it's a fair comment, I—I don't know about those things.
Selinger: All right, but in the final analysis, you had no plan to kill Mr. Joudrie.
Dorothy: No, I had no plan to kill him period ever—ever.

Dorothy had begun to cry during this exchange, and until this last remark, she had been hesitant answering Selinger, seeming to be overcome by his aggressive tone and manner, and puzzled by what he was asking her.

> Selinger: So would that be a fair characterization of your evidence then, is that these combinations caused your blackout and that you had no intention to kill your husband?
> Dorothy: I had no intention to kill my husband ever.
> Selinger: All right.
> Dorothy: Never.

Now, Selinger said that in her evidence on Friday she "described seven incidents of physical confrontation between yourself and your husband from 1959 to Kentucky in 1978. Is that fair?" Dorothy acted, not surprisingly, as though she felt caught. In her testimony, her "evidence," on Friday, Dorothy had given—O'Brien had asked her to give—examples of incidents of abuse in her marriage, but now Selinger was, apparently, treating these examples as the whole story of abuse in her marriage, and he was asking her to agree or not with what she had said, and in the process, he seemed to be misconstruing her "evidence." She seemed to realize this, but she could not disagree with what she had said on Friday. Early in this cross-examination, O'Brien interrupted Selinger, saying, "She can answer the question in her own way. . . . It doesn't have to be yes or no." For a few seconds, Selinger reworded his questions, but it wasn't long before he was again demanding answers that were either yes or no.

> Dorothy: If you have the facts, I guess that's right, yes.
> Selinger: All right, and that would have been between 39 years ago and 18 years ago, right? Kentucky was 18 years ago?
> Dorothy: Yes, yes.
> Selinger: All right, and that spanned approximately 21 years, right?
> Dorothy: Yes, I believe—I believe you're correct, yes.

Selinger referred to the "incident in Kentucky" as a "watershed" for both Dorothy and Earl, and he asked Dorothy if that was a fair comment. Dorothy asked him what he meant by "watershed." He meant, he said, that both Dorothy and Earl understood that this was "a serious situation."

> Dorothy: Oh, yes, it was a very serious situation.
> Selinger: For both of you, right?

Dorothy: For both of us, yes.
Selinger: And that you both agreed that it would never get physical
again; is that correct?
Dorothy: That's what we agreed on, yes.
Selinger: Okay, and that, in fact, you agreed that you [meaning
Dorothy] would not be as aggressive and confrontational as you had
been before; is that a fair comment?

Dorothy hesitated, apparently thinking carefully about what Selinger
was saying. She said that they both wanted to make things better. She said,
"I—I said that if he ever hit me again that I would leave him, but . . . "

Selinger: All right, and after you returned to Calgary, after this incident
in Kentucky, he never hit you again.
Dorothy: Well, that isn't exactly true.
Selinger: Well, I mean that's what you told your counsel, didn't you on
Friday?
Dorothy: Well, I . . .
Selinger: Ma'am, isn't that what you told your counsel on Friday?
Dorothy: Well, I—I don't know. I can't tell you exactly what I told him,
but basically, Earl did not hit me again, right.

Dorothy said this as if she were defeated, but obliged to submit to
Selinger's authority. Selinger offered to read aloud her evidence from
Friday. She said that would not be necessary. Still, she agreed reluctantly,
"I guess I said he didn't hit me again, yes."
During this discussion, Dorothy seemed to be thinking about what,
exactly, she had said on Friday, and I suspect that Selinger surprised her
when he asked her then, without a second's hesitation, if she lived up to
her part of the bargain that she would not be aggressive towards Earl.
"Well, no, I guess I didn't always," she said.
"In fact," Selinger said, Dorothy had some difficulty recalling what
started the arguments with Earl, "way back when in your relationship."
I wondered about the logical sequence of these questions, and I also
wondered how people who had not heard Earl's testimony could understand what Selinger was doing—that he was suggesting that Dorothy
caused the violent incidents. But Dorothy agreed that, "yes," she did not
always remember what had started the arguments. Selinger went on to
suggest that after they returned to Calgary the arguments did not stop,

and that she continued to be antagonistic, and confrontational, and "generally upset," and that she had said herself, "from way back in the relationship . . . 'I did scream.'"

Dorothy had become very upset, at first denying what Selinger said, then agreeing, but qualifying her response: "Yes, but it isn't like you're saying it."

During this discussion Selinger had not allowed Dorothy to include Earl in what she said. He corrected her whenever she said "we tried," "we wanted," "we thought." He wanted her to talk about herself.

Now he turned her attention to Earl. He asked her if Earl is an "intense individual when he's dealing with his work." Dorothy agreed that he is. Is he a "focused person" and "self-absorbed" when he was working? Dorothy agreed. Would she "characterize him as being insensitive to your needs and maybe not communicative"? She agreed. Did she "generally" have to initiate conversations with him because he was preoccupied? Dorothy hesitated, and said, "as long as you're just saying generally."

> Selinger: Well, I—isn't it a fair comment that he would—that you had to initiate most of the conversations with him?
> Dorothy: No, I don't think that's a fair comment. I don't think so.
> Selinger: He didn't pay enough attention to you, so you would escalate the matters; isn't that correct?
> Dorothy: I don't think that's correct. I really don't. I don't—I didn't think that way. I didn't think that way.
> Selinger: And if he didn't respond to you that you would get more exasperated and more confrontational, ma'am.
>
> . . . . . . . . . . . . . . . . . . . . . . . . . . . . . . . . . . . . . . . . . . .
>
> Selinger: Wasn't, ma'am, the ultimate frustration the fact that he left you in 1989, and you could not get over it?
> Dorothy: He, in 1989—and I remember it extremely clearly, when he left, he told me he wasn't leaving me. He was just moving out, and he didn't want me to let anybody know, and we continued to go out together, and we—and I didn't tell anybody that he had gone.

Many people, and perhaps some members of the jury, did not believe Dorothy when she said this about Earl. But the business executives sitting in the gallery, and their wives, know that separation and divorce are not acceptable in the conservative corporate community. The people at the top are most likely those who have traditional marriages. When Earl told Dorothy to keep their separation secret, he was probably thinking of himself.

Selinger: Because you were embarrassed, ma'am?
Dorothy: I wasn't embarrassed, but I thought if we didn't tell anybody we might get back together because he wasn't telling anybody either.
Selinger: I'm suggesting to you that that frustration continued until at least 1995; isn't that correct, ma'am?
Dorothy: Mr. Selinger, I was not constantly frustrated. I was constantly remembering the good times my husband and I had. I didn't even think about the bad times until I've had to bring them up since—since this incident, and I never thought about the bad times. I only remember the good times.

"Let's deal with that then, ma'am," Selinger said.

I could not tell if Selinger was being overtly sarcastic, but he seemed to be determined to show what he considered to be evidence of Earl's not wanting "to get back together." And he was also challenging Dorothy's denial of what really had been happening in her life. Selinger had a list. He began with the Caribbean cruise they took together in late January or early February 1990. Dorothy had bought the tickets for this cruise before Earl left their home to live alone in October 1989, but he had decided to accompany her nevertheless. Selinger pointed out to her that when they returned, Earl said that he had had a terrible time. Next, he reminded her of a retirement party in Edmonton in May 1990, when Earl chose to stay alone, in a different room from Dorothy's. Then, when they were in Kingston at Colin's graduation from Queen's University, Earl insisted that they stay in separate rooms in Colin's house. After the graduation, when they arrived back in Toronto, after having discussed with her during the journey how she thought they could get back together again, Earl did not want to spend the weekend with her. He left her, alone, at her hotel. Selinger said that Dorothy had told, also, about their staying together at an ATCO party in Phoenix in 1991. The awkward exchange that ensued, and Selinger's insistence that Dorothy must publicly admit to her sexual relationship with Earl, caused her to break down with exasperation, frustration, and sadness. But Selinger did not take pity on her: there were no gentle pauses, as there had been when O'Brien examined her, allowing her a moment to gather herself together.

Selinger pressed on to the "the issue of the cards" Earl sent to Dorothy—one in 1991 and two in 1993. Selinger referred to these cards as the "only contacts of a personal nature" that she had described when O'Brien examined her, that "gave you feelings that he wanted to get back together with you." Dorothy reacted: "I don't think that's correct at all."

> Selinger: Okay.
> Dorothy: I think that there—I mean, I don't have—I think I have other things. I don't—I don't think we put everything of 40 years in evidence, and also I have—I had—I had conversations with him at—and we had good conversations together over that period of time, and it wasn't all—and those cards, you just can't say that I just had those three cards, because that isn't all I had.
> Selinger: And, ma'am, you had good counsel. He would have put the case before the jury of all the incidents that were relevant.
> Dorothy: There are every—everyday things that happen between two people that aren't necessarily things that you can—that you can bring up and—and hand to somebody and say this is—this is evidence, because it doesn't happen that way. It just doesn't happen that way. It isn't like that. It's not like that. You're making it sound like it's—like—like, we had good conversations about Carolyn's wedding. We had good conversations about lots of things, and it's not like you're putting it. I can't tell you. It's just not like that, and I can't help it. It isn't like that. I'm sorry.

So here is the difference between truth and theatre, the difference between life and a trial in a courtroom. And ironically, the person who explained this to all of us is a woman who cannot see her own life clearly because she wants to remember only the good and happy times.

But there were no pauses for reflection. Selinger wanted to talk about "indicators," which he said would show that "Mr. Joudrie had absolutely no interest in returning to you." The first was that Earl moved out of their home in October 1989. Then, Dorothy left their family home and moved into a "condo" in October 1990. The next year, Earl presented Dorothy with three "scenarios," making it clear that if he were to choose the one he wanted, there was no room in it for Dorothy. Earl moved to Toronto in August 1991, and soon after that Dorothy began the process of a legal separation. At the time of the separation, she received a financial settlement of $1.9 million. Dorothy had objected to almost everything Selinger said up to that point, and some of her responses were contradictory, revealing her denial of what had been happening in her marriage. But now she objected with a vehement "No!"

Selinger asked, sarcastically, "He just gave you the $1.9 million?" But he let Dorothy explain that she and Earl had agreed that she should have her own money, which she could manage herself. He also gave her time to explain her position about money during her marriage, that, for example, she felt guilty about spending it. In the process of this discussion, Selinger revealed an aspect of himself we had not seen until then.

> Dorothy: . . . And when you say he gave me that money, that money wasn't just his, it was mine, too.
> Selinger: I'm sorry. I'm sorry, ma'am, if I characterized it as that, that certainly is absolutely correct. You're entitled to every penny of that, and I'm not being facetious either.
> Dorothy: I'm sorry, I'm just—it wasn't—and my husband and I, we never fought about money. That was the one thing we never fought about. When I—when we started out, we had $25 between the two of us.
> Selinger: Right.
> Dorothy: And my money was his and his money was mine, and I just can't stand listening to this.

Earl said, during his testimony, that Dorothy was very responsible about money, that she was never on a budget, that she had free access to their money, and that it was she who looked after paying the bills. But he seemed unaware that he contradicted the impression that there were no problems between them about money, and he also revealed his lack of insight about Dorothy's position as his wife, when later in his testimony he gave an example of Dorothy's behaviour that would annoy him and start a fight between them. He said that Dorothy was "tremendous at preparing nice dinners." He would compliment her on the dinner and the children would join in with their compliments, and Dorothy would say, "Well, it really doesn't matter. Your father paid for it." So it was apparent that Dorothy felt exactly as most wives do who are dependent on their husbands—beholden. And despite her family's praise of her homemaking skills, she saw them, at least some of the time, as having little or no value when compared to her husband's business accomplishments. Partly because she and Earl were so competitive, it is not difficult to imagine that directly or indirectly he reminded her of the discrepency in the value of their respective contributions to their life together. He, in his superior position, simply assumed that he was free to come and go as he pleased, to meet his business obligations; to travel all over the world; to be away from home for weeks at a time; and when he was at home to expect consideration and silence and privacy when he wanted to work, a charming and sophisticated and capable hostess when he wanted to entertain, and bright, healthy, well-behaved children when he wanted to show off his family.

During the preliminary hearing, Selinger asked Guy if there was ever an issue between his parents about Dorothy's access to money. Guy said that money was always an issue in their family. Whether or not Guy was responding, specifically, to Selinger's question, I don't know. I do know, however, that studies of the upper socio-economic class show that money is almost always "an issue." Lewis Lapham, editor of *Harper's* magazine, and who, as he says, was "brought up among people who owned most of what was worth owning in the city" of San Francisco, tells about how important it is among wealthy people to keep up with the Joneses. Among people with money, says Lapham, "Nobody ever has enough."[63] There is little doubt that the Joudries belonged to a socio-economic group who were sensitive about just how they should exhibit their wealth, and at the same time establish their position in relation to their corporate friends and associates. The days when Dorothy thought five dollars was extravagant to cover her bruises with make-up—for two days—were gone. Now, the choice between a red Jaguar and a Lincoln town car was not a matter of money, but of good taste. Dorothy seemed to have the impression that her red Jaguar attracted the wrong kind of attention, people thought that it was flashy or gauche, it was "like waving a red flag," she said—the same reaction I had had to Earl's white Cadillac. So she chose the more conservative Lincoln, an appropriate car, she decided, for a wealthy matron. Selling her Mazda was incidental.

More important, however, Dorothy's response to Selinger reveals the classic despair and discomfort of the wife of a wealthy man, and of all wives who do not have careers or money of their own. She devoted her entire marriage to helping her husband make money. Yet, she feels guilty, as she said, about spending the money. At the same time, she knows that the money is as much hers as it is his. Since the day she stopped teaching, in 1961, she has never earned, independently from her husband, a regular paycheque with her name on it. That is the issue about money. It is a problem she shares with many other women. It is a problem she never resolved—and it is little wonder that she "just can't stand listening to this."

Having let Dorothy make her explanation, Selinger continued with his "indicators." The next indication that Earl did not want to continue their marriage was that he began to see Lynn Manning in the fall ("Thanksgiving") of 1991. Dorothy saw Lynn and Earl together at a barbecue in the summer of 1992. In April of 1993, Earl started divorce proceedings. Then, in September 1993, Earl told Dorothy that he was "moving in" with Lynn Manning in Toronto. Another "indicator," was that Dorothy went "alone" on a trip to the Far East in January 1993. Then Selinger asked, "Is it not also another indicator when you delayed the divorce through two more marriages [of their children] that you didn't realize the divorce was going through?" Dorothy understood, if some others did not, what Selinger meant.

> Dorothy: I told him—I told him I would give him a divorce. I did tell him that.
> Selinger: Right, and he told you at Guy's wedding, in fact, that he was proceeding with the divorce; is that not correct?
> Dorothy: I'm not sure he told me at Guy's wedding. He told me.

Another "indicator" was that, in January 1995, Dorothy made up a package of Christmas letters because, Selinger said, "you stated that you would probably not be together again."

At first, Dorothy said "Yes," that all the children had packages of the Christmas letters, and she thought "that I—Earl and I should have them also, because it was our life together for the whole time. That it was a—it was like a history of our family, and so I—I thought I was doing really well, and I decided—to put together the album for him and myself." Selinger asked her again if she did this because they would not be together again. Dorothy said, "That wasn't the reason. The reason I did it, I did it because I thought he should have them—the things that I had and the children had."

> Selinger: All right. Now, ma'am, given all these 13 indicators that I've just pointed out in the last 10 or 15 minutes, would these not give you strong indicators that, in fact, Earl was not getting back together with you?
> Dorothy: Of course.

But Selinger was not finished with indications that Dorothy knew that her relationship with Earl was over. He reminded Dorothy that at "that barbecue in the summer of 1992" she had introduced a gentleman who was with her as her fiancé. Dorothy was outraged. "No. that is not true. That is not true. [The gentleman] never asked me to marry him. I had no intention of marrying him." Selinger said that she had told her brother-in-law, Keith Joudrie, and also Earl, that she intended to marry this man. Dorothy said that she knew that Earl had said this in court, but she was vehement that it was not true.

Then Selinger introduced a discussion of Dorothy's drinking. At first Dorothy agreed with Selinger's account of her drinking, but when he suggested that she drank "daily," or "almost daily," she objected.

> Dorothy: Look, I have admitted that I am an alcoholic, and I've admitted that I was drinking, and I cannot tell you how many drinks I had a week. I cannot tell you how many days of the week I drank.

Dorothy said that both she and Earl drank, and that Earl poured very strong drinks. She agreed that she and Earl argued about her drinking, that Earl sought counselling for both of them in 1988 because of her drinking, and that she agreed to cut back on her drinking, but because she did not know she was an alcoholic then, she did not promise to quit. When Selinger repeated a story Guy had told about her forgetting that her car had slipped into a ditch one winter night, and that she did not know how it had got back into her garage, she became angry.

> Selinger: Is that a fair comment?
> Dorothy: No, that is absolutely not true. You said you wanted the truth in this courtroom.
> Selinger: Yes, absolutely. You tell me.
> Dorothy: And unfortunately, I have to say that my son did not tell the truth that day in court.

Dorothy told about that night and made it clear that she had not forgotten what happened to her car. Selinger reminded Dorothy that her daughter, Carolyn, had said that "you can handle your liquor pretty good during the day, but you belted it back in the evenings." Dorothy said, correctly, "She didn't say I 'belted' anything back in the evening. She was very—she didn't say anything in that way at all." But Selinger continued to tell about humiliating incidents related to her drinking, which he ended by asking her if she remembered a meeting with her children between

Guy's wedding on December 10 and Christmas 1994, when the children asked her to do something about her alcohol problem. She said she could remember saying, at this meeting, that she would really try not to drink.

The discussion of Dorothy's drinking ended with a long series of questions during which Selinger asked her if she had been given any neurological tests to determine if she had any brain damage because of her history of drinking. Dorothy said that she completed all of the tests the psychiatrists and psychologists gave her, but that as far as she knows, she did not have tests to determine if there has been any brain dysfunction because of her use of alcohol. In his brief rebuttal after Selinger's cross-examination of Dorothy, O'Brien asked Dorothy if she refused any of the tests offered to her by the various doctors who examined and treated her. She said that she had not refused any tests.

After the lunch break, Selinger began a discussion of the handgun— that Dorothy had said on Friday that she purchased it in Phoenix in November of 1992. He noted that this would have been her first trip to Phoenix after having seen Earl and Lynn Manning at the barbecue during the summer of 1992. Dorothy seemed not to be aware of the connection Selinger was making. She said that she went to Mandall's—the gun store—to enquire about guns, "'cause I really didn't want to have a gun." Then she told, just as she had on Friday, about buying the gun and practising shooting it. She said that it was very noisy in the basement where people practised shooting.

> Selinger: How did your little Saturday Night Special compare to the other guns as regards the noise, ma'am?
> Dorothy: Well, I couldn't tell. I couldn't tell how noisy it was at all.
>
> . . . . . . . . . . . . . . . . . . . . . . . . . . . . . . . . . . . . . . . . . . . . . . .
>
> Selinger: The small—that gun is quite small and easy to handle for you compared to one of the big guns?
> Dorothy: Oh, I guess so, yes. I didn't practise with a big gun.
> Selinger: Easy to put in your pocket and conceal?
> Dorothy: Well, no, he suggested—he suggested that I buy this black fanny pack thing so I did that and that's where it went.

Dorothy seemed quite innocent and unaware of what Selinger was implying as he asked these questions. He asked her if she went back to "test fire it again," and she said that she had gone back the following March when she was in Phoenix, and that she may also have gone back again in November 1993. She agreed with Selinger that she had brought the gun into Canada inadvertently in her car in May 1994. It was under the front seat, "on the passenger side."

> Selinger: You intended to take it back down to Phoenix, right?
> Dorothy: Yes, I did. I didn't intend to bring it up for starters.

. . . . . . . . . . . . . . . . . . . . . . . . . . . . . . . . . . . . . . . . . .

> I was horrified when I found it in the car.
> Selinger: You didn't really need a gun in Canada, did you? In Calgary?
> Dorothy: Well, I didn't really need a gun in Canada 'cause guns aren't used like they are in the States. The people are using guns all the time and—in my area as well.
> Selinger: But not at Bearspaw? [Dorothy's neighborhood in Calgary]
> Dorothy: No, no, I didn't need a gun in Canada.
> Selinger: So, why didn't you unload it, ma'am? You had it loaded and ready to go?
> Dorothy: Well, I never took it out of the pack at all. I just—when I found out I had it I thought, well, I got to put this somewhere and I put it in the bottom drawer in my bedroom and I never even opened it or looked at it or did anything with it.
> Selinger: Now, when you say you put it in the bottom drawer in your bedroom can you—if you were in the kitchen?
> Dorothy: Yes.
> Selinger: I suggest that you have to go through the kitchen, down the hallway, through the bedroom to get to the dresser? 'Cause it's at the far end of your bedroom; is that not right?
> Dorothy: Well, it doesn't—it's not very far to go if that's what you're trying to say.
> Selinger: Right.
> Dorothy: You just come out from the kitchen, go around the hall and it's right after you've gone through the door of the bedroom.
> Selinger: It's on the other side of the bedroom; is that right?
> Dorothy: It's by the window.
> Selinger: So if I was to give you a distance in a straight line would it be from here to the end of the courtroom? Probably?
> Dorothy: I would say so, yeah.
> Selinger: All right. So you would have to walk that distance to get it and then, of course, walk that same distance to get back to the kitchen if that's where you started from, right?

Dorothy: Yes, that's true.

Selinger: And when you're in the bedroom you would have to bend over, lean down, pull the drawer out, take the gun out?

Dorothy: I believe that's what I'd have to do.

Selinger: And, in fact, if it's in the fanny pack and the fanny pack was closed you'd also have to open the fanny pack; is that right?

Dorothy: That's what I have to do.

This slip of the tongue, from the subjunctive mood to the indicative, is the first, and very tentative indication, that there was any connection at all in Dorothy's mind between this discussion about the gun and her shooting Earl.

Then there was another interesting exchange between Selinger and Dorothy about which we had heard nothing, until now, during Dorothy's testimony and cross-examination.

Selinger: Did you have prior meetings with Mr. Joudrie? Did you have a prior meeting with him, for instance, before Christmas at your house?

Dorothy: Well, he says we did but you know, I can't seem to really recollect that we had a meeting, and I've been trying to remember what day it was and when it was but I haven't seemed to be—Christmas is very—the wedding and everything was very upset—you know, was a big upset and there were a lot of things that went on and I thought I just talked to Earl at the wedding. But I can't—I can't recollect that.

Selinger: Do you have a tendency to forget things if things get quite busy, ma'am?

Dorothy: No, not really.

Selinger: Well, you wouldn't say that the meeting didn't take place?

Dorothy: I'm not going to say that the meeting didn't take place, but certainly I can—I thought after the wedding he left and went back to Toronto.

Selinger: So when Mr. Joudrie says that you had a meeting where he came to your house and there was a discussion about Guy and about the children generally and about the divorce in your living room area that that—you can't recall that at all? Is that what you're saying?

Dorothy: Yeah, that's what I'm saying because—

Dorothy asked Selinger if she could tell about the events, and incidents, and the "upset" as she had called it, between Guy's wedding and Christmas. And she did.

"So, like, it seemed to me," she said, "that I would have remembered that Earl had come and I don't remember him coming at all. I don't remember talking to him then at all. And I was—I—it was news to me is what it was, okay?"

Selinger asked her if events with her husband are "generally forgettable." Was she suggesting that?

Dorothy said, "No, they're not. Events with my husband—they're not forgettable. They're very important. And so maybe he has the time wrong on it, maybe he didn't come then. Did he have—did he say when he went back to Toronto or where he went after the wedding? Because I stayed in Banff after the wedding, and I thought he had returned to Toronto after the wedding."

Selinger ignored her questions. He had made his point that there were lapses in Dorothy's memory before the day of the shooting. He wanted to talk now about that day, and he asked her about her arrangements with Earl to come to get the certificate for the house and the other things she had gathered together for him on January 21. Dorothy said that she telephoned Earl to find out when he was coming because, "I'm not saying this nastily or anything, but I always waited for Earl, all the time. . . . I never knew lots of times when he would be coming or if we'd be going some place or whatever, but I did a lot of waiting."

Selinger pressed on, suggesting implicitly that Dorothy's story about moving food from one freezer to another was an excuse to explain why she had left her car outside the garage. Selinger seemed to have difficulty understanding the security system in her house, and he suggested that it was strange that after she knew that Earl would arrive any minute, she locked the outside front door and asked him to come into the house through the garage. Selinger took her through the sequence of events and the conversation after Earl arrived, Dorothy's inability to remember shooting him, and their conversation after Earl asked her to call 911. When Earl told Dorothy to call the police, she said, initially, "I can't," but after Earl said "that he loved me and he always loved me and always had looked after me [and] . . . it isn't what you think with Lynn," she started to call the police.

Selinger asked Dorothy if she has had any counselling to help her to remember the events of that morning. Dorothy said that she could not talk about the shooting incident at the Betty Ford Center. "But—I did talk about it with Dr. Weston the whole time. . . . I mean, I saw Dr. Weston every day and he was trying to help me remember."

Selinger: And you can't possibly remember anything else than what you've told us here?

Dorothy: I've tried—if you can't believe how hard I've tried to remember what happened that day. And I find that—I'm finding it very difficult because when I got—when I was at the preliminary hearing I heard what I said to all these people and I knew I had to have shot him because I was the only person there and so I didn't have and—

Selinger interrupted Dorothy to ask her if her psychiatrists explained to her the meaning of a dissociative state. Dorothy said that the psychiatrists did not talk to her about that for a long time, "because I don't think I was capable of even dealing with anything like that. I was just trying to get help to find out what was wrong with me. . . . Like, I don't understand. I cannot believe—I'm an intelligent woman and I can't believe that this could happen to me."

But Selinger was concerned that she could, in fact, remember some things. He wondered how she knew to tell the EMS operators, when she talked with them on the telephone, that the gun in question was a handgun, when there was also a shotgun in the house. Dorothy could not answer this: "I didn't know what I shot him with but I had to assume that I shot him with a gun."

"Well," Selinger said, "couldn't you also assume, ma'am that he somehow got shot by somebody else or that he had another gun? . . . Why did you respond so clearly, 'handgun'?"

"Because I wanted them to get there, I guess," Dorothy said.

But what had prompted these questions from Selinger, suggesting that someone else might have shot Earl? To whom was he referring when he asked "or that *he* had another gun?"

Selinger also wanted to know, when Officer Boudreau asked her to show them the gun, why she took them directly to her bedroom dresser and took out the handgun.

Dorothy: From what I've heard in the preliminary hearing, sir, I hate to differ with you, but I have listened at the preliminary hearing and this hearing with the policeman.

. . . . . . . . . . . . . . . . . . . . . . . . . . . . . . . . . . . . . . . . . . . .

And they said they talked to me for quite a long time and they said—I don't remember saying these things very well. I was very upset. And they

said that I had . . . they said I said my husband told me not to say any-
thing, right?
Selinger: Yes.
Dorothy: And they also said—they also said that—they finally said if you
can show us the gun, you know, we would be able to help your husband.
Selinger: Exactly?
Dorothy: And so—
Selinger: And you went and showed them the gun?
Dorothy: I did, but the only place I knew to look for the gun was where
it had been before. I didn't know if it would be there. I didn't know if it
was back in the drawer, but that's the only place it had been and so that's
where I took them.
Selinger: Okay.
Dorothy: And it was there.
Selinger: Would that be a surprise to you, ma'am?
Dorothy: I was—everything was unbelievable.

. . . . . . . . . . . . . . . . . . . . . . . . . . . . . . . . . . . . . . . . . . . .

And that's where I had kept the gun, so that's why I went there. I didn't
know if it was going to be there.
Selinger: How did you know that that was the gun that was used to
shoot your husband?
Dorothy: Well, as I said, I'm the only one there.
Selinger: Yes.
Dorothy: I don't know—I mean—I don't know how you can ask me
these questions 'cause I don't—I didn't know—I didn't remember shooting my husband but I know he was shot.

As Selinger asked these questions he seemed to be very belligerent.
Dorothy tried to answer reasonably and politely, but the persistence and the
repetitious nature of the questions made her desperate. She wept, and put her
head down on her arms as she leaned on the edge of the box. But Selinger
kept on. He wondered how she would know "in this robotic state" that her
husband had not changed his will. "I didn't know that," Dorothy said.

Selinger said, "I suggest to you . . . that you had planned this whole
effort and, therefore, when you were in the robotic state you recalled your
plan and told him that you were going to stuff him in the car and dump
him in the ditch."

"That's what he said, but I didn't remember that. And, anyway, what
was the car doing out in the driveway if I was going to stuff him in the
car. It's a stupid idea. It's an absolutely idiotic idea," Dorothy said.

Selinger: It wasn't mine, ma'am.
Dorothy: Well, it wasn't mine either.

Selinger asked Dorothy, "You weren't drunk at the time of this incident were you?"

"No," Dorothy said, "I don't think I was, anyway."

Finally, Selinger suggested that Dorothy was not in a dissociative state on the morning of the shooting, that she "never entered the robotic state." She said, "I don't remember anything that happened." He continued his attack, ignoring her responses, saying that this "robotic state" could not have come from physical confrontations "because they ended in 1978," and that it could not be the result of emotional confrontations because "you were the main instigator of those confrontations."

Dorothy, desperate and angry, said, "I don't agree with you whatever you're saying."

Selinger suggested that "this robotic state" could not have been triggered by her realization that a divorce was imminent because she had known for years that there would be a divorce. He suggested that she planned the shooting from the time that she brought the gun to Calgary in May of 1994. He suggested that she chose the gun because it was small and easy to conceal and relatively quiet.

Dorothy said, "I disagree with you completely."

Selinger suggested that she knew that the divorce would take place after Guy was married.

Dorothy said, "Well, I had agreed to the divorce, right?"

Selinger suggested that she called Earl on the pretext of wanting to give him this "memorabilia and the certificate of title," and that she left her car outside the garage that morning in order that she could "complete this dastardly deed on the concrete floor in the garage."

"I did not do that," Dorothy said.

Selinger suggested that she locked the front door so that no one would disturb her while she was "doing the deed or cleaning up afterwards." And, he suggested, "you had the handgun ready to use, either on your person or in the utility room." He suggested that she deliberately shot Earl in the back "in an area where, if the bullet had gone directly through, [it] would have struck vital organs."

Dorothy said, "I didn't know where he was shot and I didn't know how many times he was shot . . . And I didn't find that out until somebody told me that he was shot six times in the back."

"I suggest further," said Selinger, "that when you saw him on the floor looking up at you, you leaned over him and shot him directly in the chest at close range." When he still didn't die, she asked him "how long is it going to take you to die?"

"I didn't say . . . I mean, I can't say my husband's a liar, and he says that's what I said. But I cannot believe that I would say that," Dorothy said.

Selinger continued to suggest, "that you told him that you would put him in a car and dump him in a ditch."

Dorothy said, "Again I don't remember saying that, but he said that so I can't call him a liar."

"I suggest that you started cleaning up the bullets in anticipation of him actually expiring."

"That's so wrong," Dorothy said.

Selinger suggested, "You were surprised that he was still not dead and Mr. Joudrie used his best negotiating skills in order to get you to call 911 . . . by telling you that he loved you and by telling you that Lynn was not that important, and that he would always be with you."

> Dorothy: Well maybe he was lying when he said that.
> Selinger: Maybe he was, ma'am. I suggest to you that you wanted to remain Mrs. Earl Joudrie not because you love him, but because you could not bear to lose the social standing you had maintained for 40 years.
> Dorothy: I did not lose my social standing. I was doing a thing here in Calgary as Mrs. Earl Joudrie on my own. Earl was down in Toronto doing his thing. And I was not using him for all that time for any social standing. I was—I had 250 people at my house on the 18th of December and it wasn't with his assistance. It was on my own.
> Selinger: Thank you ma'am. I have no further questions.

Selinger, and some others as well, may have thought that Dorothy, especially in her final remarks, had proved his theory. But Selinger's proposal that Dorothy cherished her social standing so much that she was driven to try to murder her husband by the possibility of losing it was too far-fetched for some observers. Also, Selinger had failed to show intent: he could not solve the mystery of the gun and how Dorothy, according to Earl's account, had the gun in her hand seconds after Earl got up from the table to leave the kitchen. And I am convinced that there are other things that we do not know about what really happened on that Saturday morning.

Selinger did suggest, reasonably, that Dorothy's rage and her determination to take revenge on Earl were so strong and that these emotions had existed for so long, that they carried her through the mental and emotional trauma of her "dastardly deed," even if she could not remember doing it. It was not easy to follow Selinger's argument, but if listeners— and especially the jury—persisted, they could see that Selinger had tried to provide the motive for her actions.

The flaw in his argument, for me, was his attempt to diminish the extent and the importance of Earl's abuse of Dorothy. Diminishing Earl's abuse weakened Selinger's argument that Dorothy acted out in rage and a desire for revenge because she did not want a divorce. Dorothy's account of the abuse, and Earl's revelation of himself during his testimony, and especially during O'Brien's cross-examination of him, were disturbing and convincing evidence of the serious violence Dorothy had endured for years, and which had not ended in 1978. In fact, Earl's determination to abandon Dorothy and replace her with her younger cousin and former "friend" was, no doubt for Dorothy, a continuation or perhaps a culmination of his abuse of her. But I was naive. On the day that Selinger crossexamined Dorothy, and defended Earl, and both explicitly and implicitly blamed Dorothy for much of Earl's abuse of her, I had no idea how accurately Selinger had measured the prevailing attitudes in our society, and its general lack of understanding of wife abuse.

It seemed to me that Selinger had been playing with fire in his aggressive attack on Dorothy. He might have incited the same kind of rage that he suggested caused her to shoot Earl, and perhaps that was what he was trying to do, hoping that in the process she would reveal what she says she cannot remember. In fact, he did make her angry, but the anger did not help her memory. Also, the quality of her anger was hardly comparable to the mean force of power and authority that Earl demonstrated when Noel O'Brien provoked him. Selinger might have triggered another dissociative state, rendering Dorothy incapable of conscious action. It would not be the first time that this has happened to a defendant in the courtroom. Dr. O'Shaughnessy, when he testified for Dorothy as an expert witness, cited such an incident. Instead, Selinger's attack caused Dorothy to use what experts who treat abused women call survival skills. She had "managed" other crises, other attacks, and she managed this one. Finally, almost a year after her divorce, and just three days since she announced to the court that she had "got rid of Earl," she assured Jerry

Selinger, the jury, and everyone else in that courtroom, that she knows herself as Mrs. Earl Joudrie. I thought of her telling me that she has trouble remembering even her own name. If some people saw Selinger's cross-examination as a victory for Dorothy's side in this legal battle, and for Noel O'Brien, it was a sad victory.

# The Experts

. . . the justice system and the psychiatric system have a
natural affinity with each other because both prefer
diagrammatic, black-and-white, instantly comprehensible
renderings of reality to the messy, difficult tangles of truth.
                Wendy Lesser, *Pictures at an Execution:*
                *An Inquiry into the Subject of Murder*[64]

The law surrounding the defence of automatism is
unsatisfactory in a number of areas. As is the case with any
defence which lends itself to the introduction of psychiatric
opinion evidence, a defendant who raises automatism
gambles on the outcome of the inevitable "battle of the
experts" which must ensue. The odds on coming out a
winner are decidedly stacked against him. He may hit the
jackpot and be acquitted outright, although he is more likely
to be found insane, drunk or 100 per cent responsible.
                Marc E. Schiffer, *Mental Disorder and the*
                *Criminal Trial Process*[65]

Earl Joudrie, who was present in court only when he testified, claimed,
in a prescient and contradictory statement to the press before the jury had
reached a verdict, that he was not troubled about the outcome of the trial:
"I'm not looking for vengeance at all. I'm just hoping that if Dorothy
needs treatment, she gets some. If she's acquitted, she's acquitted. But
some son-of-a-bitch shot me six times and somehow that seems to have

been forgotten in this whole mess. There's something unfair about that."[66] Earl was very upset that some "son-of-a-bitch" shot him six times. But already, before the jury had made a decision, Earl declared his membership in a society that, despite the *Lavallee* decision in 1990, can barely tolerate the possibility that a battered wife might be acquitted on a charge of attempting to murder her husband because she may be justified, as a reasonable person, in defending herself from him. Yet, he was apparently willing to think, and implicitly to assume, that his former wife might be sick and in need of "treatment."

Earl did not suggest that he, himself, may need treatment; that now, especially, as he plans to begin a new marriage,[67] he might need some help to manage the possessive, jealous, controlling, and physically violent behaviour he exerted over the first woman he chose to share his life. Noel O'Brien deserves credit for trying to show that there is something wrong with Earl. But very few people seemed to pay attention.

It was not only in the 1940s and 1950s that girls were told, "Be good, sweet maid, and let who will be clever." To often, even today, a "good girl" is expected to take on the burden of her disappointments, whatever the cost. She is expected not to complain when her husband controls her by his jealousy, by keeping her waiting, by demanding his level of taste in dress and food and style and performance as a wife and a hostess, by insisting that she conspire with his silence about his health and about whatever else he chooses not to tell others, by moving her and their children across the continent to aid in his aspirations for success. A "good girl" is expected not to complain, or even confide in anyone else, when her husband leaves her alone at home with the children most of the time, resents her demands on his attention when he is preoccupied with his work, diminishes her and insults her in public, frightens her and threatens her by shouting and swearing and punching holes in walls and knocking down doors, and beats her up many times—on at least one occasion so severely that a reliable witness thought that he would kill her. A "good girl" is expected not to be angry and aggressive, and certainly not to try to kill her husband, by shooting him six times.

But a "good girl," if she is as severely abused by her husband as Dorothy Joudrie was, may become anxious, depressed, self-destructive, incapable of acknowledging the reality of her existence—even her own identity—and in extreme cases she may act out violently against her husband, suddenly releasing her suppressed rage and desperation and loss and terror in what psychiatrists call a dissociative state of mind, and lawyers, a state of automatism. Even "good girls" who reach this extreme stage are often sentenced to jail for a very long time if a jury decides that they are guilty. If a jury finds them "not criminally responsible" because of a "mental disorder"—the new term in the Criminal Code for "insanity"—they may be sent to a mental hospital, under the disposition of a Provincial Board of Review, for an undetermined length of time, where, Earl Joudrie apparently believes, they will get "treatment."

There were five expert witnesses at Dorothy Joudrie's trial. Dr. Joyce Wong testified for the Crown about the seriousness of Earl's bullet wounds, where they were on his body, and that four bullets remain in his body. She said that his life would have been threatened had he not received treatment. Sergeant David Kessler, an RCMP weapons expert, testified for the Crown about the power and potential danger of the semi-automatic Beretta pistol that the police took from Dorothy's home. He said that when the gun was seized, six bullets had been fired and one bullet remained in the gun. He held the gun, which he assured the court was not loaded, as he discussed it. In fact, he got down from the witness box to demonstrate, dramatically, for the jury, how one of the bullets shot into Earl's upper body was fired from between three and twelve inches away from his chest as he lay on the garage floor. Kessler began to kneel down on one knee, aiming the gun in his hand, at the floor. Observers were startled, not just by what he was telling us, but by his graphic demonstration of what he alleged had happened. Justice Lutz interrupted his pantomime. It was the only time during the trial that Lutz, in the presence of the jury, became agitated and impatient, insisting that Kessler be more concise and less elaborate in his explanation. But Kessler had left no doubt in the minds of anyone in that courtroom about the determined actions of the person who shot Earl Joudrie. Contrary to what Earl believes, the people in the courtroom, and certainly the jury, were not allowed to forget that "in this whole mess" he was shot six times.

Noel O'Brien, knowing the risks he was taking in his defence of Dorothy, chose two psychiatrists to give expert evidence at the trial. Dr. Roy O'Shaughnessy, associate professor and chairman of forensic psychiatry at the University of British Columbia, was the first to testify. O'Shaughnessy appears to be in his early to mid-forties. His demeanour is cool—too cool, I thought sometimes as I watched him sitting inside the bar before he testified. At one point he held up a popular paperback novel to show his colleague, Dr. Alan Weston, what he had chosen as a diversion while he was here in Calgary. This was a friendly gesture. But the other people inside the bar, and especially his colleague, were too preoccupied with the task at hand to give the book much attention. O'Shaughnessy redeemed himself somewhat for me during his testimony, and especially during his cross-examination by Selinger, when his careful distance, his apparent attitude of a man simply doing his job, disappeared.

O'Shaughnessy spent a total of five hours with Dorothy on two separate days in January 1996. He had read the transcripts of the preliminary hearing, the reports from the Betty Ford Center, Earl's statements to the police, the Christmas letters, and the transcript of Dorothy's calls to the Emergency Medical Services on the day of the shooting. He reviewed Earl's testimony. He was present during Selinger's cross-examination of Dorothy. It was O'Shaughnessy's opinion that Dorothy was in a dissociative state at the time of the shooting. He said that she would have no conscious awareness that shooting a gun was wrong in a legal sense. He said that he believed that in this state she could not form the intention to kill. O'Shaughnessy referred several times to Dorothy's "massive denial" of her real-life situation, saying that she saw her life through "rose-coloured glasses," that she had no sense of her identity except as Mrs. Earl Joudrie, and that her belief that she and Earl might be reunited was like a "magical wish." O'Brien asked O'Shaughnessy to explain the difference between rage and a dissociative state. O'Shaughnessy said that they are very different: for example, a person may be so angry she cannot speak, but in a dissociative state there is a disruption of the person's awareness of her surroundings. He said that it is possible, however, for rage to lead to a dissociative state. When normal emotions of anger, hurt, and sadness are "just placed on the back burner," then nothing is complete, especially when all of it is covered over with drinking. O'Shaughnessy suggested that Dorothy was acting out the rage that was there while she was shooting Earl, but there was no "affect." During the shooting, according to Earl, Dorothy was "calm" and "detached." There was no expression of anger or rage, and this absence of emotion is an indication of a dissociative state. O'Shaughnessy believed that during her conversation with Earl that Saturday morning, Dorothy realized that their marriage was over. This realization "triggered" her dissociative state. O'Brien asked O'Shaughnessy if it is common for abused women to deny. "All the time," O'Shaughnessy said. He also said that Dorothy showed no evidence of a psychiatric disorder apart from her alcoholism.

Selinger seemed to leap with both feet into his cross-examination of O'Shaughnessy, demanding to know immediately if, on the morning she shot Earl, Dorothy was in a state of "non-insane automatism." O'Shaughnessy said, "That's a legal term. I'm able to determine her dissociative state at the time." And O'Shaughnessy continued to be cautious as he answered Selinger. But his manner and tone of voice were sometimes politely defensive throughout the cross-examination. He said that when he thinks of Dorothy's hair appointment and her plans for dinner that day, it seems "unlikely" that she had planned what Selinger called a "cold-blooded, calculating and vindictive act." He said that he thinks she is not still a "high risk." He said, when Selinger asked him, that neurological tests were unnecessary because Dorothy's condition is "not organic."

Dr. Alan Weston, director of outpatient services in forensic psychiatry at Bow Valley Centre, a Calgary hospital, was O'Brien's second psychiatric expert. Weston's expression, as I watched him sitting inside the bar for several days, seemed rather stern, but his manner on the witness stand was quiet, assured. He received his medical and psychiatric training in England, and he has had extensive experience in forensic psychiatry in Canada. He is a professor emeritus at the University of Calgary and at the University of Saskatchewan. He has tendered evidence in court for both the Crown and the defence at least twenty times a year over a period of thirty years. Weston began treating Dorothy on January 24, 1995, and during the fifteen months between the shooting and the trial, he continued to see Dorothy regularly. He sat near Dorothy, near the prisoner's dock, during Earl's testimony. Dorothy seemed not to be apprehensive as Weston began his testimony.

What Weston said was similar in most respects to O'Shaughnessy's evidence, but for me it seemed to carry more authority, perhaps partly because of his age and experience, and also because he has treated Dorothy for some time. He believes that Dorothy was in a dissociative state as she was shooting Earl, and that this state began when Earl got up to leave the kitchen. He believes that she is not mentally ill, and that a recurrence of a dissociative state is very unlikely if she continues to deal with her problems and does not drink again. He said that she needs help to resolve her problems, but that there is no need for her to be hospitalized. He said that she does not need drugs, and that she has not been taking medication while she has been in his care. Weston suggested more than once that Earl's testimony about Dorothy's behaviour that Saturday morning—for example, the comments Earl says she made while she was shooting him—may not be reliable. He said, "I have only seen Mr. Joudrie on the witness stand. He is a very tough person." He did not interview the children because, he said, they did not want to talk with him. It was apparent from what he said that he supports Dorothy, and that he sees her as a normal person who succumbed, temporarily, to a dissociative state of mind.

Selinger seemed so antagonistic during his cross-examination of Weston, and especially in his repeated insistence that Weston should be able to point out exactly when the dissociative state began and exactly when it ended, that observers in the courtroom began to react with impatient clucking and whispering. Weston met Selinger's challenges calmly and logically, and sometimes with disdain. Justice Lutz did not interfere, but Selinger seemed to be aware of the reaction in the gallery and he stopped his attack long enough to tell the court that "it is not my intention to ambush" the witness. Nevertheless, when O'Brien used his few minutes of rebuttal time, after Selinger had finished, to dissipate the tension and confusion, and to clarify some issues to the advantage of the defence, there was a collective sense of relief—not necessarily because everyone agreed with O'Brien's defence, but because he had restored a sense of civility, and order, and logic. I was not able to measure the effects on the jury of the chaos of Selinger's cross-examination of Dr. Weston. They were remarkably poker-faced, keeping their thoughts to themselves.

Dorothy became visibly very upset during Selinger's cross-examination of Weston. She seemed to be protective of Dr. Weston and to see Selinger's attack as a personal affront. As we all left the courtroom for the afternoon break, she said to Noel O'Brien and Dr. Weston, "It's too much!"

Before Dr. Julio Arboleda-Flores took the stand as Selinger's rebuttal witness, O'Brien talked quietly with Dorothy as she sat in the prisoner's dock. O'Brien apparently was trying to prepare her and reassure her. Arboleda-Flores has an impressive background of education and experience in medicine and forensic psychiatry, not only in Canada, but internationally. He has worked with the World Health Organization at the United Nations. He received his M.D. at the National University of Colombia, and his training in psychiatry and forensic psychiatry in Canada. He also has a Ph.D. in epidemiology. Despite his quite pronounced accent, his self-confidence and his animated gestures and facial expressions clarify and enhance his speech. Selinger's first question to Arboleda-Flores was not easy to understand, but implicitly, it seemed to be "Help!"

Arboleda-Flores turned to the jury, and looking directly at them, he presented a lecture on the meaning of memory, forgetting, dissociation, a dissociative state, intoxication, and finally, his impressions after he examined Dorothy Joudrie "about two weeks ago"—two or three days before the trial began. He had the complete attention of every juror. He said that Dorothy suffers from "mild alcoholism," but that she has other "difficulties": elements of paranoia, post-traumatic disorder as a result of the years of abuse, anxiety, tension, depression, and thought deprivation—"seeing the world in rosy colours." He said that this was more than the "massive denial" O'Shaughnessy and Weston had described. He said that Dorothy told him when he saw her that "We should not be there in court. My family doesn't want it. I don't want it"—suggesting, he said, that she denies the seriousness of what happened. I was startled initially by this information, but thinking about what Dorothy said, I realize that it confirms her conscious dissociation from her actions, and even from an emotional reaction, afterwards, to what she did.

Arboleda-Flores said, "she has suffered badly." Because Dorothy did not give him enough details, for example about her drinking, he "needed to see the victim." So he also saw Earl. He did not tell how, exactly, Earl enlightened him about Dorothy's drinking, or anything else. Arboleda-Flores placed much emphasis on his claim that seventy percent of alcoholics have suffered organic brain damage, and he said that he has a "hunch" that Dorothy has brain damage. He said that post-traumatic stress disorder also causes changes in the brain. He returned repeatedly to the fact that Dorothy has had no neurological tests to determine the extent of the brain damage which, he suggested, probably exists.

Looking directly at the jury, Arboleda-Flores said that if he were to accept that Dorothy was in a state of automatism, it would be "insane automatism." Unlike the other two psychiatrists Arboleda-Flores was not averse to using legal terms. Here was his response to the defence: a surprising agreement that yes, Dorothy was in a state of automatism when she shot Earl. But the shadow over this unexpected bonus for the defence was that Arboleda-Flores believed that her mind was not, in all other respects, normal, as O'Shaughnessy and Weston claimed. He added that the jury could use Section Sixteen of the Criminal Code and find her not criminally responsible because she is "insane"—because she could not appreciate what she was doing, along with the fact that she had been drinking. Then he agreed with Selinger that if the jury chose to disregard the psychiatric evidence, they might find that Dorothy had some degree of alleged criminal responsibility when she shot Earl. I was surprised that O'Brien did not object or that Justice Lutz did not intervene in this exchange.

Noel O'Brien, in his cross-examination, asked Arboleda-Flores directly, "Do you believe that at the critical moment she was in a dissociative state?" Arboleda-Flores said, "Correct. The question is what caused it." He said that the cause cannot be determined without neurological tests. Nevertheless he continued, saying that he had two theories: "the big gulp theory"—Dorothy's alcohol consumption that morning, her alcoholism generally, and the organic damage she may have suffered from it; and "the bad news theory"—her realization that her marriage was over. Or, he added, the cause could be a combination of the two. Arboleda-Flores said that he believes that Dorothy's depression, anxiety, and alcoholism could become serious. He said that her treatment should be clinical therapy. Finally, when O'Brien asked him if he had concerns of a recurrence of trouble "if the jury finds this way," Arboleda-Flores said, "Yes—emotionally, socially, psychologically." And he added, "Fifty percent of murders are committed by people who are drunk."

The jury listened to, and seemed to understand every word Arboleda-Flores said. I was bothered by the fact that his evidence was based on "hunches" and "theories" and what might be, if certain tests had been completed. Was it his long experience as a forensic psychiatrist, his seniority, that gave him the luxury to guess with impunity? Perhaps his "diagnosis" was as reliable as that of the other two psychiatrists and he was simply candid enough to use words the others had avoided. Dr. Weston had incited Selinger's objections to the credibility of his diagnosis of Dorothy when he said that studies of dissociative states in particular, and psychiatry in general are still undeveloped. But no one challenged Arboleda-Flores. O'Brien must have been enormously relieved that this expert for the Crown had agreed with the defence that Dorothy was in a state of automatism when she shot Earl. But the difference between non-insane automatism and insane automatism, except that there is a penalty for one and not the other, seemed to me to be a mystery none of these three experts had resolved satisfactorily. As some of the regular observers at the trial began to speculate that the jury would probably go with forced treatment rather than prison, the murky, dangerous waters of a mental hospital began to seep into my imagination. For many people, the important issue now seemed to be that Dorothy Joudrie might escape going to prison and having a criminal record—what they considered to be suitable punishment—and this possibility angered them. One woman, forgetting or disregarding Dorothy's many years of volunteer work in all of the cities in which she has lived, was quite exasperated. She said, "I think she's going to get off without even any community service!"

When I left the Court of Queen's Bench that day I continued to see the faces of the jury as they listened to Arboleda-Flores. I lay awake that night thinking about the three psychiatrists, three men, all of whom testified compassionately on behalf of a woman in trouble. How would the jury weigh their respective opinions, I wondered. How would the jury apply what these experts had said to the Dorothy Joudrie they saw from day to day at her trial—as she listened to other people talk about her, as she testified on her own behalf.

Dorothy Joudrie spent her adult life existing inside a carefully learned and practiced veneer of femininity, wifely devotion, gentility, maternity, efficiency, silence, and unmistakable signs of her social position and class—her expensive homes, cars, clothes, hair styles, even her perfume. By the time the trial began, although it was not apparent to me during the first day or two, the veneer had become brittle, it had begun to crack and blister, drawing away from the woman underneath. There were moments during her trial, and especially during her testimony, when I thought I saw glimpses of the real Dorothy Joudrie: her pride, courage, strength, intelligence, her capacity to endure, to survive. But these qualities were tempered by her vulnerability, her emotional pain, and more than anything else, by the impression I had, watching her, that she was simply lost—buffeted from one day to the next by the support of her lawyer, her psychiatrist, and a few kind words from other professionals and some spectators on the one hand, and on the other, the aggressive attacks by her former husband, two of her children, the Crown prosecutor, and some of the press, whose photographs of her sometimes were almost grotesque.

Of her five character witnesses, four of whom were women, and all of whom testified to the lack of violence in her character, only two of the women had known Dorothy throughout most of the years of her marriage. All of these witnesses were convincing in their affirmation of her peaceful disposition and her generosity, and the man spoke out courageously, without having been asked, about the label "socialite" which inevitably appeared in media stories about her and which he said "irked" him and was an offence to her. To his credit, the word "socialite" began to disappear after his testimony. But I wondered, and I think others did too, if these character witnesses had been asked if they knew Dorothy Joudrie intimately, what they would have said.

I began to wonder if I were in Dorothy's position, who I would suggest could be character witnesses for me. I could think of five people who could testify to my general disposition, but I could not think of five people, without including some of my immediate family, who know me really well, who know me intimately.

Most of us know very few people really well, and we could count our "closest friends" on the fingers of one hand. According to Carolyn Joudrie, her mother is a gregarious person. While I believe it was very important for Dorothy to be able to say that she has many good friends, I think she is quite unaware of how hard she has worked to keep people from knowing her well—and to keep from knowing herself.

I am sure Dorothy could never have imagined so raw an exposure of herself as she experienced at her trial. And it was all the worse because it was often as much of a revelation to her as it was to the people in the courtroom. I think very few people appreciated the emotional trauma Dorothy suffered during this unavoidable public revelation of herself. One or two journalists who attended the trial, and who knew that I wanted to write about her, warned me that I would have difficulty because she is "shallow" and "lacking in insight." I took their comments seriously; in fact, from what I had seen of Dorothy, I agreed to some extent with what they said. But I saw these characteristics as symptoms of her emotional trauma. Also, I thought that I saw signs that Dorothy was beginning to see herself more clearly than she ever had before, but that often she drew back from these revelations, not only because of her practiced denial, but because the shock at what she saw simply prevented her embrace of it.

Several times during the trial I thought of Elizabeth Bishop's poem "The Prodigal."[68] This poem is indirectly about Bishop's alcoholism, but also about the prodigal's (and Bishop's) "shuddering insights," which like "the bats' uncertain staggering flight" were "beyond his control,/touching him. But it took him a long time/finally to make his mind up to go home." Unlike the biblical prodigal, who was welcomed home by his forgiving father, Elizabeth Bishop did not have a "home" in the usual sense. Her father died when she was an infant, and her mother, who never recovered from her husband's death, was in and out of hospitals during Bishop's early childhood and was finally confined to a mental hospital until her death.

Bishop was almost obsessed, throughout her life, with the fact that she never had a home. But in this poem, going "home" means also, I think, making up one's mind to face and accept the "shuddering insights." And I wondered, as I watched Dorothy at her trial, while everyone around her was working to determine her fate, if she was struggling to make up her mind, perhaps for the first time in her life, to see and know herself.

All of the experts agreed, as Earl had suggested they might, that one way or another Dorothy needed help, treatment, to mend the damage. But no one suggested that he, Earl, needed anything. Dorothy was the problem, society's problem—the same society that taught her how to be a good girl, and a lady.

# The Verdict

The judgments of the courts are meant to reinforce social
rules and values. To achieve this end, the public has to believe
that jury verdicts are statements about the truth of actual
events, not mere probabilities. If that belief is ever lost, a
society based on the rule of law would ultimately collapse
into anarchy.

. . . . . . . . . . . . . . . . . . . . . . . . . . . . . . . . . . . . . . . .

"The truth?" Facher said, smiling, one day after court.
"The truth is at the bottom of a bottomless pit."
Jonathan Harr, A Civil Action[69]

On the third Monday of Dorothy Joudrie's trial, May 6, 1996, defence
counsel Noel O'Brien and Crown prosecutor Jerry Selinger presented their
closing arguments. Long before ten o'clock, the waiting area outside the
courtroom was crowded with people impatient for the clerk to open the door,
and when she did, the usual polite determination to get into the courtroom
gave way to silent shoves and pushes from a few people who knew where they
wanted to sit, and who had not expected to have to compete with others for
what had become their usual place. I, too, wanted to sit in my usual place,
but my obsessive nature had brought me here in time to be near the beginning of the line. Within a very few minutes, the room was full.

Noel O'Brien stood quietly beside Dorothy, resting his elbow on the
side of the prisoner's dock, waiting in a practised, casual manner, not

speaking unless she spoke to him. His presence near her was undoubtedly reassuring to her, and it was also symbolic of his position in relation to her. At one point, as she spoke, she shook her head. She must have been anticipating what lay ahead in the next few hours, and particularly listening to Jerry Selinger's argument. Perhaps, also, she was amazed at the number of people who had streamed through the door. When Justice Lutz appeared, he said that counsel would present their summations today, and that tomorrow he would direct the jury. Then, the jury would be sequestered as they deliberated the verdict.

O'Brien began his argument by noting immediately that because as a matter of law he must speak first, he cannot rebut what the Crown prosecutor says. He said that the defence does not have to prove that Dorothy Joudrie was in a state of automatism when she committed the acts with which she was charged, but that the Crown must prove, beyond reasonable doubt, that she was fully aware and not in a state of automatism. He pointed out that automatism does not imply a robotic state, but simply a lack of awareness. He said that Dorothy's "massive denial" of the reality of her life, which existed throughout her marriage, continues today, and that this was evident during her testimony. As he reviewed the testimony of all of the witnesses, he emphasized the "reliable" testimony of Elizabeth Griffiths, an independent witness, whom Selinger did not question, because she was telling the truth. O'Brien placed great emphasis on the psychiatric evidence. Both of his expert witnesses, Dr. Roy O'Shaughnessy and Dr. Alan Weston, said that Dorothy is not mentally ill, and all three psychiatrists, including Dr. Julio Arboleda-Flores for the Crown, came to "exactly the same conclusion": Dorothy was in a dissociative state at the time of the shooting. O'Brien was very critical of Selinger, to whom he referred, using the acceptable courtroom etiquette, as "my friend," while diminishing Selinger for not having asked Earl any questions about the gun, and saying that Selinger had "a huge bag of suggestions" but no real evidence to support a guilty verdict. Also, O'Brien said that the only evidence to find Dorothy not criminally responsible because of a mental disorder is Dr. Arboleda-Flores' "hunch" that Dorothy could have organic brain damage, and this is not enough. She is entitled to a verdict of not guilty.

O'Brien concluded his argument dramatically, pausing for effect, and articulating his words carefully. He emphasized the years of abuse Dorothy has endured. Despite having criticized part of Arboleda-Flores' expert testimony, because O'Brien seemed to recognize the profound effect this forensic psychiatrist had had on the jury, and also the extraordinary fact that he had agreed with the two psychiatric experts for the defence about Dorothy's dissociative state, O'Brien said that Arboleda-Flores' evidence, "is so, so important to this case." O'Brien ended his argument with a dramatic put-down of Jerry Selinger. O'Brien reminded the jury that it was Arboleda-Flores, Selinger's expert witness, who said, "This woman is suffering badly."

Jerry Selinger read his final argument. He said that his "partner" was eloquent, but that the jurors' duty was to see "justice done" and that they are the final judge. He said that the Crown must prove every element beyond a reasonable doubt, and that while his charge is that Dorothy Joudrie is guilty, the verdict is up to the jury. They should let their conscience be their guide.

Selinger described Dorothy as a vindictive, enraged, violent woman who was prepared to shoot her estranged husband that January morning if he told her that he was proceeding with their divorce. He repeated Earl's report of Dorothy's statements as she was shooting him. He noted, also, that she did not take the advice of the EMS operator to apply pressure bandages to Earl's wounds as they waited for the police and the medical services to arrive that day.

Selinger suggested that the jury could reject the "opinions" of his forensic psychiatric expert, Dr. Arboleda-Flores. He said that research on dissociative states is not yet well developed, and he urged the jurors, again, to use their common sense. He said that these expert witnesses are no better able than the jury to make a judgement. He added that if they did decide to accept the psychiatric evidence, they should remember Arboleda-Flores' opinion that Dorothy should have neurological tests, that she needs continued counselling, and that her violent behaviour could recur.

As he had during his cross-examination of Dorothy, Selinger emphasized the seriousness of her drinking problem, and he said that she could have lost her memory for a number of reasons, and not automatism at all. He questioned her credibility. Selinger said that the jury should leave to the direction of Justice Lutz Dr. Arboleda-Flores' sudden announcement of Dorothy's "insanity." Selinger concluded his argument by telling the jury for the third time that they may simply want to use their common sense, before what they learned during the past two weeks. In doing so, they may find that the accused is guilty as charged—which he believes is a just and appropriate comment.

On Tuesday, the Honourable Justice Arthur M. Lutz addressed the jury. Until this day we had heard almost nothing from this man, who, for more than two weeks, had presided over Dorothy Joudrie's trial. The little that we had seen and heard of him suggested that he is quiet-spoken, dedicated to the law, and cautious. He 'was never officious, and his facial expression was almost always pleasant and confident. I had found his biography in the archives at the Court of Queen's Bench and discovered that he was born in 1937. He belongs to Dorothy's generation, our generation. Although Lutz has been the presiding judge in several controversial cases in Calgary, he is not well known among lay people.

But if Justice Lutz had not asserted himself until this moment in Dorothy's trial, except by always being late, he made up for it now. For almost six hours, he read his address to the jury—quickly, and in a voice that was flat, passionless, devoid of almost any inflection, and so quiet that it was barely audible. During the first twenty minutes or so, the jury sent him several notes, probably asking him to speak up so that they could hear, but he laid the notes aside without reading them, and proceeded without interruption. I was astonished by this performance. I strained to hear what he was saying, and to take notes. No one in this room had the courage, or thought that they had the authority, to stand up and say, "Stop! We cannot hear you!" We sat there like sheep, submitting without protest to the control and authority of a powerful institution in our society. We felt compelled to be silent.

Justice Lutz began by telling the jury that they must follow the law as he determines it, and that their decision must be based solely on evidence presented in the trial. A few minutes later, he said that if they did not agree with what he considers facts, it is their right to disagree, and that they are not bound to believe everything people say in the witness box. He urged the jurors not to express an overt opinion at the beginning of their deliberations.

Justice Lutz explained direct and circumstantial evidence, guilt, and intent, which is required in all criminal cases to find guilt. Then, he proceeded to discuss the entire trial, and what he had heard as evidence. As he repeated Earl's testimony, Dorothy shook her head, apparently in amazement at some of the things Earl had said. When he repeated some of Carolyn's testimony, Dorothy was obviously upset, but she sat silently. I noticed as I watched her then that she was holding a small teddy bear in the palm of her left hand. The bear was her charm or amulet, and as I saw her holding it gently, stroking it unconsciously with her thumb, I realized how dramatically she had let down her guard, her lady-like veneer, since the beginning of the trial. She was no longer attempting to hide her vulnerability, her fear.

When Justice Lutz reviewed the expert evidence of the three psychiatrists, he warned the jury to remember that these views are hypothetical. Two psychiatrists for the defence had testified that Dorothy was in a dissociative state, or a state of non-insane automatism. While automatism and mental disorder are often intertwined, Justice Lutz said, they are two separate things. As he recalled the evidence of the Crown's psychiatric expert, it was evident that he saw it as contradictory: Dr. Arboleda-Flores had said initially that he saw no indications that Dorothy was psychotic. Later in his testimony, Arboleda-Flores said that her inability to see her life realistically was more than denial, and was "thought disorganization," and that she had suffered a major trauma which could last, and could recur. Arboleda-Flores had said that if Dorothy was in a state of automatism, he would consider it insane automatism. Justice Lutz said that if the jury agrees with the defence's argument of non-insane automatism, they should find Dorothy not guilty on all charges. But, he said, the Crown's psychiatric evidence was that Dorothy was suffering from a mental disorder, and that if the jury agrees with that evidence, she should be found not criminally responsible. Finally, if the jury finds that Dorothy was acting consciously and voluntarily—with intent—when she shot her estranged husband, she is guilty of attempted murder, aggravated assault, and use of a weapon. Justice Lutz pointed out that the jury's findings determine the verdict, not the ramifications of it.

At 5:30 p.m. the jury was dismissed to begin their deliberation. Most of the people in the gallery went home. The journalists and some of the regulars stayed. We did not expect a verdict that evening, but juries have been known to come to a verdict in two or three hours, and we did not want to be absent if that happened. After we had seen them driven away to their hotel for the night, we too, left.

I had not been outside all day, and I was surprised to discover, when I left the Court of Queen's Bench, that Calgary was in the throes of a May snowstorm. After the first day or two of the trial, I had decided that the cost of parking downtown was more than I could manage and I began to drive to the suburban LRT station near my home and take the train. Walking to the train from the courthouse that evening was not too difficult, because the pedestrian traffic had cleared the sidewalks downtown of most of the snow, if not the ice. But when I got off the train I had to wade through three inches of unbroken snow and ice to get to my car. What did this reveal about me, I wondered, cross and agitated, that I was more concerned about the state of my not new, but much beloved Italian leather shoes than my freezing ankles. My car, at the far end of the dark, nearly empty parking lot, was covered with ice, the doors frozen shut. It must have been fifteen minutes before I managed to open the door of the hatch-back and crawl up to the driver's seat and finally, the warmth of the motor, and my pushing and pulling, allowed me to open the front door, and to scrape enough ice from the windows to see my way home. The next day, all of us who came to the courthouse were wearing our winter coats, boots, woollen hats, and gloves. But I can't remember anyone remarking on the weather.

It was a long day. We sat together in the waiting area, drinking coffee, reading newspapers, filling spaces in our notebooks, talking about where to get the best coffee beans and fresh fish in Calgary and Toronto and Montreal, telling tales about our children, our dogs and cats, and quite personal experiences we would not normally share with strangers. It was like being aboard a ship, suspended in time. And while it was Dorothy Joudrie who was on our minds, we said very little about her. When the jury was taken out for their supper, some of us ventured out too, and discovered that the snow was gone. It was May again. I walked out with a young journalist who lived nearby and who had decided to go home, taking a chance that there would be no verdict tonight. I stopped at a restaurant not far from the courthouse and was both comforted and rejuvenated by a bowl of hot spicy soup and a fresh green salad, but I enjoyed, especially, sitting alone, in the crowded, noisy room. I saw some of the other "regulars" there, and I think they saw me, but we made no effort to acknowledge each other or to talk. These few moments were a strange little escape into the real world, and we knew that we would be together again in a matter of minutes. At about nine o'clock we watched the jury being chauffered swiftly away for another night in their hotel. One of the experienced journalists for a daily paper drove me home that evening. We had talked often during the trial, sharing our observations, and discussing the daily reports, and we did talk for a few minutes during the drive about Dorothy. But while I know that this journalist is very conscientious, and her stories are accurate and well written, I suspected that she was beginning to think ahead to her next assignment, and I didn't want to prolong a discussion of a story that would soon be behind her. We did not speculate about the verdict.

On Thursday morning there was a restlessness among those of us who had waited at the courthouse. The local journalists came up from their press room occasionally to ask if we had heard any signs from the jury. Very few people left the courthouse for lunch. Shortly after two-thirty, we heard applause in the jury room and within a minute or two, a firm knock on their door. They had deliberated for twenty-one hours.

We gathered ourselves together quickly and lined up at the door of the courtroom for the last time. We had only one thing on our minds, and I was both surprised and embarrassed when the clerk of the court, having waited until we were in line, and assuming the tone of a schoolteacher speaking to children, announced that no one would enter the courtroom until we had returned every chair to its proper place and picked up the "garbage"—a few empty coffee cups and the odd chocolate bar wrapper or empty potato chip bag. For a moment we were stunned, not only by the authority of her command, but also by our own thoughtless behaviour. None of us wanted to leave our place in line. I cannot remember now which good people hustled around, quickly moving the two or three chairs, and picking up the few pieces of garbage.

It was only minutes before the courtroom was full. I saw a few people I had not noticed before—two or three men in business suits, for example. Earl's brother, Keith, and his two step-sisters were there, but none of the Joudrie children was present. Earl was not present. Dorothy had spent the past two days with a friend in Calgary and she appeared within about ten minutes. She was very pale, and she was obviously frightened. She was asked to stand in the prisoner's dock as the forewoman of the jury read the verdict: "We find that the accused committed the acts alleged against her, but is not criminally responsible on account of a mental disorder." Dorothy leaned on the rail of the dock, put her head down on her hands and sobbed.

Justice Lutz warned the jury that their deliberations—everything that was said in their discussions—must be secret. They must tell no one.

Noel O'Brien stood immediately, and tried to persuade Justice Lutz to enter a not guilty verdict. Jerry Selinger objected, and Justice Lutz agreed with him, that while Dorothy will not have a conviction entered against her, the jury's verdict should not be extended to a finding of not guilty. He said that there will be no other entry than "not criminally responsible." Dorothy continued to stand, weeping quietly, and not seeming to understand the implications of this verdict. Justice Lutz said that Dr. Weston, who is a member of the Alberta Board of Review, will admit Dorothy to the Provincial Mental Hospital in Edmonton for a two-week assessment, following which the Board will hold a disposition hearing. Dorothy may remain at liberty until she enters the hospital, but she must have no contact with Earl Joudrie, and she must present herself to Dr. Weston within two days.

By this time Dorothy had sat down on the bench in the dock. O'Brien had had no time to speak to her. Now he turned to her, and for about a minute, he stood three or four feet away from her, looking at her. His face was flushed, and it seemed to me that he was trying to come to terms with his own mixed emotions, probably of both relief and disappointment, and at the same time to decide how he could help her. Finally, he said, "Dorothy you are not guilty. You are free." I don't know how many people heard him say this. In light of what we had just witnessed, at first I was stunned by what he said. But gradually I realized that what he had told Dorothy was essentially true; that it was what he believed she needed to hear now; and that he would explain her situation to her when he thought she could understand it and bear it. He came to her side to support her. About an hour later, in his office, in the presence of journalists and Dorothy, O'Brien explained that the Board of Review can do one of four things: order her to stay in the provincial hospital for treatment; order her to attend the hospital on an outpatient basis; order her to receive treatment from a psychiatrist or a psychologist, or both, outside the hospital; or let her go, free of the bail conditions set earlier, and/or free of any recommendations for counselling.[70] This information was also essentially true. Dorothy would learn soon enough what assessments and dispositions really mean, and the power of autonomous Provincial Boards of Review.

But now, I think O'Brien hoped that Dorothy could face the many journalists who were pressing against the bar, wanting to talk with her, to ask her questions. The journalists from radio, television, and the press also wanted to talk with him and with Selinger. The journalists were relentless; they needed their stories. Keith Joudrie was furious, and so also were some other spectators. Some of Dorothy's friends pressed through the crowd to embrace her, congratulate her, and wish her well. The courtroom and the waiting area were chaotic. I knew that I should stay, to be able to record my reaction to this spectacle. But I was shocked and repelled by it. I wanted to escape. When I discovered the newspaper and television photographers outside the brass doors of the Court of Queen's Bench, waiting to get pictures of Dorothy and O'Brien and Selinger, I simply continued to walk to the train. I was overwhelmed by my realization during the past few moments that from my point of view, despite the fact that Dorothy had not been found guilty of any criminal act, she had not been found innocent. This was only the end of one phase of her fate and the beginning of the next.

# Part Three

# After the Trial

# Aftermath

Money and power used to buy thicker walls; because no one
could see inside his home, a CEO could do whatever he
wanted there. He could, like Earl Joudrie, put his fist
through walls—or into his wife's face. But slowly, other
people are beginning to peek inside. And sooner or later,
some of them will act to protest what they see.
        Mike Woloschuk, "Silence of the Lions,"
        *Elm Street*[71]

In Alberta, and in some other parts of Canada, the uproar about the jury's
verdict in Dorothy Joudrie's trial was deafening. Dorothy was scarcely aware
of this because she was preoccupied. But in headlines across the country, she
was the Calgary socialite who had shot her estranged husband six times, and
because of her money and the eleven women on her jury, she had got off—
she had just walked away. I am quite sure that some other patients in the
provincial mental hospital, when she arrived there after the trial ended, let
her know what they thought about her, and also that there were at least a
few people on the staff, who despite their professional training, could not
hide their personal biases and judgements about her. During the trial, Dr.
Arboleda-Flores said he believed that Dorothy suffers from some elements
of paranoia. I thought at the time, and I still do, that if she believes that people are critical of her, and of what she did, and of the decisions that have
been made about her, her judgement is quite sound. This is not paranoia; it
is not an aberration of her mental functioning; she is not imagining it.

Although the word "automatism," whether sane or insane, was not in her jury's verdict, everyone assumed that the "mental disorder" in the verdict meant insane automatism. I was troubled by this at first, and I needed to read again what Justice Arthur Lutz had said. His directions to the jury were that if they found that they agreed with the Crown's psychiatric evidence, and this included mental and emotional problems that may have contributed to a state of insane automatism at the time of the shooting, they should find Dorothy not criminally responsible—which they did. "Not criminally responsible on account of mental disorder," or the abbreviated NCR, is a common term in law and forensic psychiatry. But most lay people are not familiar with this term. It's little wonder if Dorothy was confused and frightened when her verdict was announced.

Kirk Makin, justice reporter for *The Globe and Mail*, in his article about Dorothy's verdict two days after her trial ended, quoted several prosecutors and defence attorneys whom he had interviewed. He quoted Robert Martin, a law professor at the University of Western Ontario, who worries that more and more women are being "acquitted of violent crimes." Martin compared Dorothy's case to Karla Homolka's twelve-year manslaughter sentence in the torture-murders of Kristen French and Leslie Mahaffy. Martin said, "We seem to be developing one system of justice for women and another for men. I am concerned about the extent to which this idea that women are incapable of wickedness has suffused our legal system."[72]

During the summer of 1997, I talked with a former judge in Calgary who had the good sense not to compare Dorothy's case to Karla Homolka's, but he did say that the prevailing attitude now is that it is all right for women to kill, but not men. I was astonished, and asked him if he really believes this. "Absolutely," he said. I think his saying this to me at the beginning of our conversation was partly a reaction to my wanting to write about Dorothy, which he could not understand, and to most vocal female advocates for other women, who he thinks are not concerned about the "real problems in society" such as "child poverty." I agreed with him that child poverty is a real problem, but I added that wife battering is also a real problem. He said that he doesn't know if this is true or not, in Dorothy's case: "Everybody *claims* abuse." The real problem in Dorothy's case, he believes, is that she is an alcoholic, and "alcohol causes people to do these things." I wondered what he thought had caused Dorothy's alcoholism. Also, I wondered how he was able to determine the veracity of

Dorothy's alcoholism, but not that she was abused. But he had moved on. He said that the public is in bad shape: there is a belief in zero tolerance; a search for revenge; an acceptance of vigilante justice, and what he called "voodoo justice," instead of concern for real problems. I was relieved to be able to agree with him to some extent, and we skirted the edges of these complex and troubling issues with relative comfort, avoiding Dorothy, specifically. I wanted to discuss especially the public's desire for vengeance in Dorothy's case, but I decided that he probably would agree with me, if not for exactly the same reasons, and I didn't want to prolong his attack on Dorothy and Earl and, indirectly, on me. He had said that he took no interest at all in Dorothy's trial, and he considered it the least important trial in the past ten years. Nevertheless, as we ended our conversation, he agreed with me that Dorothy's being committed to a mental hospital for an indefinite period of time was the "worst possible sentence."

A former Ontario prosecutor, Brian Gover, told Kirk Makin that the public is sometimes too cynical after "a circus-like celebrity trial. The public needs to know that just because a case is sensational and involves prominent public figures, it doesn't mean justice got skewed." But Gover added that prosecutors should take any defence very seriously. "You can't simply assume a jury will see through a defence one might consider far-fetched."[73] When I asked one criminal lawyer if he considered a verdict of insane automatism, and specifically Dorothy Joudrie's verdict, far-fetched, he paused, and then he said, "Well, obviously the jury didn't think so." Dorothy's jury heard credible psychiatric evidence from both the defence and the prosecution to support automatism, and if some of them thought that it was "far-fetched" it was surely no more so than the prosecution's argument that this woman was driven to try to murder her husband simply by her rage and fear at the possibility of losing her social position now that her husband had decided to divorce her. Makin quoted Dan Brodsky, a Toronto defence lawyer, who said, "No question about it—this was a compromise verdict. Saw-offs happen every day in our courts. The jurors in this case were just not going to let Mrs. Joudrie go scot-free."[74]

While the public and private discussions about Dorothy's verdict continued for two or three weeks, I was interested that we heard almost nothing from the corporate world. Most of these people were silent, publicly at least. One exception, two days after the verdict, was a news story in the business section of the *Calgary Herald*. Gordon Jaremko and Anne Crawford interviewed Earl Joudrie "as he headed out of Toronto to a newly acquired country cottage for a quiet weekend." The story confirmed Earl's decision to take a leave of absence as chairman of Canadian Tire, because he needs the rest, and noted that he "remains chairman of Gulf Canada Resources Ltd., and Algoma Steel Corp., as well as a director of seven other firms in Calgary, Toronto and Edmonton." According to Jaremko and Crawford, the "corporate and financial community's verdict" on Earl Joudrie is that "he has lost no stature."[75] During Dorothy's trial, Gordon Jaremko interviewed, for the *Calgary Herald*, several corporate leaders—Bobbie Sparrow, Peter Lougheed, Don Mazankowski, Bob Blair, and others—and all of these people defended or praised Earl's business skills and/or his character.[76]

Earl's reaction to the verdict was predictably guarded, while express-ing concern for his (not their) children's pain and suffering. He said: "The jury has made a decision which I must accept with equanimity. It is over. I greatly regret that this proceeding was so terribly difficult for my chil-dren. I presume the court will ensure that Dorothy receives proper care and treatment."[77]

A few weeks after Dorothy had been admitted to the provincial mental hospital, David Coll, "Oil & Gas" columnist for *Calgary downtown* wrote:

> Fifteen months later [after the shooting] with the best defense her hus-band's erstwhile, hard-earned dollars could buy, the jury finds her "not guilty by reason of insane automatism." [sic]. . . . Dorothy walks with the proverbial slap on the wrist. In this instance, it amounts to a visit to the friendly neighborhood shrink.
>
> . . . . . . . . . . . . . . . . . . . . . . . . . . . . . . . . . . . . . . . . . . . . . .
>
> No matter what talents Earl Joudrie brings to the boardroom table through his numerous directorships, we have witnessed the destruction of a great (albeit one-dimensional) man.
>
> Dorothy, "the hostess with the mostest," "Robo-wife," "the silver-haired socialite," "the gunslinging grandmother"—to quote my favorite four-second references—saw to that. Whether she was "disassociative" [sic] at the times [sic] matters less than the fact that her Beretta only holds six cartridges in its clip and that she was a poor shot.[78]

Not all business reporters were as vicious, and as careless, as Mr. Coll. On Peter Gzowski's weekly *Morningside* Business Report on May 22, 1996, his three regular business columnists, Jennifer Wells, Teresa Todesco, and Don

Campbell discussed the corporate world's reaction to Earl. All three columnists agreed that corporations appeared to be "circling their wagons" around Earl, protecting him, but that it is difficult to know what is really happening. Gzowski expressed surprise at the rallying around of the business community, particularly such people as Peter Lougheed, Bobbie Sparrow, and Ron Southern, all three of whom he said he has met, and from whom he seemed to have expected something else. The three columnists agreed that if corporations thought that their share values would be affected they would do something about Earl's position as chairman of the boards of Canadian Tire, Gulf Canada, and Algoma Steel, and his presence on the boards of several other corporations. What concerned me about this discussion was that everyone accepted the belief that Earl's abuse of Dorothy ended twenty years ago, and "does everyone not have a skeleton in their closet?" Jennifer Wells did express some discomfort with this attitude, and Don Campbell wondered, "if the abuse were more current? . . . " One of the women interrupted him: "But what is current is what we do not know."[79] I wondered why they did not know; why they had not taken the trouble to find out; why they had simply accepted what Earl said. I wondered how they would define abuse.

In the fall of 1997 I talked with Don Campbell about the *Morningside* discussion and he said that he remembers it well. He said, "I have modified my views since then," and that he no longer believes that Earl's abuse of Dorothy should be excused. He thinks it is very important that the whole story be told. We discussed a group of Alberta women who protested Earl's chairmanship of the board of Canadian Tire and Earl's subsequent "stepping down" as chairman of the board in the fall of 1996.[80]

Despite considerable effort, I was able to talk with only one of the corporate leaders Gordon Jaremko had quoted. Bob Blair, former Nova Corp chairman, is retired now, but he was very gracious when I spoke with him, and he said he appreciated my wanting to confirm what he said about Earl in 1996; nevertheless, he said that he would stand by his earlier comment that Earl Joudrie is "a solid guy."[81] The others are well protected from people like me by unlisted telephone numbers, and one faithful, committed secretary, whose scorn was audible when I explained why I wanted to talk with her employer. My calls to these people were not returned.

I am convinced that only Earl knows what really happened that Saturday morning in January 1995—and that Dorothy cannot remember shooting Earl, or exactly what happened before she began to shoot him.

For more than forty years Dorothy had worked very hard, and at great cost to herself emotionally and physically to comply with the complexity of her own need, and her husband's demands not to tell, to be silent, to deny the reality of her life with him. So it is not surprising that she cannot remember the most dramatic and violent moments she has ever experienced. Selinger could not show intent on her part to murder Earl. Although O'Brien provided strong evidence to show that Earl's abuse of Dorothy had never stopped, he did not argue that she acted, consciously, in self-defence. When I asked O'Brien if he believes that Earl was telling the truth about the day Dorothy shot him, O'Brien said, "We'll never know, Audrey—we'll never know."[82]

I think that the jury's verdict was thoughtful; courageous, in light of the criticism they must surely have known they would face; and reasonable, considering what they had seen and heard during the trial. Armchair critics, who did not attend the trial, or all of the trial, cannot make a fair judgement. Everything that took place in that courtroom was important. Apart from the psychiatric testimony for both the defence and the Crown, and especially Elizabeth Griffiths' testimony, which obviously influenced the jury, there were many subtle, unrehearsed revelations. I think, for example, of Dorothy's obvious shock as she listened to the tape of her conversation with the Emergency Medical Services, and to the testimony of the police officers; of Earl's revelation of himself as O'Brien cross-examined him; of Dorothy's reactions when Selinger discussed the gun.

Despite my cynicism about the revelation of truth in a trial, I think that both Dorothy and Earl revealed important aspects of themselves during their testimony. I am very critical of Earl, primarily because of his abuse of Dorothy, but also because of what he revealed about himself from the witness stand, and what he said to journalists outside the courtroom. Because the prosecution wanted to diminish the extent and importance of Earl's brutal treatment of her, Jerry Selinger made no effort to explain what may have caused Earl to become the kind of man who treats his wife as Earl treated Dorothy. Selinger, wanting to focus the jury's attention on Dorothy's aberrant behaviour, insisted that she incited Earl's abusive treatment of her, and some people believed him. Many of the same people who believe that she was responsible for the abuse also believe that she got off scot-free, and that women can get away with anything. Earl is known as "the plumber," "the fixer" in the corporate world, and he often sits at boardroom tables in strained, tense situations, where he must argue strategically, carefully, with other people who are critical of him. But he has never, apparently, leapt up from his boardroom chair, grabbed his opponent by the hair, slammed him or her against the wall, and punched them in the face. He knows that he cannot do that. Such behaviour is not acceptable. He would be charged with assault. But this is what he did to Dorothy—many times. He did this to her because he could. Not only is he stronger than she is physically, but he knew that it was very unlikely that she would charge him with assault, and until recently even if she had, her charge probably would not have been taken seriously. I wonder if Earl realizes that his treatment of Dorothy makes it very difficult for some men and women to sympathize with him. If there is something in Earl's background that caused him to believe that he had the right to control his wife and to beat her we heard nothing about it. But his behaviour on the witness stand as O'Brien cross-examined him showed everyone in the courtroom that when he is threatened he is quickly defensive and incited to anger. Dorothy's shooting Earl threatened his life, and eventually, because of the revelations during the trial, it also may have threatened his career and society's opinion of him. Having observed his need to be in control, I am sure that he tried to do everything in his power to influence the legal decisions that were made about Dorothy. How he did this and what he did, or if he managed to do anything, I do not know. Earl's most striking revelation of himself, for me, was his self-pity. His shedding tears for himself was all the more dramatic, when it was compared to Dorothy's behaviour throughout the trial. Allowing himself the luxury of this pathetic display seemed to me to be a shocking act of manipulation.

During the trial Dorothy was faced repeatedly with the fact that she has denied the reality of her life. All of us in the courtroom heard this so many times, and saw it so plainly when she testified, that we became used to it. But for Dorothy, the relentless diagnosis of her impression of her entire marriage must have been excruciating. How humiliating it must have been to be told over and over that all along she had been deceiving herself! O'Brien said very pointedly during his final argument that her testimony was clear evidence that this denial still exists. She said more than once about her marriage that she didn't remember the bad things, she only remembered the good things. Once or twice when Dorothy was asked to tell about the good things, she seemed almost at a loss for words, and I wondered if some of the bad things that O'Brien encouraged her to tell the jury had begun to interfere with her attention to the good things. It seemed to me that she was beginning, finally, to see her marriage realistically.

Immediately after the trial she said, "I never complained. I never told anybody I had a hard life. I didn't complain about it . . . ever. I have never said one word against my husband until this week. I guess that's what happened to me . . . I didn't say anything."[83]

It is very difficult for most people to understand that in the conscious mind, denial can be so deep that facts are not just forgotten: they do not exist. I am quite sure that knowing that she tried to kill Earl, but having no recollection of doing it, terrifies Dorothy, and perhaps at the same time it is a relief to her. I suspect that when Dr. Weston examined her after her bail hearing and discovered how thoroughly during her marriage she learned the intricacies of denying the reality of her life, how practiced her conscious mind has become at suppressing what she does not want to know, and how severely Earl abused her—all that, combined with the reports from Earl, the EMS, and the police about her demeanour that January morning, he realized that her not being able to remember what happened was a more complex form of forgetting than that which some other people experience after such a traumatic event. O'Brien told me that it was because psychiatrists said that Dorothy was in a dissociative state that morning that he chose a defence of automatism.[84] Automatism is used infrequently as a defence, and it is risky and controversial, but it is not new in Canadian law.[85] When the EMS and the police testified about that morning, and as Dorothy listened to them and tried to put together the shocking fragments of what had happened, it was quite apparent that she had no vision of the whole event in which to place them. When Earl related his account of what Dorothy said and what he said during and immediately after the shooting, Dorothy was extremely distraught. She knew that she could not necessarily trust what Earl said, but at the same time, she did not want to say that he was lying. She said more than once, "I can't call my husband a liar." During these discussions of the shooting, whether they were directed by O'Brien or Selinger, Dorothy's confusion and her general emotional distress added to my impression of her honesty, and her vulnerability. When she told about her first memories after she had shot Earl, how she saw his face, "ashen," and "wrinkled" and she stood in the middle of the garage and thought, "What have I done? I'm going to go to jail," she was not denying what she could see that she had done in those repressed moments of "cool" and "detached" rebellion and self-protection—in an act so terrible she cannot remember how she did it or even how she could have thought to do it.

Dorothy's inability to remember what happened that morning makes some of her story a mystery still. I am sure that this was a concern for the jury and the reason that they found Arboleda-Flores' psychiatric evidence more acceptable than that of the other two psychiatrists. I agree with O'Brien and his two psychiatric experts that Dorothy's hair appointment in the morning, and her arrangements to have dinner with her friend that evening make it very unlikely that she was also planning to shoot her husband. It is possible, as the psychiatrists testified, that the onset of her automatism was Earl's confirmation that he was proceeding with completing their divorce. Dorothy's telling about feeling forlorn, and alone, and sad was very convincing. But apart from the fact that suddenly attacking Earl by shooting him was extraordinary behaviour for Dorothy, how did she get the gun into her hand? I agree with Jerry Selinger that there was not time for her to walk to her bedroom, open the dresser drawer, unzip the black purse, remove the gun, and get back to the kitchen while Earl put on his coat, which was on the back of his chair, and walked the few feet to the door of the garage—if that is what Earl did. It is possible, I suppose, that something Earl said when he phoned to tell Dorothy that he would be at her home shortly, caused a "dissociative state" to begin to take hold then, and that she put the gun in a cupboard in the utility room, which is between the kitchen and the garage, or on her person, before he arrived. When she told, during her testimony, about doing something in the utility room as she waited for Earl, she seemed uncomfortable, and disturbed that she could not remember what she was doing there.

Dorothy could not remember a meeting with Earl in her home between Guy's wedding and Christmas, and Selinger taunted her with this, attempting to point out that her memory was not reliable before January 21, or that she was lying about the shooting. But Selinger never explained, and neither did Earl, the purpose of their meeting in December, and what happened when they were together that day. What caused Dorothy to forget that meeting, I wonder. She may have been drinking quite heavily then, but her drinking did not cause her to forget other things. She remembered another difficult meeting during that period, with the children, and the discussion then about her drinking. The memory of that meeting was unpleasant for her and she was reluctant to discuss it, but she did not forget it.

I have wondered if, as he left the kitchen that Saturday morning, Earl neglected to take with him the mementoes Dorothy had collected for him and she objected to this, and the two of them had a confrontation that frightened her. Earl said that he paid little attention to these things. He only glanced at the photographs, and he did not read any of the letters. Dorothy told, as well, of his lack of attention to the things she had gathered together for him. O'Brien implied, but he did not say, that the Christmas letters and the other things Dorothy had collected may not have dropped from Earl's hands onto the garage floor when he fell, suggesting that they remained in the kitchen where the police photographed them later.

A subject that arises repeatedly, when I have discussed that day with others, is the gun. (People do not know, or they forget, that Dorothy had had her father's shotgun and ammunition for it in her house for years.) Some people believe, and they cannot be convinced otherwise, that Dorothy deliberately smuggled the gun into Canada. I believe that as she said, she brought it into Canada unintentionally, and that it would not necessarily be difficult for her to do this. When I think about the gun, I remember Dorothy telling about it in her testimony. When she told about her friends advising her to get a gun, about her going to the gun store in Phoenix to buy it, and then her returning twice, at least, to practise shooting it, she seemed to be embarrassed, even guilty. It was apparent that buying a gun was something that caused her discomfort from the beginning. The most dramatic moment, when she told about getting the gun, was her exchange with the man in the store after she had practised using it. Dorothy suggested that she should unload it. She remembered that the salesman said to her, that if "someone is doing something to you," she would not have time to stop and load the gun.

But if Dorothy seemed uncomfortable and embarrassed when she told about buying the gun and bringing it to Canada and not taking it back to Phoenix, her manner was completely different when Selinger pressed her into a hypothetical discussion of how she got the gun into her hand on the day of the shooting. Selinger was very specific when he described the distance from the kitchen to the bedroom and then to the dresser, and how she would have to open the drawer and open the purse and take the gun back to the kitchen. But throughout this discussion Dorothy seemed to be absolutely innocent, completely unaware of any connection between what he was saying and her having used the gun. If this was, in fact, what she did that morning, Selinger's proposal to her about it had no effect on her whatsoever, except that she was as puzzled as he that she could have done this.

As I watched her and listened to her I was quite convinced that we would not find out, from Dorothy, about the gun. And Selinger did not ask Earl one question about how Dorothy may have got the gun in her hand.

If, in moments of extreme rage and fear, she named the "someone" the gun salesman in Phoenix mentioned to her, I am quite sure she could never have admitted it to anyone, including herself. But she kept the loaded gun in her dresser drawer in Calgary, in a place where it could—and did—provide her with protection from someone who was doing something to her, someone who had been doing something to her since she was fifteen years old.

# Meeting

They were pretty girls, easy-limbed and pleased with
themselves; anything could have been anticipated on their
behalf. They showed such promise; people wished them well
and were excited by the prospect of their having great,
perhaps unqualified joy in their lives . . . absolute happiness
devoid of responsibility, as only a woman would be able
to. . . . It was not really expected that either girl took this too
seriously. . . . It was not really expected that either girl would
have control over her own fate.

Robb Forman Dew, *Dale Loves Sophie to Death*[86]

In September 1997 I invited Dorothy to have lunch with me at a restaurant in downtown Calgary, a pleasant and comfortable place where I
thought that we could talk quietly. I told her on the telephone that I did
not want to press her for disturbing details, but that I wanted to tell her
why I was interested in her story, and give her an opportunity to ask me
questions if she had any. I told her that I wanted to talk with her partly as
a matter of courtesy. And this was true. But Dorothy has learned, obviously, that people who want to interview her might use any excuse to get
her attention and more information about her. She had declined my suggestion that we might meet at her home with a definite "No."

Because she had a choir practice at two o'clock, we arranged to meet
at eleven thirty. It was a glorious September day, warm, sunny, a deep blue
autumn sky. When I entered the restaurant, Dorothy was there, being

seated at a table she may have chosen near south windows—a bright, cheerful corner of the large room. She was talking to the waiter and she greeted me pleasantly—poised, slender, and attractive in a vivid print dress with an electric blue jacket and matching shoes. As we prepared to order, she chatted with the waiter, and I saw that her politely officious manner was a means of self-protection, of hiding her apprehension and nervousness. I thought how practiced she is at this almost unobtrusive, gracious control, not only of herself, but of the situation generally. As we began to talk, I realized that she had thought carefully about this meeting, that she was directing the conversation, telling me things she wanted me to know.

She told me that when she came home from the hospital she discovered that she had breast cancer, and that since the malignancy was removed she continues to see cancer specialists. When I commented on her loss of weight, she explained that it is a symptom of Graves disease, a disease of the thyroid gland, which causes hyperthyroidism. She said that other symptoms, which affected her teeth, bones, hair, and eyes, became apparent while she was in the mental hospital, but that the staff there dismissed them as part of her "psychiatric condition." Now, she is receiving proper treatment. She held out her hands to show me her artificial, bright red finger nails. They cover her own nails which, she said, are brittle and crumbling away. These new colored nails are quite elegant, but they change the character of Dorothy's hands, which I had noticed throughout the trial. This discussion of her health prompted her to tell me about her experience in the mental hospital. She said that she went to the hospital on her own.

"Literally?"

"Yes. I drove myself there."

Dorothy talked at some length about the five months during which she was locked behind the doors of the forensic unit at the provincial mental hospital. I was shocked by what she told me—that she received no treatment, that there is little compassion on the part of some of the staff for any of the patients, and especially that she did not know until an hour before she left that she had been released. But we agreed that because the most recent disposition of the Review Board is that she is still, officially, "subject to detention" there, now was not the time to discuss this publicly. I thought bitterly of this new, urgent demand for silence. She said, quite candidly, that it was her money that got her out of the hospital. O'Brien called seven doctors to testify before the Board on behalf of Dorothy at a cost of $50,000. Throughout this discussion she had no unkind words, none, about the other patients. She told me about her current therapists, now that she is out of the hospital. She has confidence in them; they understand her; she relies on them.

When she came home from the hospital a friend who had collected the newspaper clippings during the trial and after the verdict gave them to her to read.

"Why," she asked, "are people *interested*?"

"Because you are a woman, and a woman who was abused by her husband," I said. "Because of your money. Because of Earl's position in the corporate community."

She said then that Earl's corporate position is no longer as secure as it was, that corporations deal with such situations quietly, privately. What is important to Earl is that he is at the top, but promotions are no longer offered with the enthusiasm he has known in the past.

She wanted to tell me that she knows that shooting Earl was "wrong—people cannot do that," but that she still cannot remember what happened that morning, except that her conversation with Earl, before she shot him, "*was* a quiet conversation." She talked about Earl—that during the summer she had found some old "love letters" from him in which there were many examples of his "jealousy," and signs that there were negative and dangerous aspects in their relationship even then. She said that she can hardly believe, now, that she could not see this clearly at the time. She talked about Earl and Lynn, the new Mrs. Earl Joudrie, with bitter humour.

We reminisced briefly about our years in elementary school. I hoped to talk about ourselves, as women in our sixties now, and I remarked that during her testimony at the trial she had said almost nothing about her relationship with her mother. Dorothy seemed surprised. She said that her relationship with her mother was "good, a wonderful relationship." Then, without elaborating about their relationship, she told me about her mother as a young teacher and how she had met her father; that during the war, when her father was in the RCAF and working with the Americans in Iceland, her mother had taken in boarders; that after the war her father had attended the University of Oregon to get his Ph.D. Could she not separate her mother and her father? Did she not want to discuss her mother? I couldn't tell. I said that her father must have been away from home for some time. "No," she said, "He was not away very much."

I tried again to encourage a discussion of herself and women. I said that while I did not want to write a feminist tirade, I did want to write about women of our age, and women's position in society. Dorothy picked up the word "feminist." She said, vehemently, "I really hate all that stuff." Then she said, I think because she believed it was contradictory to what feminists would think, "Women abuse men. They do." I agreed that this can happen, but I reminded her that in a physical confrontation the relative size of a man and a woman places the woman at a serious disadvantage and in danger, as she knows. She agreed.

"But it's a power struggle," she said.

"Yes," I said. "Yes it is."

I knew that if I continued this discussion I would betray my proposal of a pleasant conversation. I did not want to disturb the insights she may be developing in her psychotherapy now. Also, it would take me too long to explain carefully, and without inciting an argument, my concerns that men still have more power than women in our society, my concerns about women of our age, about women who are abused, about women in Dorothy's position. And in any case, it seemed to me that Dorothy did not want such a discussion. Perhaps she is not ready for it. Perhaps she will never be ready. I wondered then, and I have been haunted since by the possibility of this: that while Dorothy is being encouraged to see that she did not cause Earl to abuse her, and, in fact, that his violent abuse of her was "abnormal," she is also being helped, perhaps very subtly, and not with malicious intent, to see herself and her actions as having been abnormal as well—her long and complex complicity in a power struggle with Earl, and her acting, finally, to end it. Without knowing what really happened that January morning in 1995, and in the light of more than forty years of Earl's physical and emotional abuse of her, if she was frightened and believed she was in danger, I'm not convinced that her actions were "abnormal."

I was quiet for a few moments, wondering how to proceed. Dorothy changed the subject. She talked about having begun to write a book in which she would tell her story. I was delighted to hear this, and said so. I encouraged her. She asked me what a person needs most to write a book and to get it published. I hesitated, not being an expert on this subject, and then I said that possibly what one needs most is endurance. We laughed.

Dorothy told me that she came to this restaurant during the trial and a waiter spoke to her quietly, saying, "We want you to know that we support you." For that reason, she was glad to come here again. She told me that she has, still, "many good, faithful friends," and that during her months in the hospital she had 143 visits. Her friends brought her gifts of food, soap, hand cream. She received hundreds of letters. Now people phone her asking for advice. She told me about one of the patients who had been released after so many years of confinement that he was almost incapable of surviving in a society he could barely recognize.

As we got up to leave the restaurant, I said that I was grateful to her for agreeing to talk with me. She said that she was relieved, that she had been nervous about our meeting, despite Noel O'Brien's having told her that he thought that I would be sympathetic.

Both of us basked in the sun and warmth as we walked along Eighth Avenue, back to our cars. We were preoccupied now with a rather superficial conversation, and our desire to part gracefully, and as I turned to speak to her, I realized that Dorothy is taller than I. I remember her being slightly taller than average when we were children, but during the trial she appeared to be shorter somehow, diminished. Now, as we walked together side by side, it seemed to me that she has regained her stature physically. Her setting off directly from our lunch to attend a choir practice is typical of her physical and emotional energy, and her determination to resume an active social life despite her sensitivity to people's attitudes about her and the legal limitations on her activities. At the corner we parted pleasantly, but without ceremony, and said that we would keep in touch with each other.

# Unit 3-1

"The people there are just forgotten."
Dorothy Joudrie[87]

$A$s I sit here at my work table, I have a vista, across the upstairs hall, through the master bedroom, and out its window into the back garden. This extraordinary late fall, brilliant with sun and colours, has been more beautiful than any other I can remember. Two weeks ago, in late October, the bright gold leaves on the birch tree dominated the garden. Now, most of those leaves are gone. The ornamental crab apples are frozen and drab, and the intense red of the mountain ash berries provides the last colour. In the mornings the lawn and the dark bare branches of the trees are streaked with frost. Signs of winter have begun. A robin who broke his wing when he flew into our window about a month ago sits most days in the mountain ash that grows through our deck. We worried about him at first, because soon after his accident his friends took off for the south, leaving him behind. The wildlife people tell us that he can survive the Calgary winter, and that some robins stay, but they suggested that we put out suet and worms and a special cat food for him. We haven't seen him eating these delicacies, but he still perches high in the tree, fluffing out his feathers for warmth, and he seems to be watching us as we sit at the kitchen table and move about in the house. His wing has mended, but not properly. It does not fit neatly against his body. Occasionally he makes successful forays to other trees in the garden, but obviously he knew that he could not fly thousands of miles. Three bluejays are there this morning, teasing him, and showing off. Their cheekiness pleases me, and their hoarse, sharp announcement of their presence draws me to the window to watch them. I like having them there. I love their colour. But I'm protective of the robin. I wonder what the robin will do when the waxwings arrive and settle together in their dozens for a feast of berries. About once a week three or four magpies come and threaten the robin. I rush out and try to shoo them away. They ignore me, or talk back to me, and sometimes they seem to think they threaten me, as well.

———————

In mid-October, when I realized that a year had passed since Dorothy had been allowed to leave the Provincial Mental Hospital in Edmonton, I wondered why I was putting off visiting the hospital—something I was determined, but reluctant, to do. I had wanted to visit Dorothy while she was in the hospital, but she did not encourage me to do that. She did not say so, but I realized that anyone who wanted to interview her there might exacerbate her vulnerable position in her pending appeal of the decision of the Board of Review. Perhaps the reason for my reluctance now was partly that I do not know what Dorothy's relationship is with the clinical director of forensic psychiatry at the hospital, Dr. John Brooks. I have no doubt at all about the relief she must have experienced when she knew that she could go home, but because the Board decided at her most recent hearing in May 1997 that she is still subject, at their discretion, to detention at the hospital, even though at that time she had lived at home for seven months, I know that her relief has been less than perfect. The Board's disposition in May included eight conditions on her behaviour. I was frustrated by the final "whereas" clause: "And Whereas the Alberta Review Board is not of the opinion that Dorothy Day Joudrie is not a significant threat to the safety of the public."[88] It would seem that since they had allowed her to live away from the hospital, they must believe that she is not a "significant threat" to the public. But this was not the case apparently. If I were Dorothy, I would have wanted a clarification of the grammar, the double negative, in this statement. I am sure that those people who received copies of the disposition, including Dorothy and Noel O'Brien, and the various journalists who reported it, read that statement, as I did, more than once.

When I asked Dr. Brooks, about three weeks ago, if I could visit the hospital, I was concerned about Dorothy's sensitive position now. Thus,

I told him that I did not want to discuss Dorothy, specifically, or the Board's disposition with respect to her. I said only that because I am writing about her and her trial, I would like to see for myself where she was confined for five months. And he agreed to let me do this. I'm sure he knew that, in fact, I would like to discuss Dorothy and the Review Board, but he accepted, without comment, my offer to refrain from doing so. It is possible that he would have welcomed such a discussion, and perhaps even an opportunity to defend Review Boards. But the subject never came up, because he, a practising psychiatrist after all, allowed me to ask the questions, to direct the conversation. When Dorothy was still in the hospital, Dr. Brooks told a reporter from the *Calgary Herald*, "Our job is to get people better and make sure they're safe to be released. There is no element of punishment. We are not a limb of the department of justice."[89] I wanted to challenge that statement, but I did not.

My husband went with me to Edmonton, to keep me company on the drive—actually to help me if I needed him, and to suffer through what he thinks is my bad driving. But he read and slept part of the way, so perhaps my driving skills are not quite so bad as he says. We arrived early, of course, for my three o'clock appointment with Dr. Brooks. I parked in the visitor's parking lot outside the front door of the Forensic Pavilion, and as we sat together in the car we were facing the small staff parking space, across the narrow road. The tamarack trees there were dark gold, and shedding their needles. The ground was covered with needles, which were slippery as I walked on them later. A red squirrel played in the tree in front of our car, running up and down the trunk, aware, it seemed to us, that he was being admired.

This natural beauty diverted our attention from the three staff cottages on our right, which must have been built in the early 1920s. They have a strange, dated and shabby gentility now, in their mild art deco style, but they were probably quite respectable then, when they would have been on the edge of the hospital property, facing away from it. When we arrived, I drove around the grounds, a quarter section of land in northeast Edmonton, on which there are forty-four buildings, including sixteen staff residences. I wanted to see one of the older buildings, which was, and still is known, Dr. Brooks told me, as "Number Five Building."

I worked in that building, as a ward aide, during the summer of 1953, just before I turned eighteen. I had been accepted into the B.Sc. nursing program at the University of Alberta, and I thought I wanted to be a psychiatric nurse. I wonder now how I was able to endure the job. It was a horrifying experience. I knew nothing at all about mental illnesses, and I was left alone, day after day, with groups of women, some of whom were very ill, to feed them, bathe them, supervise them.

On ward 5-C, where I worked, there were several separate areas. There was an infirmary for elderly women who were senile, women who were physically ill, and others who were being treated with insulin shock therapy. In another area, there were women who spent their days idly in a "day room," a few of whom washed and waxed and polished endlessly the battleship linoleum. These "day room ladies" ate their meals locked in a "dining room." The noise of their shouting to each other and to themselves was deafening. Women who were too disturbed—or too healthy—to take part in the noisy fray sat silently, picking at the unappetizing food, trying not to attract attention to themselves. These "day room ladies" slept in a dormitory of rows of beds placed not more than three feet apart. In one large room, which was called "the veranda" and furnished only with wooden benches pushed against the outer wall, about twelve women stood or paced back and forth all day. Occasionally a woman would stand on a bench to deliver a loud, deluded tirade to the other "veranda ladies," who paid no attention. One or two women huddled in the corner or lay on the cold cement floor. These "veranda ladies" wore no clothes at all. There were not enough staff to take them individually to the bathroom or to be bathed. The same water from a hose that the staff used to wash the walls and the floors three times a day, washed them. This means of "bathing" these women was not officially acceptable, but it was overlooked because of the staff shortage. There was one registered nurse on the ward and the rest of the staff were ward aides, like me, who had no training at all, none.

Other women, "the violent ladies," lived in "side rooms," small cell-like rooms, sometimes furnished with a bed or a mattress, but more often bare. They, like the "veranda ladies," were given their meals in three battered, tin bowls—one for the main course, one for dessert, and one for tea, piled on top of each other, topped with two slices of bread, and slipped quickly inside the door which was unlocked for this moment. About an hour later, the ward aide unlocked the doors of the side rooms, one at a time, to pour on the floor a pail full of hot water and creosote, and squeegee out with the grey-brown liquid, the uneaten food, the urine and feces. There were benches in the dark corridor between the side rooms. Twice a week when we arrived at seven o'clock, the benches would be occupied by women from other wards, who sat in terrified silence waiting for at least three hours for their electric shock treatment at ten o'clock—after the doctor had enjoyed his morning coffee and a smoke. This doctor seemed to appear and disappear without notice. The other patients ignored him. He was not someone with whom they wanted to talk. The superintendent of the hospital, when he appeared two or three times during my hours of duty that summer, was accompanied every step of the way to the door of a patient who for some mysterious reason had his private attention. The charge nurse was there to protect him from "day room ladies" desperate to ask him the one important question on their minds. When could they go home?

I was afraid of the violent patients in the side rooms, but as often as I could, I worked in that corridor because being there I was also allowed to help with the shock treatments. The patients who received these treatments were more receptive of comfort and support, more lucid and willing to talk about themselves, or just take part in a conversation. I thought, or imagined, that I saw improvement in the mental state of some of these women as the weeks went by. The treatment itself upset me, but I concealed my reaction and concentrated on trying to allay the fears of the patients. This was years before I knew about the dangers of electro-shock convulsive therapy.

There were no tranquilizing drugs, as we know them now, in those days. Some patients were given a sedative called paraldehyde to drink. It had a sweet, sickening odour which seemed to cling to them for hours after they had taken it, and as we entered the building each morning, the smell of paraldehyde, urine, and cooked cabbage was suffocating. The walls seemed to breathe that collection of odours, which I have never forgotten. And I have never forgotten some of the patients—even their names. My experience that summer served me well. I learned that I could never be a nurse: I had neither the physical nor emotional stamina to cope with the day-to-day care, and the sudden crises integral to nursing, and especially psychiatric nursing. I continued to want to work with people who are troubled, as those people were, and I did, for several years, but not in an institution that seemed to me to belong in the Dark Ages.

As my husband and I drove past Number Five Building that afternoon, I saw that it had been painted bright yellow, the heavy metal mesh was gone from the windows, which are clean and shiny, and the building seemed smaller than I remembered. Dr. Brooks told me later that it is empty now. He said that in the 1970s, when he first came from Newfoundland to work at this hospital, he, also, worked on ward 5-C. I told him that I had night-mares for twenty years about my experiences in that building, but I did not tell him that my worst nightmares were variations on the theme that I had lost my keys and knew that I could not get out, that I would never get out. I can't remember now if I actually said to him that I think Number Five Building should be bulldozed into the ground.

I am sure that Dorothy was never able to look objectively at even the outside of the Helen Hunley Forensic Unit. Naming the building, when it was opened in 1982, for one of Alberta's former lieutenant-governors, was a rather dubious honour, it seems to me, especially in light of the weighty and questionable responsibility lieutenant-governors took with respect to the people who were confined there. Before amendments to the Criminal Code, in 1993, lieutenant-governors did not have to give reasons for deci-sions they made about persons held under what were called then, lieu-tenant-governor's warrants. There was no requirement for records of the proceedings that determined these decisions, nor was there provision for hearings in which persons found not guilty on account of insanity could make submissions. Boards of Review have replaced lieutenant-governor's warrants, and lieutenant-governors are no longer part of the disposition process. Boards of Review are required to give reasons, keep records, and allow appeals of their proceedings. But like lieutenant-governor's warrants before them, they function autonomously.[90]

The outer appearance of this dark red brick structure, set in among the shrubs, poplars, and conifers typical of that region of Alberta, is decep-tively benign. As my husband and I looked at it closely, we agreed that it is a bunker-style design, and that there are probably low ceilings in its interior, the set-in windows not allowing much light to enter. We were correct in assuming this.

A brochure[91] tells about the pavilion, which "provides quality care to individuals who have come into conflict with the law and may be suffer-ing from a mental disorder." It says that the building was designed, archi-tecturally, as a "secure hospital," and each of its seven units is in a "pod design for maximum observation." There are "secure" courtyards, occupa-tional therapy facilities, school classrooms, a gymnasium, an auditorium, a chapel, exercise rooms, a swimming pool, a beauty parlor, and full clin-ical laboratory facilities. There is a Remand Unit, for court-ordered psy-chiatric assessments to determine whether a person is unfit to stand trial, or not criminally responsible (NCR); an Intensive Care Unit, for acutely psychotic or disturbed psychiatric patients; a unit that provides assessment and treatment for sex offenders; a unit for young offenders; and the Rehabilitation Program, Unit 3-1, where Dorothy was, and the unit I was visiting. I saw and heard no signs of the other units. Dorothy must have been in another unit, probably the Remand Unit, during the period of her assessment. Dr. Brooks offered no information about her assessment. The brochure says that Unit 3-1 provides "ongoing psychiatric care to patients who are no longer in the acute phase of their illness, with the goal being their safe reintegration into the community." It is a "minimum security unit." Almost all of the patients on this unit are of NCR status. The brochure adds that because NCR patients come under the jurisdiction of the Board of Review, "both patients and staff must work within the boundaries placed on the patients' freedoms by the Board of Review. Because of this, NCR patients may remain in hospital for an indeterminate period of time." Thus, the power of the Board of Review is clear.

Along with the "congenial, therapeutic environment," the design of the building, according to the brochure, "allows for the supervision of forensic patients and monitoring of visitors and other users of the facility." This is the function of a forensic psychiatric assessment and treatment centre. But most people who heard or read about her jury's verdict, and even the jury, did not realize, I am quite sure, that Dorothy Joudrie would be confined in a place such as this, even for a two- to six-week assessment. As Dorothy knows now, many people thought that because she had not been sentenced to prison, she had been given a full acquittal, and that she was free. When, or if they realized that she must be admitted to a forensic unit in a mental hospital for an assessment, and then that she was confined in the hospital for an indefinite period of time, well, whatever they might imagine about mental hospitals, she was not in jail. Dorothy told me that she did not read the press reports during and immediately after the trial. So she did not see, then, at least, Don Braid's column in the *Calgary Herald* the day after the verdict was announced. It was Braid who expressed his outrage during the trial that Earl was being treated by some as if he were a criminal, and not the victim of a crime. The reaction to what Braid said caused him to rethink his opinion, apparently. He redeemed himself somewhat in his column after the verdict. He quoted "one local defence lawyer" who, referring to Dorothy's forthcoming disposition by the Alberta Board of Review by its former term, said, "I wouldn't wish a lieutenant-governor's warrant on my worst enemy."[92]

As I went into the security office, just inside the main door of the Forensic Pavilion where Dr. Brooks had said he would meet me, I tried to imagine Dorothy's arrival there. I remembered her telling me that she arrived at the hospital alone. Straight ahead of me was a glassed-in area, with closed, locked doors beside it, closing off passage to and from Unit 3-1. Uniformed security staff are responsible for "peripheral security." They are able to unlock the doors from a panel inside the office, which is less alarming for visitors or newcomers than waiting for a staff member to fumble through the handful of keys we used to wear strapped to the belts of our uniforms. But this barricade was like the entrance to a prison. Through a small circular opening in the glass, I told one of the security guards that I had an appointment with Dr. Brooks, and he asked me to give him my purse and present some photo I.D. I had left my purse in the car, so I went outside to get my driver's licence. After I returned, Dr. Brooks' secretary came through the locked doors, with the smooth assistance of the security guards, to tell me that Dr. Brooks had been detained, and that he would be with me shortly.

I sat on one of the sturdy chairs arranged in rows in shallow alcoves on both sides of the entry. The chairs are upholstered in the department store decorator colours that prevail throughout this unit—oatmeal, navy, pale rust. I wondered how quickly Dorothy, with her practiced eye, reacted to the decor—an aspect of the "congenial" atmosphere in this part of the hospital. A group of three patients, whom we had seen raking leaves, came into the building, and after the doors were unlocked, allowing them to enter the unit, a female security guard checked them, thoroughly, with a metal detector. Their conversation with all of the security staff was pleasant, and there was laughter as they talked casually. The patients were middle-aged men, but they acted like modest, well-behaved children—and they were treated like children.

I waited only a few minutes. Dr. Brooks, a soft-spoken, thin, small-boned man, with greying hair, appeared to be tired and rather pale, but his eyes were bright and animated, and his manner was courteous, pleasant, unobtrusively alert. His limp handshake bothered me, but perhaps he was taken off guard when I offered my hand as I introduced myself. Stronger men than he have shaken my hand in a similar manner, and I've often wondered if they shake hands like this with other men. I was not checked with the metal detector, but Dr. Brooks gave me an identification tag to wear. He listened carefully as I spoke and asked questions.

He took me in to what appeared to be a staff room and introduced me to a young woman, Bev, who is the program manager on Unit 3-1, and who he said would accompany us as we walked through the unit. Both of them described the various areas to me and they complemented each other's descriptions as we talked. They explained that the staff on this unit wear their own clothes, not uniforms. I saw the swimming pool, which was deserted; the small chapel, also deserted, and wondered if Dorothy ever attended services there; and the dining room, which I said seemed very small, and they told me that there are two sittings at meals. I saw the lounge, which is divided into two areas—smoking and no smoking—and the small alcoves, one in each area, in each of which there is a caged budgie bird, and where a patient can sit alone if he or she chooses. A man sat in one of these alcoves, resting his elbows on his knees, his head bowed, looking desolate. It struck me that he was only a few feet away from the other patients, and that being "alone" in this open unit was probably impossible. Seeing this man prompted me to ask if the patients are heavily medicated. Bev said that they are, but added that they are being treated with a view to eventual discharge. I said that some of these patients must have been here a long time. She agreed. "How long?" I asked. She looked at Dr. Brooks, the ceiling, sighed, and said, "Twenty years?"

I noticed a telephone on a table near the lounge, and I asked if patients were allowed to use the phone whenever they wished. Both of my chaperones said "Yes." "Are the calls monitored?" I asked. Only when a patient is bothering their family or someone else with repeated calls, in which case their calls are limited, they said. I wondered if it was from this phone that Dorothy called me, and I thought how little privacy anyone had when they used this telephone.

I saw the little kitchen area where patients can make snacks, and where someone had recently made coffee, which left a pleasant aroma. Dr. Brooks said that some of the patients walk out to a supermarket nearby to buy food which they prepare here for themselves. I wondered how many patients have this privilege. My observations as we walked among them suggested that they are few.

By this time, what seemed most apparent to me was that the whole day area, which was clean, if not lavishly furnished—I can't remember noticing any books or magazines, but there may have been some—seemed small, even claustrophobic. Although it was fairly large in square feet, because of the various areas designed for different functions, the patients seemed to be crowded together. If more than one or two wanted to watch TV, for example, they needed to sit side by side. There was no space that was entirely shut off from the rest. Then I realized what a "pod" meant. For the first time, I noticed the control desk, or what, in a general hospital, would be called the nursing station. Like the security office, it was enclosed behind plexiglass, and from it, the staff, who were gathered there, could see everything.

The empty bedroom Bev and Dr. Brooks showed me, when I asked to see one, was almost the size of many children's bedrooms in middle-class homes, but it seemed small, and stark, and empty. It had in it a single bed, a wardrobe, and a hospital-style bedside table. The window was low enough that a person could see outside while they were lying in bed, and the view was the trees and shrubs surrounding the building—a not unpleasant view. There were no bars or heavy wire mesh on the windows. Dr. Brooks said that patients could bring things from home to make their bedrooms more attractive and personal. I asked if patients could lock their doors when they were in the bedrooms. He said no, the only lock was from the outside, and that was used rarely. I thought of how Dorothy must have felt when she went to bed at night, among her fellow patients, all of whom were diagnosed as suffering from a mental disorder, and had committed serious crimes, and one of whom had assaulted Dorothy and broken her nose.

There were six or eight patients in the lounge while we were there, but they were not reading, or doing anything purposeful, or even watching the coloured television. Perhaps they were diverted by us, and especially by the presence of Dr. Brooks. Most of these patients seemed to me to be resigned to their existence here. I wondered how quickly this happens. They must reach a point when they realize that there is no alternative but to succumb to their helplessness, that they do not know how long they will be here, and this must have been part of what frightened Dorothy. Whatever emotional problems she had then, she was not mad. But she was surrounded—literally locked in—with a kind of madness that was not unlike that with which she had lived for years: the unpredictable authority and power of her husband's behaviour. Now, I suspect, from what she has told me, she saw a similar kind of madness, not in the other patients, for whom she seemed to have a strong sense of compassion, but in some members of the judicial and medical systems; in the manner in which she was treated, and not treated, by some members of the staff in this forensic unit; in what seemed to be the arbitrary authority of the Provincial Review Board. I thought of her saying to me, on the telephone, "This is the scariest place I have ever been,"[93] and I know that she told others the same thing. I thought of my reaction after her verdict, which was that I would rather go to jail than be committed to a mental hospital for an indefinite period of time.

Bev went with the patients to a meeting, and Dr. Brooks and I continued to talk for a few minutes. It was a strange, desultory conversation: about the forensic unit; the terms sane and insane automatism; his choosing to work in forensic psychiatry; my having worked, untrained and innocent, at this hospital many years ago; the similarities and differences between this facility and the forensic units in Calgary hospitals where Dr. Arboleda-Flores and Dr. Weston work. Dr. Brooks seemed relaxed, and I was comfortable talking with him, but it was what we did not say that was on my mind, and perhaps on his as well. I am quite sure that he sensed my emotional reaction to this place, and that my trying to imagine what being here for five months—or twenty years—must have been like for Dorothy and the other patients made me feel weak. Quite soon, I thanked him for allowing me to visit, to see this unit. We returned to the security office where I took off my identification tag. The locked doors were opened for us. I shook Dr. Brooks' hand again, and left.

I opened the outer doors with relief, anxious to get away. We drove into the sunny countryside, and within minutes we were in busy, traffic-filled streets, among ordinary people who were driving home to ordinary family dinners. We stopped at a small restaurant on the South Side, and every detail of our surroundings seemed exaggerated to me: the linen tablecloths; the stylish cutlery; the good, colourful paintings on the walls; the music; the lively conversation around us; the perfectly cooked pasta, giant shrimps, tomatoes, spinach, basil. I turned to look through the window beside me and saw that it was dark now. I thought of Dorothy and the other patients eating their suppers in that little dining room. I thought of how many times in her life Dorothy has stood alone, at the extreme edge of the real world.

# As the Earth Tips Slowly toward the Sun

Dorothy stood up and found she was in her stocking feet.
For the Silver Shoes had fallen off in her flight through the
air, and were lost for ever.
          L. Frank Baum, *The Wizard of Oz*[94]

I woke up just after five o'clock this morning. I was glad to be awake early, and I got out of bed quietly, shutting the bedroom door, hoping that my husband would not wake up and that I could sit alone for a while at the kitchen table. The steam rising now from my cup of hot, strong coffee, in the cool kitchen, reminds me of how I take for granted the luxuries of my daily existence, my ordinary life.

As I sit here at the table—a large, sturdy, pine table we found in Quebec—I think of the woman who, more than a hundred years ago, tightened her meat grinder against one end of it, making grooves in the soft wood that have become more visible with time and use during the more than thirty years it has been ours. She was up this early every day, beginning her domestic chores, doing everything from scratch, necessary labour we can hardly imagine today.

This table is the centre of our home, where our family gathers for meals and conversation. Individually, we all have used it for marking students' papers, writing letters, doing homework, working at serious and exciting summer projects. We also have sat here together for difficult, sometimes tearful discussions. I put my sewing machine on this table in the days when I made my clothes, and I still do, when I struggle reluctantly to alter trousers or jeans. We have dozens of photographs of our family and friends sitting here at meals. My husband enjoys taking these pictures and we complain, but we all love looking at this recorded history of our lives. We never cover the table with a cloth; we use place mats so that we can see and touch the gold wood. What we put on the table marks the months of the years: blossoms from the fruit trees, lilacs, and early blue bachelor buttons in May and June, then the cosmos, sweet peas, daisies, marigolds, blur the months from July until mid-September, when autumn leaves begin to be part of the gathered colours. Lighted candles, fruit, and vegetables—apples, oranges, persimmons, a squash, an imperial aubergine—mark the dark months, and holly and evergreen boughs, Christmas. This morning, gold kumquats on a white plate keep my attention away from the window and the still dark January morning. In a few minutes the sky will show signs of a new day, of light. For reasons I have never understood, the dark months of November and December have always been difficult for me. Christmas seems to compound the strange melancholy that grips me despite the promise of the winter solstice. The release begins now, in late January, when I exaggerate the slight change day by day as the earth tips slowly toward the sun.

From what I have learned about Dorothy Joudrie, I know that Christmas for her has always been an important, if not a perfectly happy time. But she worked hard to make it happy, as wives and mothers are expected to do. Of all of mothers' duties, I think Christmas is one of the most difficult. It is our job to create peace, contentment, pleasure, love, and affection within our families. The burden of this unrealistic responsibility is overwhelming for many women. How did Dorothy manage this all those years? How did she hold inside herself, silently, the pain and loneliness, and worse, the fear she must have felt?

———————

Dorothy was granted an absolute discharge from the jurisdiction of the Alberta Board of Review on October 20, 1998. The Board decided that after a detention of five months in the Helen Hunley Forensic Unit at the Provincial Mental Hospital in Edmonton in 1996, and after having lived during the past two years in her own home but at the same time subject, at the Board's discretion, to further detention in the hospital, Dorothy is no longer a "significant threat" to the safety of others.

The announcement caused a flurry of media attention: newspaper stories of her discharge, a television interview with Hana Gartner on

CBC's *The Magazine*, a lead editorial in *The Globe and Mail*. The news stories told about Dorothy's relief, her new freedom, her continuing therapy, and her outspoken but at the same time restrained criticisms of the Helen Hunley Forensic Unit, and the long, frightening months of her "incarceration," as she calls it, "in that place."[95] Most of the news stories were factual and reasonable, expressing an attitude that seemed enlightened compared to some of the stories we had read during and after the trial. The editorials and some of the letters to editors were different. Many of these people continue to believe that the defence of automatism was a hoax. The same people believe that Earl's abuse of Dorothy ended almost twenty years before she shot him. Moralists proclaimed again that all people who commit crimes must be made to take responsibility for their actions. I looked for some thoughtful consideration of what society will do with a new approach to problems of spousal abuse, the Battered Woman's Syndrome, the increasing authority of psychiatric experts in the courtroom, the federal Self-Defence Review. But I found none. I thought that Dorothy would be upset by some of the publicity. I was. But she seems not to be, perhaps partly because many people have gone out of their way to write to her or speak to her, telling her that they support her, that they are glad that she is free now, and that they wish her well.

---

I chose to write about Dorothy Joudrie partly because she represents what could have happened to me, and does happen to other women in a society that too often still does not listen to women, or even acknowledge that what we say is worth hearing, especially when we challenge traditional authority. The reaction to Dorothy Joudrie's experience is evidence of this.

Dorothy was on trial for attempting to murder her husband. In the beginning there was justification for the fact that she was the focus of attention. At the time of her trial it was she who appeared daily in the news photographs as she entered or left the court house. But as the trial progressed, and when, finally, we knew about the extent of Earl Joudrie's physical and emotional abuse of her for almost forty years, the reaction was shock, but also restraint, and on the part of some, disbelief. Elizabeth Griffiths broke through this guarded reaction very dramatically when she told of witnessing Earl's brutal abuse of Dorothy in Toronto. But even Elizabeth Griffiths' credible testimony seemed to fade as the world around Dorothy remembered particular aspects of Earl's testimony, and the public pronouncements of both women and men who are threatened by the ugly facts of spousal abuse, and by changes in traditional values, institutions and the law. They were asking the same kinds of questions they had asked at the time of the shooting: "Who does Dorothy Joudrie think she is?" "Look how the wealth and privilege provided for her by the husband she almost killed got her off?" "What is wrong with *her*?"

For the most part, it is people who did not attend the trial who ask these questions. They did not hear the testimony of three psychiatrists—two for the defence, one for the Crown. They did not hear the testimony of the police, Carolyn Joudrie, Elizabeth Griffiths, and both Earl and Dorothy. They did not see the jury as they watched and listened to the judge, the lawyers, the witnesses, Earl and Dorothy, and asked for help to define "not criminally responsible," which was, in the end, their verdict. The people who ask these questions do not know, or seem to care, that Earl's mental and emotional abuse continued up to and during Dorothy's trial. Mental and emotional abuse is terrible when it is combined with threats, throwing furniture, punching holes in walls, knocking down doors, and especially when it is exerted by the same man who slammed her against walls, punched her in the face causing black eyes and a broken nose, pushed her over furniture, dragged her by the hair, and kicked her until she could not walk. When Dorothy talked with me about the way she and other patients were treated in the mental hospital, she said, speaking from experience, "Mental and emotional abuse is the worst."

Dorothy's trust in Noel O'Brien and her reliance on his good judgement may have had its foundation in the perspicacity he demonstrated during the first few minutes he talked with her after her arrest on the day of the shooting. He asked her outright, and he was the first person to do so, if she had been abused by Earl.[96] Throughout the trial O'Brien never allowed the jury to forget the importance not only of the effects on Dorothy of Earl's abuse, but the fact of it.

———————

When Dorothy and I met to talk on the morning of January 4, 1999, at her suggestion, she came to my house. I had baked bran muffins before she arrived, and we sat at my kitchen table with the muffins and coffee. I wanted to sit in the living room, where the morning sun was bright and welcoming, but she said she was more comfortable in the kitchen.

She brought me a copy of her 1998 Christmas letter in which she tells about her discharge from the Alberta Hospital in October, her commitment to help others less fortunate than she to be assessed and treated properly when they are placed under the jurisdiction of the Board of Review, and about the births of her grandchildren. The letter is brief, hopeful, and realistic. With the letter are photographs of her son Colin, his wife, and their son, and a photo of Dorothy holding the child—a proud grandmother, and a sweet child, curious, looking straight into the camera. She was tearful for a moment when she told me that Guy and Carolyn, who live in Calgary, do not want to see her and do not invite her to visit them or their children, who were born during the past two years and whom she has never seen.

During the trial, someone told me that one of Dorothy's friends gave her a transcript of the CBC broadcast of my initial article about her. One of the reasons I wrote the article, the open letter to her, was that I remember her as a child. Several people have asked me if she remembers me. She did not recognize me or my name when I introduced myself to her at the trial. When she telephoned me from the mental hospital, in response to a letter I had written to her and said that she remembered me, that she knew who I was, I knew that she might be referring to her memory of me at her trial, or from my article. Now I asked her. She said that she is not sure, that she thinks she remembers me "vaguely," but that she cannot remember me at her house, with Ann, eating graham wafers and honey. This prompted a discussion of our collective memories of grades two and three at Queen Alexandra school in Edmonton. Dorothy had come to Queen Alex not too long before I did in March of the year we were in grade two. But by the time I arrived, Dorothy was settled, she belonged. I was an outsider, observing the others, hoping to be accepted by them. Dorothy, even then, was, or at least she gave the appearance of being, quite self-confident, a leader, a happy child. And I am sure that this is why I remember so vividly being invited to her house that afternoon. We talked briefly about Ann, Dorothy's "best friend," with whom I played occasionally, but we didn't dwell on these memories for long.

Still, since Dorothy's visit with me that morning I have thought more about both of us as children. What provided Dorothy with such self-possession, I wonder, and why was I so timid, so shy, until I was about twelve years old, and in fact, throughout much of my life. I know that my shyness and insecurity have been interpreted, more often than I like to think, as cool disdain, or arrogance.

I remember an incident when my husband and I visited my parents during the summer our older son was two years old. As my mother and I were preparing supper, we could hear my father talking quietly with his grandson in the garden. Mother and I stopped what we were doing to listen. Suddenly my son laughed delightedly at something my father said to him. "I remember your laughter when you were little sounding exactly like that," my mother said. I was quite unprepared to hear this. I did not want to spoil my mother's memory, but after a few moments I said, cautiously, that I don't recall myself laughing as a small child, or even being a particularly happy child. "Well, it's true," my mother said, "in some ways you were a sober little old woman right from the start." In some ways, I was. I think I was. But perhaps, sometimes at least, I was also a happier, more confident child—more like Dorothy seemed to me to be—than I remember now. Also, it is possible that Dorothy's energetic, apparently happy confidence was only the most visible part of her personality, and her way of coping, even then, with the insecurities and the fears every child knows.

When Dorothy and I talked this last time, I wanted to share some childhood memories with her, hoping that she would reciprocate. But I remembered her saying to someone, "I can't put my heart on a table for people to dissect." So I tried to restrain myself and concentrate on her current situation. We talked about the class prejudice that has prevailed throughout the public revelation of her private life. Dorothy talked easily about this, and told some amusing anecdotes about the "jealousy" that exists among people with money. We also talked about her drinking, the relative ease with which she managed her determination to stop, and the help she continues to get from Alcoholics Anonymous and from her therapist.

I have learned that while I can try to imagine the physical and emotional pain Dorothy has suffered, and how desperately she must have longed for relief, and peace, and safety, I cannot know the tragedy in her life. She would say, "But it wasn't all tragic." And having observed the intense and complex dynamics in the relationship between Dorothy and Earl, as I did at the trial, I would believe her. I asked her when she was here if she has begun to feel, consciously, some anger towards Earl. She hesitated for a moment, then she said, "This may seem strange to you, but I feel more angry at Lynn than I do at Earl. I still care for him."

Sometimes I think that those of us who have had good marriages—as good as marriages can be—are people for whom the romantic myth of a fairy-tale marriage was tested before we married. Like Dorothy, during the years I was at university the first time, I was in love with a young man I had known since we were children. Despite the fact that I suspected, but would not acknowledge, that he did not love me as I loved him, I think I would have married him, for most of the reasons that Dorothy married Earl. I did not marry him because he fell in love with someone else and she became his bride. The sense of loss I experienced consumed me. It was not months but years before I could even begin to feel angry at him, not just for the way he left me, but for the way he treated me throughout our relationship. Finally, I was free. I felt nothing for him—nothing at all. By the time I met my husband I still had many romantic expectations—I have told about them—but in some ways, my feet were on the ground.

Many women want to be cherished by a man, and I think that Dorothy wants this still, and that this is a perfectly reasonable desire in a woman. But first women need to respect and know themselves, and this is something women, especially women of our age, were rarely taught. Some of us learned how to do this, but it was painful, difficult, because it went against the grain of everything that was expected of us. I remember when my young man told me that no two women, and certainly no man and woman could ever have a relationship of such exquisite intimacy and trust and love as that which existed between the biblical David and Jonathan. I laughed, surprised that he could believe that men are superior to women, that men intrinsically possess good qualities women can never know. He was angry with me and quite unwilling to consider what I was saying to him. Fortunately, such a conversation probably rarely occurs between two young lovers these days. Most young women now look upon themselves and the men they love as equals, and their young men expect and want this. But some people, and certainly our society and its institutions, are lagging behind. And most of us who are older have not let go completely of the lessons we learned so well.

––––––––

Writing about Dorothy has made me aware that apart from our different economic positions in society, and the kind of men we married, there are other things we do not share. Nevertheless, Dorothy has become an important person in my life, and I realized when we talked recently that she will always be that. Do I dream about Dorothy? Yes. Always in my dreams we meet in a crowd of people. Usually, in the presence of the others, we are sitting next to each other, or just talking together. At some point in the dream, when we greet each other, or part, we take each other's hands. Dorothy's hands are strong and warm, and I feel that we are kindred spirits. I do not know what my dreams mean. Perhaps our joined hands represent the intimacy we do share in having grown up at the same time, and in the same society, a society whose expectations of women nearly destroyed Dorothy, and which are still affecting her now. Perhaps our clasped hands represent that inexplicable affirmation of self that women can give each other, and that in the years of thinking and writing about Dorothy she has given me.

Dorothy "made up," as she said, her fairy-tale marriage, but it was she, finally, who ended it. What is most sad and tragic about her fate is that she was left to act alone. Society generally, many of the people she knew, even her parents—reluctantly perhaps—when they were alive, allowed her to believe in her fairy tale, and finally, when she broke the law in a desperate act to protect herself, many of the same people criticized her, deserted her, wanted to punish her, or to mark her as a woman who was a threat to the safety of the rest of us. Few people said, publicly at least, that they saw Dorothy Joudrie as a reasonable person at the very end of her endurance. I found it ironic and sad at the time of Dorothy's discharge by the Board of Review that Earl was, apparently, consulted about his feelings of safety if she were free, and free to travel to Ontario, where he lives. I can't remember anyone asking Dorothy, at any time, if she felt safe, or if she feels safe now.

As we talked the other day, I was reminded again of the complexity of Dorothy's personality, of her strength, her courage. She is an optimist. While this characteristic has betrayed her in the past, it is also one of her most endearing qualities. She tempers her optimism with astute observations, which she relates and manages with humour and intelligence and determination—especially determination. Her generosity and compassion for others is not self-serving. If she enjoys again what some of us would consider the luxuries of her life, and her circle of friends, which includes important people in Canada, she is entitled to this comfort and pleasure.

Dorothy is not a feminist. And she knows, as some feminists, unfortunately, do not, that women are not right or good simply by the fact of their gender. Her life experience is teaching her, gradually, the importance of women's need to take control of their lives, to do everything possible to define themselves, to own themselves. Like some other women of her age,

Dorothy began to realize this when it was almost too late. If, as most of us are, she is still learning about herself, discovering the possibilities that are ahead for her, she is no longer completely lost in a fairy-tale existence she knows now was a lie.

# Notes

**Part One**
**Before the Trial**

1 Wendy Dudley and Gordon Jaremko, "Gulf Canada Chairman shot," *Calgary Herald,* January 22, 1995, A1, A2.

2 Brad Thompson, Calgary 7 News, in *Calgary Herald,* January 22, 1995, A1.

3 Daryl Slade, "Joudrie hearing set for June," *Calgary Herald,* February 1, 1995, B2.

4 Wendy Dudley and Gordon Jaremko, "Gulf Canada Chairman shot," *Calgary Herald,* January 22, 1995, A1, A2.

5 Helen Dolik and Vicki Barnett, "Accused 'had an ideal life,'" *Calgary Herald,* January 23, 1995, A1.

6 Ibid.

7 Tom Fennell with Carla Turner in Calgary, "High Society Shooting," *Maclean's,* February 6, 1995, pp. 44, 45.

8 Dolik and Barnett, *Calgary Herald,* January 23, 1995, A1.

9 Leif Sollid, "Oil Patch: Gulf Exec Back on Job," *The Calgary Sun,* May 4, 1995, News 4.

10 Fennell and Turner, *Maclean's,* February 6, 1995, pp. 44, 45.

11 Simone de Beauvoir, *The Second Sex.* New York: Alfred A. Knopf, 1957.

12 Betty Friedan, *The Feminine Mystique.* New York: Norton, 1963.

13 Sylvia Plath, "The Babysitters," *Collected Poems.* Edited with an Introduction by Ted Hughes. London: Faber and Faber, 1981. pp. 174, 175.

14 Adrienne Rich, *On Lies, Secrets, and Silence. Selected Prose 1966-1978.* New York: W.W. Norton & Company, 1979, p. 189.

15 Sylvia Plath, *The Bell Jar.* London: Faber and Faber, 1963, p. 74.

16 Daryl Slade, "Socialite's hearing adjourned," *Calgary Herald,* June 16, 1995, B6.

17 Angela Carter, *The Sadeian Woman: An Exercise in Cultural History.* New York: Pantheon, 1978, p. 5.

18 Cole Porter, "Miss Otis Regrets," *The Cole Porter Years.* Secaucus, NJ: Warner Brothers Inc., 1934, pp. 77-79.

19 Reynolds Price, *The Promise of Rest.* New York: Scribner, 1995, p. 330.

20  Michael Woloschuk, *Family Ties: The Real Story of the McCain Feud.* Toronto: Seal Books, 1996, pp. 210, 211.

21  Susan A. Ostrander, *Women of the Upper Class.* Philadelphia: Temple University Press, 1984, pp. 82, 83.

22  Evan S. Connell, *Mrs. Bridge.* San Francisco: North Point Press, 1959, p. 212.

23  Helen Dolik and Vicki Barnett, "Accused 'had an ideal life,'" *Calgary Herald,* January 23, 1995, A1.

24  Tom Fennell with Carla Turner in Calgary, "High Society Shooting," *Maclean's,* February 6, 1995, pp. 44, 45.

25  Christa Wolf, *Medea: A Modern Retelling.* Translated from the German by John Cullen. New York: PUBLISHED BY NAN A. TALESE, an imprint of Doubleday, a division of Bantam Doubleday Dell Publishing Group, Inc. 1998, p. 150.

26  Iona and Peter Opie, eds. *Children's Games with Things.* Oxford: Oxford University Press, 1997, p. 266.

27  Adrienne Rich, *On Lies, Secrets, and Silence: Selected Prose 1966-1978,* p. 190.

28  Carol Shields, *The Stone Diaries.* Toronto: Random House, 1993, p. 175.

29  Alice Munro, *Lives of Girls and Women.* Toronto: McGraw-Hill Ryerson Ltd., 1971, p. 67.

30  Dora (Isadora) Angela Duncan was born in San Francisco in 1877. She became known in America, Britain, major European cities, and Russia as a pioneer of modern dance. Wearing unusual tunics, scarves, and shawls, she danced barefoot to classical music and her free style influenced the famous ballet dancers Diaghilev and Mikhail Fokine, among others. She made her life exciting and dramatic, but it was also tragic. She was married three times; her two children drowned in a car accident; and she died in 1927 in Nice, when the long tassles of the red shawl she wore as she rode in a car caught in the wheels and caused the shawl to strangle her. Millicent Dillon, *After Egypt: Isadora Duncan & Mary Cassatt.* New York: A William Abrahams Book, Dutton, 1990.

31  Dorothy Joudrie's mother suggested that she could cancel her wedding. See pp. 203, 204.

32  Iona and Peter Opie, eds. *The Oxford Dictionary of Nursery Rhymes.* Oxford: Oxford University Press, 1996, pp. 100, 101.

33  Licia Corbella, "Socialite's trial weighty responsibility," *The Calgary Sun,* April 19, 1996, News 5.

34  Muriel Rukeyser, "Käthe Kollwitz," in Sandra M. Gilbert and Susan Gubar, eds. *The Norton Anthology of Literature by Women, The Tradition in English.* New York: International Creative Management Inc., 1985, p. 1786.

35  Kennedy Fraser, *Ornament and Silence: Essays on Women's Lives.* New York: Alfred A. Knopf, 1996, p. 53.

36  In 1990 Madam Justice Bertha Wilson of the Supreme Court of Canada made a landmark decision for women in the case *R. v. Lavallee.* Lavallee was acquitted of the charge of second degree murder in the death of her abusive partner. Madam Justice Wilson's decision was innovative, and its essence was to amend the laws regarding self-defence as they had existed in the Canadian Criminal Code until that time. For example, a woman no longer is required to behave like a "reasonable man" in defending herself. But also, her acting out against her abusive partner must be considered in light of the cumulative effects of the history of the abuse she has endured. But if this decision was

extremely important for women, its effect has been only to begin to raise the awareness of the justice system and the public generally with respect to the problems of women who kill or attempt to kill their abusive partners in self-defence. So far there is no comprehensive published research on the effects of *Lavallee*. From my own research and my discussions with Kim Pate of the Canadian Association of Elizabeth Fry Societies (CAEFS), it appears that very few women have benefited from the changes in the law.

In 1995, the federal Minister of Justice and the Solicitor General responded to the concerns of CAEFS and others by appointing Judge Lynn Ratushny of the Ontario Court of Justice to review the needs of women who might benefit from the still-developing law since *Lavallee*. In what became known as the Self-Defence Review, Judge Ratushny reviewed ninety-eight self-defence claims. Of the ninety-eight women, she recommended seven for remedial action. Of the seven, various forms of relief were provided for five women. No one was released from prison as a result of the Self-Defence Review.

See Elizabeth Sheehy, *What Would a Women's Law of Self-Defence Look Like?* Prepared by Elizabeth Sheehy for Status of Women Canada, 1995.

## Part Two
## At the Trial

37 Christina Rossetti, *Sing-Song.* New York: Macmillan Co., 1924, p. 21.
38 *In The Court of Queen's Bench of Alberta Judicial District of Calgary. Her Majesty the Queen v. Dorothy Day Joudrie, Accused.* No. 9501-1280-C6. All quotations of statements made in court at Dorothy Joudrie's preliminary hearing and her trial are taken directly from the official transcripts or drawn from my own notes. No further citations will be given for such quotations.
39 Lenore E. Walker, *Terrifying Love: Why Battered Women Kill and How Society Responds.* New York: Harper & Row, 1989, p. 76.
40 Elaine Hilberman, M.D., "Overview: The 'Wife-Beater's Wife' Reconsidered." *American Journal of Psychiatry* 137, 11 (November 1980), pp. p.1342.
41 Dorothy Joudrie in conversation with Audrey Andrews, September 1997.
42 Ann Jones, *Next Time, She'll Be Dead.* Boston: Beacon Press, 1994, p. 95.
43 Ann Jones, *Women Who Kill.* Boston: Beacon Press, 1996, p. 336
44 Christina Stead, *The Man Who Loved Children.* Introduction by Randall Jarrell. New York: Holt, Rinehart, and Winston, 1965, p. 355.
45 Alice Munro, "Friend of My Youth," in *Friend of My Youth.* Toronto: A Douglas Gibson Book, McClelland & Stewart Inc., 1990, pp. 25, 26.
46 Ann Jones, *Next Time, She'll Be Dead,* p. 164.
47 Betsy Morris, "It's Her Job Too," *Fortune,* February 2, 1998, pp. 65-78.
48 Margaret Atwood, *Alias Grace.* Toronto: McClelland & Stewart Inc., 1996, pp. 295, 296.
49 Carol Shields, *The Stone Diaries,* p. 75.
50 *Criminal Code of Canada,* R.S.C., Vol. IV, c-46, Section 268.
51 Joel Steinberg and Hedda Nussbaum were arrested in New York City in November 1987 for the murder of their illegally adopted daughter, Lisa. This notorious case of wife abuse, and child abuse and murder, was widely publicized during the trial in December 1988.

52 Ann Jones, *Next Time, She'll Be Dead*, p. 197, and note 106 on p. 273.

53 Ibid., p. 168.

54 Bob Beaty, "Nanny recalls family violence," *Calgary Herald*, May 2, 1996, B1.

55 Don Braid, "Six shots can change a life," *Calgary Herald*, May 2, 1996, B1.

56 Jerry Selinger in a telephone conversation with Audrey Andrews, July 24, 1997.

57 See note 36.

58 Ann Jones, *Next Time, She'll Be Dead*, p. 145.

59 Jerry Selinger in a telephone conversation with Audrey Andrews, July 24, 1997.

60 Kim Lunman, "The Joudrie Affair: Legal Top Guns." *Calgary Herald*, May 10, 1997, p. A15.

61 Toni Morrison, *Jazz*. Toronto: Alfred A. Knopf Canada, 1992, p. 113.

62 Rosellen Brown, *Before and After*. New York: Dell Publishing, 1992, pp. 207, 224, 367, 368.

63 Lewis Lapham, *Money and Class in America: Notes and Observations on Our Civil Religion*. New York: Weidenfeld & Nicholson, 1988, pp. 28, 30.

64 Wendy Lesser, *Pictures at an Execution: An Inquiry into the Subject of Murder*. Cambridge, MA: Harvard University Press, 1995, pp. 85, 86.

65 Marc E. Schiffer, *Mental Disorder and the Criminal Trial Process*. Toronto: Butterworths, 1978, p. 118.

66 Licia Corbella, "Forgiving but not forgetting." *The Calgary Sun*, May 8, 1996, News 21.

67 Earl Joudrie and Lynn Manning were married in a private ceremony in Toronto on July 27, 1996.

68 Elizabeth Bishop, "The Prodigal," *The Complete Poems 1927-1979*. New York: Farrar, Straus & Giroux, 1983, p. 71.

69 Jonathan Harr, *A Civil Action*. New York: Random House, 1995, pp. 236 and 340.

70 Bob Beaty and Rick Mofina, "Not Responsible," *Calgary Herald*, May 10, 1996, A1.

## Part Three
## After the Trial

71 Mike Woloschuk, "Silence of the Lions," *Elm Street*, October 1996, pp. 16-20.

72 Kirk Makin, "Joudrie Verdict Raises Issues," *The Globe and Mail*, May 11, 1996, A1, A11.

73 Kirk Makin, *The Globe and Mail*, May 11, 1996, A1, A11.

74 Ibid.

75 Gordon Jaremko and Anne Crawford, "Joudrie Taking Leave of Absence," *Calgary Herald*, May 11, 1996, D1.

76 Gordon Jaremko, "Corporate Plumber: The Business Side of Earl Joudrie," *Calgary Herald*, May 4, 1996, A1.

77 Bob Beaty and Rick Mofina, "Not Responsible," *Calgary Herald*, May 10, 1996, A1.

78 David Coll, "Hard Lessons: What we learned from the Joudrie Trial," *Calgary downtown*, June 1996, p. 5.

79 *Morningside*, CBC, May 22, 1996.

80 Don Campbell in a telephone conversation with Audrey Andrews, fall 1997.

81 Bob Blair in a telephone conversation with Audrey Andrews, fall 1997

82 Noel O'Brien in a telephone conversation with Audrey Andrews, June 10, 1997.

83 Catherine Ford, "Dance of Death Is Over," *Calgary Herald,* May 10, 1996, A23.

84 Noel O'Brien in a telephone conversation with Audrey Andrews, June 10, 1997.

85 Edwin A. Tollefson and Bernard Starkman, *Mental Disorder in Criminal Proceedings.* Toronto: Carswell, Thomson Professional Publishing, 1993, pp. 93 and 108.

86 Robb Forman Dew, *Dale Loves Sophie to Death,* New York: Farrar, Straus, & Giroux, 1981, pp. 136, 137.

87 Dorothy Joudrie, at lunch with Audrey Andrews, September 1997.

88 Province of Alberta, Canada, Alberta Review Board, In the Matter of Part XX.I, Criminal Code of Canada, and in the Matter of Dorothy Day Joudrie, 28th day of May, A.D. 1997.

89 Helen Dolik, "Behind Locked Doors," *Calgary Herald,* City and Life, May 26, 1996, p. 2.

90 Tollefson and Starkman, *Mental Disorder in Criminal Proceedings,* pp. 93 and 108.

91 Forensic Psychiatric Services, Alberta Hospital Edmonton, October 1995.

92 Don Braid, "Trial Split Calgarians Along Gender Lines," *Calgary Herald,* May 10, 1996, A23.

93 Dorothy Joudrie in a telephone conversation with Audrey Andrews, July 1996.

94 L. Frank Baum, *The Wizard of Oz.* New York: Tom Doherty Associates, Inc., 1993, p. 167.

95 Dorothy in a conversation with Audrey Andrews, January 4, 1999. No further citations will be given for comments Dorothy Joudrie made that day.

96 Noel C. O'Brien, Q.C., Bernard Cohn Memorial Lecture. *R. v. Joudrie—Automatism: Legitimate Defence or Legalized Irresponsibility,* October 26, 1998, p. 19.

# Bibliography

Apter, Terri. *Secret Paths: Women in the New Midlife.* New York: W.W. Norton & Company, 1995.

Atwood, Margaret. *Alias Grace.* Toronto: McClelland & Stewart Inc., 1996.

Barnett, Ola W. and Alyce D. LaViolette. *It Could Happen to Anyone: Why Battered Women Stay.* Newbury Park: Sage Publications, 1993.

Baum, L. Frank. *The Wizard of Oz.* New York: A Tor Book, Tom Doherty Associates, Inc., 1993.

Beaty, Bob. "Nanny Recalls Family Violence." *Calgary Herald,* May 2, 1996: B1.

———— and Rick Mofina. "Not Responsible." *Calgary Herald,* May 10, 1996: A1.

Bingham, Sallie. *Passion and Prejudice: A Family Memoir.* New York: Alfred A. Knopf, 1989.

————. "The Truth about Growing Up Rich." *MS,* June 1986: 48-50, 82-83.

Bishop, Elizabeth. "The Prodigal," *The Complete Poems 1927-1979.* New York: Farrar, Straus & Giroux, Inc. 1983.

Bogan, Louise. *The Blue Estuaries: Poems: 1923-1968.* New York: Farrar, Straus & Giroux, Inc. 1968.

————. *Journey Around My Room: The Autobiography of Louise Bogan. A Mosaic by Ruth Limmer.* New York: The Viking Press, 1980.

Braid, Don. "Six Shots Can Change a Life." *Calgary Herald,* May 2, 1996: B1.

————. "Trial Split Calgarians Along Gender Lines." *Calgary Herald,* May 10, 1996: A23.

Brown, Rosellen. *Before and After.* New York: Dell Publishing, 1992.

Browne, Angela. *When Battered Women Kill.* New York: The Free Press, 1987.

Buckley, Carol. *At the Still Point: A Memoir.* New York: Simon & Schuster, 1996.

Cameron, Stevie. *Blue Trust: The Author, The Lawyer, His Wife, and Her Money.* Toronto: Macfarlane Walter & Ross, 1998.

Carter, Angela. *The Sadeian Woman: An Exercise in Cultural History.* New York: Pantheon, 1978.

Coll, David. "Hard Lessons: What We Learned from the Joudrie Trial." *Calgary downtown,* June 1996: 5.

Connell, Evan S. *Mrs. Bridge.* San Francisco: North Point Press, 1959.

Corbella, Licia. "Socialite's trial weighty responsibility." *The Calgary Sun,* April 19, 1996, News 5.

————. "Forgiving but not forgetting." *The Calgary Sun,* May 8, 1996 News 21.

Corbella, Licia and Kevin Martin. *For Love and Money.* Toronto: The Toronto Sun Publishing Corporation, 1996.

De Beauvoir, Simone. *The Second Sex.* New York: Alfred A. Knopf, 1957.

Dew, Robb Forman. *Dale Loves Sophie to Death.* Toronto: McGraw-Hill Ryerson Ltd., 1981.

————. *The Time of Her Life.* New York: Ballantine Books, 1985.

Dolik, Helen and Vicki Barnet. "Accused 'had an ideal life.'" *Calgary Herald,* January 23, 1995: A1.

Dolik, Helen. "Behind Locked Doors." *Calgary Herald,* May 26, 1996: City and Life, 2.

Doyle, Roddy. *The Woman Who Walked into Doors.* London: Minerva, 1996.

Faith, Karlene. *Unruly Women: The Politics of Confinement and Resistance.* Vancouver: Press Gang Publishers, 1993.

Fennell, Tom with Carla Turner, "High Society Shooting." *Maclean's,* February 6, 1995: 44, 45.

Fineman, Martha Albertson and Roxanne Mykituk. *The Public Nature of Private Violence.* New York: Routledge, 1994.

Ford, Catherine. "Dance of Death Is Over." *Calgary Herald,* May 10, 1996: A23.

Fraser, Kennedy. *Ornament and Silence: Essays on Women's Lives.* New York: Alfred A. Knopf, 1996.

Freud, Anna and Dorothy T. Burlington. *War and Children.* New York: International University Press, 1944.

Friedan, Betty. *The Feminine Mystique.* New York: Norton, 1963.

Garner, Helen. *The First Stone: Some Questions about Sex and Power.* Sydney: The Free Press, 1997.

Gartner, Hana. *The Magazine*, CBC, November 9, 1998.

Godfrey, Ellen. *By Reason of Doubt.* Toronto: Goodread Biographies, 1984.

Gordon, Mary. *The Shadow Man: A Daughter's Search for Her Father.* New York: Random House, 1996.

Graham, Katharine. *Personal History.* New York: Alfred A. Knopf, 1997.

Guberman, Connie and Margie Wolfe, eds. *No Safe Place: Violence Against Women and Children.* Toronto: Women's Press, 1985.

Harr, Jonathan. *A Civil Action.* New York: Random House, 1995.

Hilberman, Elaine. "Overview: The 'Wife-Beater's Wife' Reconsidered." *American Journal of Psychiatry* 137, 11 (November 1980): 1336-47.

Hill, Anita. *Speaking Truth to Power.* New York: Doubleday, 1997.

Imbrie, Ann E. *Spoken in Darkness.* New York: Plume, 1994.

Jones, Ann. *Next Time She'll Be Dead.* Boston: Beacon Press, 1994.

————. *Women Who Kill.* Boston: Beacon Press, 1996.

Kaminer, Wendy. *It's All the Rage: Crime and Culture.* New York: Addison-Wesley Publishing Company, 1995.

————. *True Love Waits.* New York: Addison-Wesley Publishing Company, 1996.

Kaplan, Alice. *French Lessons: A Memoir.* Chicago: The University of Chicago Press, 1994.

Lapham, Lewis. *Money and Class in America: Notes and Observations on Our Civil Religion.* New York: Weidenfeld & Nicholson, 1988.

Lefkowitz, Bernard. *Our Guys.* New York: Vintage Books, 1998.

Lesser, Wendy. *Pictures at an Execution: An Inquiry into the Subject of Murder.* Cambridge, MA: Harvard University Press, 1993.

Lunman, Kim. "The Joudrie Affair: Legal Top Guns." *Calgary Herald,* May 10, 1996: A15.

Makin, Kirk. "Joudrie Verdict Raises Issues." *The Globe and Mail,* May 11, 1996: A1

Malcolm, Janet. *The Journalist and the Murderer.* New York: Vintage Books, 1990.

————. *The Silent Woman: Sylvia Plath and Ted Hughes.* New York: Vintage Books, 1995.

————. *The Crime of Sheila McGough.* New York: Alfred A. Knopf, 1999.

Meigs, Mary. *Lily Briscoe: A Self-Portrait.* Vancouver: Talonbooks, 1981.

Meynell, Viola. *Follow Thy Fair Sun.* London: Jonathan Cape, 1935.

Modjeska, Drusilla. *Poppy.* Victoria, Australia: Penguin Books Australia Ltd., 1990.

Morris, Betsy. "It's Her Job Too." *Fortune*, February 2, 1998, 66, 71.

Morrison, Toni. *Jazz.* Toronto: Alfred A. Knopf Canada, 1992.

Mortimer, Penelope. *The Pumpkin Eater.* Middlesex: Penguin Books Ltd., 1964.

Munro, Alice. *Lives of Girls and Women.* Toronto: McGraw-Hill Ryerson Limited, 1971.

_____. *Friend of My Youth.* Toronto: McClelland & Stewart Inc., 1990.

Opie, Iona and Peter, eds. *Children's Games with Things.* New York: Oxford University Press, 1997.

_____, eds. The Oxford Dictionary of Nursery Rhymes. New York: Oxford University Press, 1996.

Ostrander, Susan A. *Women of the Upper Class.* Philadelphia: Temple University Press, 1984.

Plath, Sylvia. *Collected Poems.* London: Faber and Faber Limited, 1981.

_____. *The Bell Jar.* London: Faber and Faber Limited, 1963.

Porter, Cole. "Miss Otis Regrets" (She's Unable To Lunch Today). Miami: Warner Bros. Publications U.S. Inc., © 1934. Secaucus, NJ: Warner Brothers Inc., 1934.

Price, Reynolds. *The Promise of Rest.* New York: Scribner, 1995.

Rich, Adrienne. *On Lies, Secrets, and Silence: Selected Prose 1966-1978.* New York: W.W. Norton & Company, 1979.

Rossetti, Christine. *Sing-Song.* New York: Macmillan Co., 1924.

Rukeyser, Muriel. "Käthe Kollwitz." *The Norton Anthology of Literature by Women.* Sandra M. Gilbert and Susan Gubar, eds. New York: International Creative Management Inc., 1985.

Schiffer, Marc E. *Mental Disorder and the Criminal Trial Process.* Toronto: Butterworths, 1978.

_____. *Psychiatry Behind Bars: A Legal Perspective.* Toronto: Butterworths, 1982.

Schulman, Alix Kates. *Memoirs of an Ex-Prom Queen.* New York: Penguin Books, 1997.

Sheehy, Elizabeth. "What Would a Women's Law of Self-Defence Look Like?" Prepared by Elizabeth Sheehy for Status of Women Canada, 1995.

Shields, Carol. *The Stone Diaries.* Toronto: Random House of Canada, 1993.

Shreve, Anita. *The Weight of Water.* Toronto: Little Brown Canada, 1997.

Sipe, Beth and Evelyn J. Hall. *I Am Not Your Victim: Anatomy of Domestic Violence.* Thousand Oaks: Sage Publications, 1996.

Sollid, Leif. "Oilpatch: Gulf Exec Back on Job." *Calgary Sun,* May 4, 1995: 4.

Smart, Tom. *The Art of Mary Pratt: The Substance of Light.* Fredericton: Goose Lane Editions and the Beaverbrook Art Gallery, 1995.

Stead, Christina. *The Man Who Loved Children.* New York: Holt, Rinehart and Winston, 1965.

Steinem, Gloria. *Moving Beyond Words.* New York: Simon & Schuster, 1994.

Tollefson, Edwin A. and Bernard Starkman. *Mental Disorder in Criminal Proceedings.* Toronto: Carswell, Thomson Professional Publishing, 1993.

Torgovnick, Marianna De Marco. *Crossing Ocean Parkway.* Chicago: The University of Chicago Press, 1994.

Transcripts. *In the Court of Queen's Bench of Alberta Judicial District of Calgary. Her Majesty the Queen v. Dorothy Day Joudrie.* Proceedings. Witness: Herbert Earl Joudrie, April 23, 24, 1996. Evidence: Dorothy Day Joudrie, April 26 and 29, 1996.

Trilling, Diana. *Mrs. Harris.* New York: Penguin Books Ltd., 1982.

Walker, Lenore E. *The Battered Woman.* New York: Harper and Row, 1979.

———. *Terrifying Love: Why Battered Women Kill and How Society Responds.* New York: First HarperPerennial, 1990.

Wilkinson, Anne. *The Tightrope Walker.* Joan Coldwell, ed. Toronto: University of Toronto Press, 1992.

Wolf, Christa. *The Quest for Christa T.* Christopher Middleton, trans. New York: The Noonday Press, Farrar, Straus & Giroux, 1991.

———, *Cassandra.* Jan Van Heurk, trans. New York: The Noonday Press, Farrar-Strauss-Giroux, 1984.

———. *Medea: A Modern Retelling.* John Cullen, trans. New York: Nan A. Talese, Doubleday, 1996.

Woloschuk, Michael. *Family Ties.* Toronto: Seal Books, 1996.

———. "Silence of the Lions." *Elm Street,* October 1996.

# Index

abused women, xi; and anger, 43, 65, 81, 82; in Canada: *R. v. Lavallee,* 1990, 260 n. 36; The Self-Defence Review, 261 n. 36; reaction to, 111, 112, 122-125; *see also* Part Two, At the Trial, 57-215

Alberta Hospital Edmonton (Provincial Mental Hospital), 238-247

Alberta Review Board, 238, 243, 250

Alcoholics Anonymous, 135, 136, 254

Andrews, Audrey, article about Dorothy Joudrie, ix, x; as a mother, 99; coffee with Dorothy Joudrie, 252-254; and Dorothy Joudrie in 1944, 3; dreams about Dorothy Joudrie, 255-256; expectations in 1950s, 6, 7, 73, 74; and father, 37, 99, 254; identification with Dorothy Joudrie, 34, 35; looking at women and photographs of women, 47, 48; lunch with Dorothy Joudrie, 231-235; marriage, 72-78; memories of childhood, 30-35; and middle class, 78; and mother, 32, 33, 34-37, 106-108, 254; and mother,

father, and feminism, 36, 37; name, 75; private life as a child, 33, 34; talking with women, 48, 49; visits and remembers Alberta Hospital Edmonton, 239-247; waiting, 11-13; women friends, 29, 30; wonders about interest in Dorothy Joudrie, 52-54

Arboleda-Flores, Julio, M.D., 135, 200-203, 211

Atwood, Margaret (*Alias Grace),* 117

automatism (dissociative state), 124, 133, 195, 198-202, 208, 209, 211, 220, 226, 251

Avery, Milton (*Conversation*), 119

Bailey, Dr. Patrick, 135

Battered Woman's Syndrome, 251

Baum, Frank L. (*The Wizard of Oz),* 249

Beaty, Bob (*Calgary Herald),* xiv, 123, *see also* 262 nn. 70, 77

"Be good, sweet maid," Charles Kingsley, 26

The Betty Ford Center, 134; and Neale Joudrie, 136; 198

Bishop, Elizabeth ("The Prodigal"), 204-205